The Kids' WORLD ALMANAC of the UNITED STATES

The Kids' World Almanac of the United States

THOMAS G. AYLESWORTH

Illustrated by John Lane

WORLD ALMANAC
AN IMPRINT OF PHAROS BOOKS • A SCRIPPS HOWARD COMPANY
NEW YORK

First published in 1990.

Library of Congress Catalog Card Number: 90-44293
Pharos ISBN: 0-88687-478-5 (paperback)
Pharos ISBN: 0-88687-479-3 (hardcover)

Printed in the United States of America

Cover and interior design: Bea Jackson
Cover and interior illustrations: John Lane

World Almanac
An Imprint of Pharos Books
A Scripps Howard Company
New York, NY 10166

10 9 8 7 6 5 4 3 2

Dedication
To Rochester, Indiana, and to Rochester High School,
where I learned about the American Dream

THOMAS G. AYLESWORTH is the author of over 100 books. During his tenure as senior editor and editor-in-chief of two major publishing houses, he has edited numerous books about states and cities. In addition, he has written a 17-book series on the states of the union, as well as a book on the state capitals, and books on the southwestern states, and cities such as Chicago, New York, and Washington, D.C. He also has lived for extended periods in Connecticut, Indiana, Illinois, Michigan, Ohio, and Texas, and has spent vacations in 32 other states.

Dr. Aylesworth did his undergraduate and masters work at Indiana University, and took his Ph.D. at The Ohio State University. In addition to his career as an author and editor, he has been a professor of science, writing, and education.

All writers need a lot of help in both the publishing and the creative process. To begin with, Hana Umlauf Lane came up with the idea for this book, and, with intelligent suggestions and a lot of moral support, guided me through the writing. I also want to thank John Lane and his inspired art work, and Robin Sommer, for her editorial eagle eye. Finally, I owe a great deal to Bea Jackson, who designed the book.

☆ Contents ☆

	Introduction	1
1.	Here Are the States	3
2.	Varied Heritages	31
3.	In The Beginning	57
4.	State Capitals	83
5.	Odds and Ends	98
6.	A Little Learning	111
7.	Let's Have Fun	118
8.	Written Symbols	176
9.	Living Symbols	183
10.	Some Unusual Symbols	194
11.	People, People, People	211
12.	A Little Geography	241
13.	Down on the Farm	262
	Index	267

Introduction

One of the hardest things to explain to a visitor to the United States is that we are truly *The United States*—united, yes, but separate. Most other civilized countries have one government—a national one. Their states and provinces have identical laws, and there is a national police force and a national judiciary.

But what do we have? We have states in which the county has its own court and its own police force or sheriff's patrol, and other states in which the counties have almost no powers except to maintain jails. A person can be legally dead in one state and alive in another, and vice versa. Some states have capital punishment, some do not. A felony in one state may be a misdemeanor in another. Maximum speed limits vary from state to state, as do gun laws. Ages at which one can marry, buy beer, and drive a car differ widely. The differences between one state and another sometimes seem to be more numerous than their similarities. That's what makes it so hard to explain to a foreigner. How can we really be united?

But the fact is that we are united. And, at the same time, we like our differences. That's what makes this country great—that so many different states can present a united front. So that is what this book is all about—50 dissimilar states with a single national objective: *"E Pluribus Unum,"* or *"Out of Many, One."*

☆ 1 ☆
Here Are The States

The United States is so vast and so varied that every state is unique. Whether because of its geographical features, the nature of the population, or the history of the area, each state is truly one-of-a-kind. By way of introduction, here are thumbnail sketches of our 50 separate entities.

Alabama —Pride of the South

Alabama calls itself "The Heart of Dixie," and well it should. In Civil War days, it was here that the Confederate Constitution was formulated, in Montgomery, which became the first capital of the Confederate States of America and the headquarters of President Jefferson Davis. But Alabama is also a state that looks to the future. Huntsville, "Rocket City, U.S.A.," is the center for research on rockets and space vehicles. Alabama is also a state filled with beauty, from the forests rising from the red clay soil in the north, through the pine forests and rolling grasslands of the south, to the swamps and bayous in the Mobile Delta, on the Gulf of Mexico. This football-mad state (Auburn University has won the national football championship once, and the University of Alabama has won it six times) is no longer the rural region that it once was. Today, 60 percent of its residents live in metropolitan areas such as Birmingham, Gadsden, Huntsville, Mobile, Montgomery, and Tuscaloosa.

Alaska —Our Last Frontier

The largest state also has the fewest people. So sparse is the population that each resident could stand in a separate square mile and there would be land left over. It could be argued that Alaska is the most beautiful state, with its spectacular snow-capped peaks, great glaciers, and broad valleys. Alaska, the only state to be separated from the rest of the nation by a foreign country (Canada), contains Point Barrow, the most northerly city in the country, located only 1,300 miles from the North Pole. Indeed, about one-third of the state is located north of the Arctic Circle. Alaskans are a hardy breed, as they must be in an area where temperatures may range from −76° to 100° Fahrenheit.

Arizona —The 48th State

The last of the contiguous states to be admitted to the Union, Arizona is a land of almost overwhelming beauty, with its magnificent deserts, mountains, and plateaus. The most startling area in

the state is, of course, the Grand Canyon, which is one of the
Seven Natural Wonders of the World. Arizona is a mecca for
vacationers; its climate, under the desert sun, is ideal for camping,
hunting, hiking, and other outdoor activities. The state also has
more Indians than any other. Oddly enough, although Arizona
appears ideal for the rural life, some 84 percent of its residents live
in cities and towns.

Arkansas—Under Four Flags

Arkansas first belonged to France, then to Spain, then to France
again, then to the United States, then to the Confederate States of
America, and, finally, to the United States again. It is a beautiful
state of mountains, valleys, thick forests, and fertile plains. One of
the most important industries in Arkansas is tourism. Millions of
travelers come to the state every year—many of them to visit the
hot springs in Eureka Springs and Hot Springs, or the diamond
field near Murfreesboro—the only one in the United States. More
than 99 percent of the people in this westernmost of the southern
states are native-born Americans.

California —The Land of Contrasts

California, the most populous state, is a land of contrasts, with its
high mountains, rocky cliffs, sandy beaches, redwood forests, and

barren deserts. This state, with its vast vineyards in the north, its glitter in Hollywood and Beverly Hills in the south, its tremendous farms and ranches almost everywhere, combines the Old World charm of San Francisco and the unusual lifestyles of Los Angeles to maintain its image as a truly unique part of the country. First in manufacturing, first in agriculture, it contains some of the largest cities in the nation—Los Angeles (2nd), San Diego (7th), San Francisco (12th), and San Jose (14th). Los Angeles has more people of Mexican ancestry than any other city outside Mexico, and San Francisco's Chinatown is one of the largest Chinese communities outside Asia.

Colorado —Skiers' Paradise

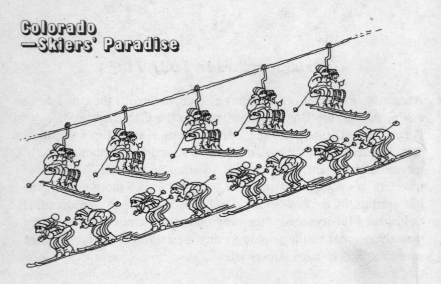

Colorado is a state of unusual natural beauty, with the scenic wonders of the Rocky Mountains and the vast plains in the eastern part of the state. It is a center for vacationers, with its cool, pleasant summer climate and its winter supply of deep powdered snow. But it is also the leading manufacturing area in the Rocky Mountain States, and a major agricultural and mining state. Indeed, the story of its gold- and silver-mining boom days has become the theme of two popular musicals—*The Unsinkable*

Molly Brown and *The Ballad of Baby Doe*. The two longest land vehicular tunnels in the United States are located in Colorado—the Edwin C. Johnson Tunnel (8,959 feet) and the Eisenhower Memorial Tunnel (8,941 feet)—both on Interstate 70. Colorado also has the highest automobile road in the country, which goes to the top of 14,264-foot Mount Evans, west of Denver.

Connecticut—New England Gem

Although only two states are smaller in area than Connecticut, it has always been a leader in industry and agriculture. Indeed, the state provided such large quantities of food, clothing, and other supplies to the Continental Army during the Revolutionary War that George Washington called it "The Provisions State." Today, the state capital, Hartford, is called the "Insurance Capital of the World," and Connecticut leads the nation in the production of helicopters, jet aircraft engines, submarines, ball and roller bearings, pins and needles, silverware, small firearms, and thread. Connecticut is a state of great beauty, with its rolling green hills, its seashores, and its pleasant little towns surrounding their village greens. Although most of Connecticut's citizens were born in the United States, Italian-Americans give the state a Mediterranean flavor.

Delaware —First of the 50

Delaware was the first state to ratify the United States Constitution, and so became the first state in the new nation. Most of its small land area is a low, flat plain, but there are rolling hills and valleys in the north. Although technically a Southern, slave-holding state, Delaware remained with the Union during the Civil War. Today, it is both a farming and an industrial region, and leads the nation in the production of chemicals. Delaware is the only state with counties divided into areas called "hundreds." It is also the only state in which the legislature can amend the state constitution with the approval of the voters.

Florida—Growing Fast

The state of Florida has grown in population at an amazing rate—from 2,771,305 in 1950 to 9,746,961 in 1980. It is also one of the leading tourist states in the country. Its sunny days, swaying palm trees, and warm ocean breezes attract travelers from all over the world. Florida has more miles of coastline than any other state except Alaska. The "Sunshine State" produces about three-quarters of the nation's oranges and almost nine-tenths of its grapefruit juice. Over the years, the flags of Spain, England, the United States, and the Confederate States of America have flown over Florida.

Georgia—Power in the South

Georgia, the largest state east of the Mississippi River, is also the leading manufacturing and business state in the South. Originally a land of farms and plantations, Georgia today has more people who live in industrialized areas than in rural communities. Still, farming is important. Georgia is a leading producer of cotton, pecans, and tobacco, and leads the nation in the production of peanuts. Most of the state is a mild, sunny land of magnolias and moss-draped trees; its features include mountains, ridges, gently rolling hills, and flat coastal plains.

Hawaii—The Youngest State

The only state in the Union that does not lie on the North American mainland is Hawaii. It is also the only state made exclusively of islands, the southernmost state, and the last t admitted to the Union. Hawaii is world-famous for its natural beauty and pleasant climate. Here are deep-blue seas, brilliantly colored flowers, graceful palm trees, and plunging waterfalls. It is also the greatest melting-pot state of the Union, with an ethnic mix of citizens including Polynesians, Chinese, Filipinos, Japanese, and Caucasians. The state includes 122 islands stretching for 1,610 miles in the Pacific Ocean. But Hawaiians live on only seven of them: Niihau, Kauai, Oahu, Molokai, Lanai, Maui, and Hawaii.

Idaho —One with a Panhandle

Idaho, one of the Rocky Mountain States, is filled with natural beauty. It has towering, snow-capped mountain ranges, swirling white rapids, peaceful lakes, and steep canyons. The Snake River rushes through Hell's Canyon, which is deeper than the Grand Canyon. Shoshone Falls, on the Snake River, are higher than Niagara Falls. Farms and ranches in this state of fertile soil produce sugar beets, wheat, and, most important of all, potatoes. Mining and forestry are also widespread.

Illinois—The Land of Lincoln

It was in Illinois that Abraham Lincoln began to practice law, entered politics, and was first nominated for the presidency. This most populous state in the Midwest had many other residents who made history—industrialists Cyrus H. McCormick and George M. Pullman, writers Eugene Field and Carl Sandburg, architects Louis Sullivan and Frank Lloyd Wright, statesmen Everett M. Dirksen and Adlai E. Stevenson. Illinois leads the nation in the production of soybeans and contains the largest beds of coal in the United States. In manufacturing, Illinois is a leader in the production of diesel engines, television sets, and many other products.

Indiana
—Hoosier Hysteria

Indiana is the premier basketball state in the nation. The first state championship in high-school basketball to be nationally televised was that of Indiana. Indiana University has won the national college basketball championship five times and the National Invitational Tournament once. Purdue University has also won the NIT once. Next to basketball, Indianians are perhaps proudest of their writers, such as Kurt Vonnegut, Theodore Dreiser, James Whitcomb Riley, Booth Tarkington, George Ade, and Dan Wakefield. Geographically, Indiana appears to be two states, with its vast prairies in the north and its high rolling hills to the south.

Iowa
—The Peaceful State

Many people think of Iowa as a land of huge farms and small cities populated by people right out of Meredith Willson's *The Music*

Man. True, it is one of the greatest farming states in the country, producing about one-fifth of the nation's corn supply and containing about a quarter of the country's richest farmlands. But it is also the state with the highest literacy rate in the nation (more than 99 percent) and one of the finest writers' schools in the country (the University of Iowa). More than 87 percent of Iowa students graduate from high school.

Kansas —The Sunflower of the Prairies

The Kansas prairies are wheat country, and the state leads the nation in that crop. Today, Kansas is a peaceful state, but it wasn't always that way. Dodge City, the "Cowboy Capital of the World," was once the world's largest cattle-market town—a dusty, brawling crossroads that was home to such legendary peace officers as Wyatt Earp, Bat Masterson, and Wild Bill Hickock. Then the conflict over slavery led to so much violence that the area was called "Bleeding Kansas."

Kentucky—One of the Commonwealths

The Commonwealth of Kentucky has long been famous for the production of tobacco and fine thoroughbred race horses. But Kentucky is also a major manufacturing and agricultural center, as well as a coal-mining state. Tourists flock to Kentucky to visit Cumberland Falls, Mammoth Cave, and Natural Bridge. More than 99 percent of all Kentuckians were born in the United States. Among the many prominent statesmen born in Kentucky were Abraham Lincoln and Jefferson Davis, the Union and Confederate presidents during the Civil War, who were born less than 100 miles apart.

Louisiana —A Bit of France

Louisiana is the home of the famous Mardi Gras celebration held in New Orleans, that charming old city with its rich French heritage. Many people from southern Louisiana are descendants of the original French and Spanish settlers, and they are called Creoles. Others, called Cajuns, are descended from French settlers who left the Acadia region of eastern Canada. In the northern part of the state, most of the residents are of Anglo-Saxon ancestry. Louisiana is one of the country's busiest commercial areas. Shipping is important, as are fishing, petroleum production, and farming. White-columned mansions, built before the Civil War, symbolize Louisiana's past glory. The world's longest bridge, the Lake Pontchartrain Causeway, crosses 24 miles of open water just outside New Orleans.

Maine—Down East

The Pine Tree State is the largest in New England, and West Quoddy Head, a small peninsula, is the easternmost point in the United States. One of the most gloriously beautiful places in the country is the "rock-bound" coast of Maine, with its lighthouses, sandy beaches, quiet fishing villages, and thousands of off-shore islands. Inland, there are sparkling lakes, huge green forests, and towering mountains. In fact, forests cover nearly 90 percent of the state. In addition to lumbering, farming and fishing are important businesses. Road signs are unique in northern Maine, where the state borders on the Canadian province of Quebec—many of them are in French as well as English.

Maryland —Home of the Crab

Chesapeake Bay, which divides Maryland into two parts, furnishes the state with several excellent harbors, as well as fine seafood. The geography of Maryland is varied, including low flatlands, rolling plains, hills and valleys, and mountains and plateaus. About half of the state is forested. "The Star-Spangled Banner" was written by Francis Scott Key as he watched the British bombard Baltimore's Fort McHenry during the War of 1812. Although Maryland was a slave-holding Southern state, it remained loyal to the Union during the Civil War. About 97 percent of the people in Maryland were born in the United States.

Massachusetts—Baked Beans and History

Even though it is the 45th state in terms of area, the commonwealth of Massachusetts has always been a national leader. The first printing press, newspaper, library, college, and secondary school in the country were established here. Massachusetts has also given the nation four presidents. It has long been one of our top manufacturing states. The historic city of Boston is a major seaport and airline terminal, and the many great universities in and around Boston make this area one of the world's great educational, research, and cultural centers. The Revolutionary War really began in Massachusetts, with the Boston Massacre, the Boston Tea Party, and the battles of Lexington, Concord, and Bunker Hill. The geography of the state includes the flat land along the Atlantic Ocean, and the terrain rises from east to west, culminating in the Berkshire Mountains.

Michigan—Two Peninsulas

Michigan is the only state that is bordered by four of the Great Lakes, and its 3,288-mile shoreline is longer than that of any other inland state. Michigan is also the only state that is divided into two peninsulas—Upper and Lower. The Upper Peninsula is sparsely settled and quite rural, whereas the Lower Peninsula contains all the large cities and towns and most of the industry and agriculture. Because of this great difference, people in the Upper Peninsula have for years carried on a tongue-in-cheek campaign to secede from the Lower Peninsula and form a proposed "Sovereign State of Hiawathaland." Michigan leads the nation in the production of automobiles, and is a leader in iron and copper mining and fruit and bean crops.

Minnesota—10,000 Lakes?

Minnesota has been called "The Land of 10,000 Lakes," but that is probably an understatement. Some estimates claim that the state has about 22,000 lakes. At any rate, Minnesota lakes cover 4,059 square miles—almost 5 percent of the state's area. Minnesota has long been a haven for Scandinavian immigrants, with thousands of people who came from Denmark, Finland, Norway, and Sweden. It is a dairy state, and almost 3,000,000 cattle graze on its rich pastures; the state makes more butter than any other and is a leader in milk and cheese production. About two-thirds of the iron ore mined in the United States comes from Minnesota.

Mississippi—Land of Southern Charm

The people of Mississippi have great pride in their state's history, and well they might. Stately pre-Civil War mansions can be found all over the state—bringing back memories of Mississippi plantation life. Monuments everywhere pay tribute to Confederate heroes. The state is a leading producer of cotton, lumber, petroleum, and natural gas. Farmland and forest-covered hills cover most of Mississippi, and more than half of its residents live on farms.

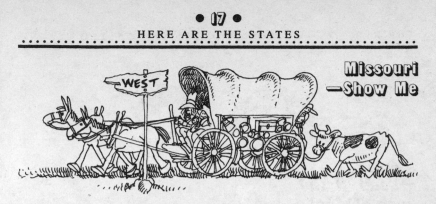

Missouri —Show Me

Missouri is the "Show Me" state, a nickname that stands for intelligent skepticism. It came into being when Missouri Congressman Willard Duncan Vandiver, in a speech in Philadelphia in 1899, said: "Frothy eloquence neither convinces nor satisfies me. I am from Missouri. You have got to show me." Missouri is a center of transportation. The nation's two greatest rivers, the Mississippi on the eastern border and the Missouri winding through the state, lend themselves to shipping. Fifteen major railroads and many transcontinental airlines service Missouri. The state is sometimes called "The Mother of the West," because it supplied so many of the pioneers who moved on to settle the land between Missouri and the Pacific Ocean.

Montana—Big Sky Country

Montana is a land of tall, rugged mountains in the west and broad plains in the east. The mountains have produced a great wealth of gold and silver, and some of the peaks in Glacier National Park are so steep and remote that they have never been climbed. On the prairies, huge herds of cattle graze. The tourist feels close to the old frontier days in Montana when he or she visits the mountains, the battlefields, the old gold camps, and the vast, lonely plains.

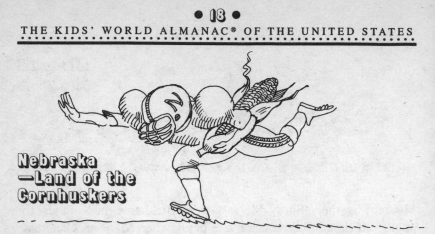

Nebraska —Land of the Cornhuskers

Nebraska is the only state to bear a nickname based on a college football team—the University of Nebraska Cornhuskers. Football at the university is so popular with Nebraskans that on Saturdays when there is a home game, the stadium, in Lincoln, becomes "the third largest city in the state," after Omaha and Lincoln. Nebraska, once referred to as part of "the great American desert," was changed into a land of vast farms by the spirit and determination of its early settlers. In the west are wheat fields as far as the eye can see. In the north-central region, huge herds of beef cattle graze on enormous ranches. In the East, corn, grain sorghum, and other crops are grown.

Nevada—And the Desert Shall Bloom

Every year, Nevada has enough tourists coming to the state to outnumber the population of any other state. Some come for the gambling, of course, but many others come for the vast tracts of beautiful deserts, plains, and mountains. Nevada is a cattle- and sheep-raising state, and most of the grains grown there are used to feed livestock. Hoover Dam, on the Colorado River, created Lake Mead, one of the world's largest manmade lakes.

New Hampshire—The Rugged State

In a way, New Hampshire can lay claim to being the first state to declare its independence from Great Britain, since the state adopted a constitution six months before the Declaration of Independence was signed. New Hampshire is a year-round tourist attraction. In the summer, visitors flock to the rugged mountains, the blue lakes, the sandy beaches, and the quiet villages. In the fall, the state is a riot of color as the leaves turn. In the winter, skiers arrive from all over the East.

New Jersey —Land of Invention

New Jersey was home to at least three of the most important inventors in American history. It was here that Thomas A. Edison invented the electric light bulb; Samuel F. B. Morse, the electric telegraph; and John P. Holland, the submarine. New Jersey is a state of industrial cities and towns, fine ocean beaches, and festive summer resorts. Even though almost 90 percent of the people live in cities and towns, the state's farms earn more money per acre than any others in the nation. New Jersey earned the nickname "Cockpit of the Revolution" because more than 100 battles were fought in the state during that war.

New Mexico —Ancient and Modern

New Mexico's capital, Santa Fe, founded in 1610, is the oldest seat of government in the country; the oldest government building in the United States, the Governor's Palace, was built in that year. It is now a museum. The oldest road in the nation, El Camino Real, runs from Santa Fe to Chihuahua, Mexico. At the same time, New Mexico is a modern state and a leader in research in rockets, atomic energy, and medicine. Its natural attractions include extensive deserts and beautiful mountains and a climate of warm, sunny days and cool nights.

New York—Cities and Farms

New York is a state of firsts. The first women's suffrage convention was held in Seneca Falls in 1848. The first president, George Washington, was sworn in in New York City in 1789. The first victory for freedom of the press—the John Peter Zenger case—was won in New York City in 1735. The first successful steamboat—the *Clermont*—was launched in New York City in 1807. New York is the greatest manufacturing state in the Union, as well as being the leader in foreign trade and wholesale and retail domestic trade. But it is also a state of fertile river valleys, forested hills, tall mountains, and sparkling lakes.

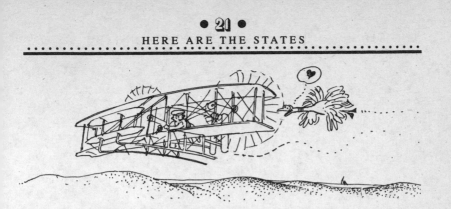

North Carolina—First in Flight

It was in Kitty Hawk, on Cape Hatteras, that the Wright Brothers made the first airplane flight in 1903. On nearby Roanoke Island the "Lost Colony" was founded by the English in 1587, 33 years before the Pilgrims landed in Massachusetts. North Carolina is both an agricultural and a manufacturing state. It leads the nation in manufacturing tobacco products, cloth, and wooden furniture. North Carolina was also a leader in being the first state to instruct its delegates to the Continental Congress to vote for independence.

North Dakota—Teddy Roosevelt's Favorite

In 1884 future president Theodore Roosevelt bought a cattle ranch in what was to become North Dakota. He loved the life of the cowboy, sometimes spending up to 16 hours in the saddle, and even helped law officers capture a band of outlaws. North Dakota today is the nation's most agricultural state: farms and ranches cover nearly all of it, from the flat Red River Valley in the east to the rugged Badlands in the west. It is also a region of coal and petroleum reserves.

Ohio—The Higher Education State

Ohio has more than 50 accredited colleges and universities. Oberlin College, established in 1833, was the first higher-education institution in the United States to enroll both men and women. Today Ohio is one of the major industrial states, ranking third in the value of its manufactured products. In addition, fertile farmlands stretch across much of the state, making it a leader in producing corn, soybeans, wheat, wine, and hogs.

Oklahoma —Boomers and Sooners

Thousands of oil and natural gas wells dot the Oklahoma landscape, and there are millions of beef cattle on its ranches. The state is also a leader in the production of wheat. It is also a manufacturing state, processing food and petroleum products, as well as glass, construction materials, and metal products. Oklahoma is the only state whose name was formed from two Indian words: *okla,* Choctaw for people, and *homá,* meaning red. The University of Oklahoma football team, the Sooners, has a fight song entitled "Boomer Sooner." This refers to the events of April 22, 1889, when the Oklahoma Territory was opened for settlement. Those who entered the territory to stake their homestead claims before the official time were called "Sooners." Those who entered legally at the appointed time were called "Boomers."

Oregon—Home of the Killer Ducks

The University of Oregon has as its mascot the "killer duck," which illustrates the maverick spirit of the state's people. Oregon has long been a leader in sound ecological legislation and forward-looking public servants. It is a beautiful state, with vast forests of evergreen trees, lofty mountains, and gorgeous seacoasts. It is the leading state in lumber production and a major producer of livestock, potatoes, sugar beets, wheat, and fruit.

Pennsylvania—Birthplace of the United States

It was in Philadelphia that both the Declaration of Independence and the Constitution—the two documents that forged the nation—were signed. Like New York, Pennsylvania is a state of firsts. The first oil well in the nation was drilled there in 1859. The first library in the colonies was established in 1731. The first fire department was founded there. Like Massachusetts, Pennsylvania is technically called a commonwealth. Instead of towns, it has boroughs, which are municipalities smaller than cities. All of the hard coal in the country is mined in Pennsylvania, and the state leads the nation in the production of pig iron and steel. Most of Pennsylvania is made up of hills, plateaus, ridges, and valleys.

Rhode Island—The Tiniest

Rhode Island is the smallest state in the Union; its total area of 1,212 square miles is only three times larger than the city of Los Angeles. But it is an important industrial state, especially in textile and jewelry production. It lies on the beautiful Narragansett Bay—an arm of the Atlantic Ocean—and is a popular vacation area, to which boaters, fishermen, and other water-sports fans flock during the summer months.

South Carolina —Queen of Battles

Two of the most important battles in the history of the United States were fought in South Carolina. On October 7, 1780, the British were defeated in the Battle of Kings Mountain, which was the turning point of the Revolutionary War in the South. On April

12, 1861, Confederate batteries bombed Fort Sumter in Charleston Harbor, beginning the Civil War. The Palmetto State is the smallest in the Deep South, and ranges from a lowland in the east, through sand hills, to the mountains in the west.

South Dakota—The Black Hills State

South Dakota is a land of low hills, glacial lakes, fertile farmland, canyons, rolling plains, and enchanting Black Hills, and the weirdly beautiful Badlands. Millions of tourists visit the state every year to vacation in the Black Hills, or to view the presidential faces of Mount Rushmore and the gigantic work-in-progress carving of Chief Crazy Horse. The history of South Dakota reads like an adventure story, filled with daring fur trappers, battles between settlers and Indians, and such colorful characters as Calamity Jane, General George A. Custer, Sitting Bull, and Wild Bill Hickock.

Tennessee—Country Music and Atomic Energy

Nashville is the country music capital of the United States, with its *Grand Ole Opry* and its many recording studios. And Oak Ridge, called the "Atom Bomb City," contains the only museum in the world devoted entirely to atomic energy. The land in Tennessee slopes from its impressive mountains in the east to its lowlands along the Mississippi River in the west. The state has a long military tradition, and its history includes John Sevier in the Revolutionary War, Andrew Jackson in the War of 1812, and Alvin C. York in World War I. More Civil War battles were fought in Tennessee than in any other state except Virginia.

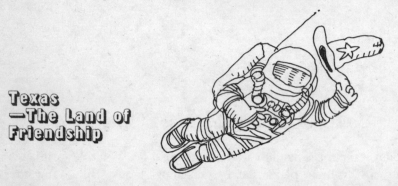

Texas —The Land of Friendship

Texans are friendly—indeed, "Friendship" is their state motto. This huge state features vast plains, rolling hills, and small mountains. Once, the typical Texan was a frontier cowboy with a 10-gallon hat, but today the state's symbol might be an oil field worker or a scientist in a laboratory. Texas is still a frontier state, but this time the frontier is the space program. It also leads the country in the production of cattle, cotton, sheep, wool, natural gas, oil, salt, and sulphur.

Utah —Mormon Country

It was the Mormons who settled Utah, turning a bleak wilderness into a garden spot and making it a cultural center as well. When the Mormons arrived, they had their own library with them. Today, the capital, Salt Lake City, with only 163,034 residents, is the smallest city in the country to boast a top-ranked symphony, dance company, and opera company. The scenery of Utah is splendidly startling. There are snow-covered mountains and beautifully colored canyons—arches, natural bridges, deserts, and the unique Great Salt Lake.

Vermont—Maple Syrup State

Vermont is the most sparsely populated state east of the Mississippi River, and it is one of the most beautiful. Every year, the spectacular Green Mountains attract thousands of skiers and other tourists. Farming is more important in Vermont than it is in the other New England states. Three-fifths of the state is covered by forests, and lumbering and wood-processing are major industries, as are the quarrying of granite, marble, and slate. Only about 34 percent of the people of Vermont live in cities and towns, and its capital, Montpelier, has fewer people than any other capital.

Virginia —Mother of Presidents

Eight presidents of the United States were born in the commonwealth of Virginia—more than in any other state. The state was in the forefront of the Revolutionary War, having produced orator Patrick Henry, commanding general George Washington, and the author of the Declaration of Independence, Thomas Jefferson. The Revolutionary War ended when Lord Cornwallis surrendered to Washington in Yorktown, Virginia. In the Civil War, more battles were fought on Virginia soil than in any other state, and the famous ironclad battle between the *Monitor* and the *Merrimack* was fought in Hampton Roads in 1862. Virginia is also called the "Mother of States," since all or part of Illinois, Indiana, Kentucky, Michigan, Minnesota, Ohio, West Virginia, and Wisconsin were carved out of the original Virginia Colony. It is a land of stately mansions, battlefields, old churches, and colonial homes.

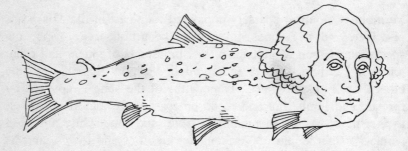

Washington—The Salmon State

Washington is the only state named for a president, and it is famous for its breathtaking beauty. There are high mountains, evergreen forests, and sparkling coastal waters. The flat semi-desert land east of the Cascade Mountains stretches for miles without a single tree. Ships from all parts of the world dock in the ports of Washington, and fishing fleets catch salmon, halibut, and other fish in the Pacific Ocean. Washington is a lumbering state, as well as a leader in dairy farming and flower-bulb production, cattle raising and wheat, fruit and vegetable crops. Grand Coulee Dam on the Columbia River is the mightiest piece of masonry in the world.

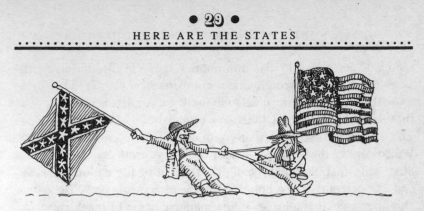

West Virginia—Miners and Mountaineers

Some historians believe that both the first and last battles of the Revolutionary War were fought in what was to become West Virginia. In 1774, in the Battle of Point Pleasant, settlers defeated Indians to gain control of the Northwest Territory. In 1782 the war's last battle occurred when the British and Indian allies attacked Fort Henry at Wheeling. The state contains some of the most rugged land in the country: there are no large areas of level ground except along the major rivers. West Virginia's beautiful mountain scenery and mineral springs attract many tourists. The state leads the nation in coal production, and is an important producer of clay, limestone, natural gas, petroleum, salt, and sand. West Virginia was created when the region refused to secede from the Union during the Civil War.

Wisconsin
—Dairyland of the Nation

Wisconsin is a state of progress and leadership in many areas. Long before other states considered them, Wisconsin had passed laws on workman's compensation (1911), teachers' pensions (1911), mothers' pensions (1913), minimum wages (1913), old-age pensions (1931), and unemployment compensation (1932). The country's first hydroelectric plant was built in Appleton in 1882. The first Ringling Brothers Circus was established in Baraboo in 1884. The nation's first kindergarten opened in Watertown in 1856. Wisconsin is the national leader in dairy products. It produces more milk than any other state, 40 percent of the nation's cheese, and 20 percent of its butter. But manufacturing is Wisconsin's chief industry. It is a leader in the manufacturing of machinery, and produces more paper than any other state. Wisconsin's more than 8,000 lakes and deep, cool north woods attract thousands of tourists every year.

Wyoming —Women Can Vote

Wyoming was the first state to grant women the right to vote. That was in 1869. In 1870, Esther H. Morris became the first woman justice of the peace in America, and in 1925, Nellie Tayloe Ross became the first woman governor. Tourism is important to the state, whose chief attractions are Yellowstone (the nation's first national park), Devil's Tower (the nation's first national monument), and Shoshone (the nation's first national forest). More than 80 percent of the state's land is used for cattle grazing, and thousands of oil wells dot the prairies.

☆ 2 ☆
Varied Heritages

Part of the reason for our diversity lies in the fact that our various states were first explored and settled by people from different European countries, among them England, Spain, France, and Russia. Add to that the influence of explorers and settlers from French Canada, British Canada, Mexico, and the Eastern states, and our states' backgrounds become a patchwork quilt. Even so, most of our states have kept their special heritage alive and visible. So here they are—all 50 of them, plus the District of Columbia, which, although not a state, is too important to ignore.

Alabama
Possibly the first European to arrive was a Spaniard, Alonso Álvarez de Piñeda, who sailed into Mobile Bay in 1519. Certainly the first to explore the region was another Spaniard, Hernando de Soto, who entered the interior in 1540. Cherokee, Creek, Choctaw, and Chickasaw Indians were living there at the time. Then, in 1702, the French arrived and began to establish settlements. Pierre Le Moyne, Sieur d'Iberville, and Jean Baptiste Le Moyne, Sieur de Bienville, founded Fort Louis on the Mobile River. Mobile itself was founded in 1711. After the French and Indian Wars, France gave the territory to Great Britain. During the Revolution-

ary War, Spain, which was on the American side, captured Mobile; after that war, the Mobile region was a part of Spain. In 1795, except for the Mobile area, Alabama became part of the United States after a treaty with Spain. Mobile was captured by the Americans during the War of 1812, and the entire region was now a part of the United States. The Alabama Territory was organized in 1817, and Alabama became a state in 1819.

Alaska

The first Europeans to sight Alaska were the Russians. Czar Peter the Great commissioned Vitus Bering, a Danish sea captain, to explore the North Pacific region in 1725; the men of the expedition discovered only St. Lawrence Island in 1728. In 1741 Bering and the Russian explorer Alexei Chirikov led another expedition that sighted Mount Saint Elias and landed on Kayak Island. At the time, there were Eskimos, Aleuts, and four other Indian tribes living in Alaska. The men of the second expedition brought sea otter furs back to Russia, and the Czarist government chartered the Russian-American Company, a trading firm, in 1799. By the 1850s, Russia was no longer interested in the declining fur trade and sold Alaska to the United States for $7,200,000—about two cents an acre—in 1867. Alaska was under federal control until 1884. After the Alaskan gold rush in 1899 and 1903, settlers wanted their own government, but the Alaska Territory was not created until 1912. It took until 1959 for it to become a state.

Arizona

During the 1530s, Spaniards in Mexico began to hear stories of vast quantities of gold to be found in what would become Arizona. In 1539 and 1540, expeditions came into the territory on a fruitless search for that metal. They found only the pueblos of Apache and Navaho Indians. It wasn't until 1692 that Europeans began to move into the area, when Father Eusebio Kino, a Spanish priest, established missions there. Eventually, he would found 24 of them. In 1752 the Spanish established a fort at Tubac that was the first European settlement in Arizona. When Mexico won its independence from Spain in 1821, Arizona became a part of Mexico, but in 1848, after the Mexican War, it became part of the United States along with New Mexico. Arizona was occupied by federal troops during the Civil War, and the Arizona Territory was established in 1863. It became a state in 1912.

Arkansas

Probably the first Europeans in the Arkansas region were the Spanish explorer Hernando de Soto and his men. After discovering the Mississippi River in 1541, they explored to the Ozark Mountains. At the time, the area was populated by the Caddo, Osage, and Quapaw Indians. Two French explorers, Father Jacques Marquette and Louis Joliet, traveled down the Mississippi to the mouth of the Arkansas River in 1673, and the Mississippi Valley, including Arkansas, was claimed for France by Robert Cavelier, Sieur de La Salle, in 1682. He called it Louisiana. The first permanent European settlement, Arkansas Post, was established in 1686. Spain was given the land west of the Mississippi, including Arkansas, in 1763, but France regained it in 1800. When the United States bought the region in 1803, as part of the Louisiana Purchase, Arkansas became part of the United States. In 1812 Arkansas was incorporated into the Mississippi Territory, and in 1819, the Arkansas Territory was established. Arkansas was admitted to the Union in 1836.

California

Probably the first European to sight what is now California was a Portuguese explorer in the employ of Spain, Juan Rodríguez Cabrillo, who discovered San Diego Bay in 1542. At the time, the area was populated by Hoopa, Maídu, Yuma, Miwok, Modoc, Mohave, and other Indian tribes. Then came an English sea captain, Sir Francis Drake, who was sailing around the world. He claimed the land for England in 1579, calling it New Albion. Spain feared losing the territory to England and sent explorers to penetrate the region. Beginning in 1769, missions and forts were established, and by 1776, the Spaniards had traveled as far as Yerba Buena (now San Francisco). Meanwhile, the Russians were coming south from Alaska; in 1812 they built Fort Ross on the northern California coast. They did not leave California until the early 1840s. In 1822, after Mexico won its freedom from Spain, California became a Mexican province. As a result of the Mexican War, it became part of the United States in 1848, and achieved statehood in 1850.

Colorado

It was the Spaniards who first explored what was to become Colorado, in the 1500s. They were looking for gold, and left when they didn't find any. At the time, the area was populated by Arapahoe, Cheyenne, Comanche, Kiowa, Pawnee, and Ute Indians. Eastern Colorado was declared part of the Louisiana territory of France in 1682, but in 1706 it was claimed by Spain. Still, most of Colorado became a part of the United States in 1803, with the Louisiana Purchase. The western part of the state was still under Spanish rule, but when Mexico won its independence from Spain in 1821, that part of the area became Mexican, only to be taken over by the United States in 1848 after the Mexican War. The Colorado Territory was created in 1861, and Colorado joined the Union in 1876.

Connecticut

It was Adriaen Block, a Dutch explorer, who first visited what was to become Connecticut in 1614. He sailed up the Connecticut River and claimed the territory for the Dutch. But the earliest permanent settlers were Englishmen from Massachusetts, who arrived in the 1630s. Many of these were searching for political and religious freedom, and, in 1639, they adopted the "Fundamental Orders," calling for government based on the will of the people. This document has often been called the first written constitution. Hundreds of Connecticut men joined the Patriot forces in the Revolutionary War, and the colony passed a resolution favoring independence from England in 1776. Representatives from Connecticut were signers of the Declaration of Independence, the Articles of Confederation, and the Constitution. The former colony became a state in 1788.

Delaware

The English explorer Henry Hudson was probably the first European to arrive in what was to become Delaware: he sailed into Delaware Bay in 1609. He was followed in 1610 by Captain Samuel Argall of the Virginia Colony, who also sailed into the bay. But it was the Dutch who first settled the area, in 1631. They were driven out by the Indians, and the Swedes followed in 1638. The Dutch still claimed the territory, and, in 1656, they regained control of the district. In 1664 the English captured the region and ruled it as part of the New York Colony until 1673, when the Dutch recaptured it. The next year, the Dutch returned it peacefully to the English, who gave the Delaware region to Pennsylvania in 1682. In 1701 Pennsylvania gave the area a separate legislature, but it wasn't until the Revolutionary War that Delaware became completely independent. Men from Delaware signed the Declaration of Independence, the Articles of Confederation, and the Constitution, and the old colony became a state in 1787.

District of Columbia

During the early 1700s, Scottish and Irish trappers and farmers settled in the swampland where the District of Columbia was to be. At the time, a few scattered Powhatan Indian villages were there. In 1790 a bill was passed to locate a federal city on the banks of the Potomac River, and George Washington was asked to select the spot. He chose the site in 1791, and asked a French engineer, Major Pierre C. L'Enfant, to survey the area and lay out the city. This man chose a flat-topped hill as the site of the United States Capitol. The first sessions of Congress were held in the unfinished Capitol Building in 1800. Although Washington was captured and partially burned by the British during the War of 1812, the District was rebuilt and hasn't stopped growing since.

Florida

Juan Ponce de León, the Spanish explorer, lured on by tales of a fountain of youth, explored what was to become Florida in 1513. At that time, Calusa, Tagesta, Timucuan, and Apalachee Indians lived in the area. Ponce de León claimed the territory for Spain, named it, and returned home. He revisited Florida in 1521, but died as a result of wounds he received in an Indian attack. Several other Spaniards came to Florida, and some settlements were established. But over the years, the English were settling north of Florida and the French were building colonies to the west. In 1762 the British captured the island of Cuba, and the next year Spain traded Florida for Cuba. The English ruled Florida until the Spaniards, who sided with the Americans, marched into West Florida in 1779, during the Revolutionary War. Spain regained control of all Florida without American opposition in 1783. During the War of 1812, Spain let England use Pensacola as a naval base, and Andrew Jackson led his American troops into Florida, capturing the city. Then came the Seminole Wars, and Spain turned Florida over to the United States. Florida became part of the U.S. in 1821, the Territory of Florida was organized in 1822, and statehood came in 1845.

Georgia

The Spanish explorer Hernando de Soto passed through what was to become Georgia in 1540, and Spain claimed all of what is now the southeastern United States. But England also claimed the Georgia region, and in 1639 it became part of a land grant made by King Charles I of England. James Oglethorpe of England and some 120 colonists arrived at the site of present-day Savannah in 1733. War broke out between the British and the Spaniards in

1739, and Georgia became part of Great Britain. But the idea of independence from England was already becoming popular in the colony. Representatives from Georgia signed the Declaration of Independence, the Articles of Confederation, and the Constitution, and Georgia became a state in 1788.

Hawaii

Although it is possible that Spanish, Dutch, or Japanese explorers stopped at the Hawaiian Islands in the 1500s, it was not until Captain James Cook of the British Navy arrived in 1778 that the rest of the world heard of them. At the time, the islands were inhabited by Polynesians. The natives were friendly to Cook and his men for the two weeks they were there, but when they returned late in 1778, a quarrel broke out, and Cook was killed the next year. Soon, traders, explorers, whalers, and missionaries arrived, and in 1842, the United States recognized the Kingdom of Hawaii, as did England and France in 1843. In 1893 a bloodless revolution occurred, and the Republic of Hawaii was set up in 1894. In 1898 Hawaii was annexed as a U.S. possession. The islands became an American territory in 1900, and statehood followed in 1959.

Idaho

The American explorers Meriwether Lewis and William Clark were the first non-Indians to explore what was to become Idaho in 1805. At the time, the area was populated by Nez Percé, Coeur d'Alene, Pend d'Orielle, Sho-shone, Kutenai, and Bannock Indians. The first trading post was built on the shores of Pend Oreille Lake in 1809. Settlers began to arrive, especially farmers, ranchers, and sheepmen. The Idaho Territory was established in 1863, and it was admitted to the Union as a state in 1890.

Illinois

Probably the first non-Indians to arrive in what was to become Illinois were the explorers Father Jacques Marquette and Louis Joliet, who came from French Canada. They traveled along the western boundary and north on the Illinois River in 1673. At the time, the area was peopled by the Indian tribes of the Illinois Confederacy—the Cahokia, Kaskaskia, Michigamea, Moingwena, Peoria, and Tamarosa. French priests continued to enter the territory, setting up missions for more than 100 years. In 1717 Illinois became a part of the French colony of Louisiana. But in 1763, after the French and Indian Wars, France was forced to cede the region to England. When George Rogers Clark of Virginia and his frontiersmen captured Kaskaskia and Cahokia from the British in 1778, Illinois became a part of Virginia. The Illinois region was given to the national government in 1784; in 1787, the area became part of the Northwest Territory. Then, in 1801, it became part of the Indiana Territory. Finally, it was made the Illinois Territory in 1809, and in 1818 was admitted to the Union.

Indiana

The first known European to come to what would be Indiana was the French explorer Robert Cavelier, Sieur de la Salle, in 1679. He returned in 1680 and explored much of the northern part of the territory. At the time, the region was populated by only a few hundred Miami Indians. French fur traders followed, beginning in the 1720s. But the French traders were competing with British fur traders, and in 1763, after the French and Indian Wars, Indiana became part of British territory in the New World. During the Revolutionary War, Virginia troops under George Rogers Clark captured Vincennes in 1778, losing it in 1779 but recapturing it the same year. After the war, Indiana was part of the Northwest Territory of the United States. The Indiana Territory was created in 1800 with its capital at Vincennes; it included the present states of Indiana, Illinois, and Wisconsin, plus part of Michigan and Minnesota. In 1816 Indiana joined the Union as a state.

Iowa

The first non-Indians to visit what was to become Iowa, Father Jacques Marquette and Louis Joliet, the French explorers, arrived in 1673. At the time, Illinois, Iowa, Miami, Ottawa, Sioux, Omaha, Oto, and Missouri Indians lived there. In 1680 Robert Cavelier, Sieur de la Salle, the French explorer, sailed down the Mississippi, claiming the Mississippi Valley, including Iowa, for France. Still, no permanent settlements were made until the 19th century. Iowa became part of the United States as a result of the Louisiana Purchase from France in 1803. In 1812 Iowa became part of the Territory of Missouri, and in 1821, when Missouri became a state, Iowa became part of the unorganized territory of the United States. In 1834 it became a part of the Territory of Michigan, in 1836, of the Territory of Wisconsin, and in 1838 it was the Territory of Iowa. Finally, in 1846, it became a state.

Kansas
Francisco Vásquez de Coronado, the Spanish explorer, led his men into what was to become Kansas in 1541. The area was populated at the time by Kansa, Osage, Pawnee, Wichita, Arapahoe, Cheyenne, Comanche, Kiowa, and other Indian tribes. The Spaniards were looking for gold, but left when they found none. The French came in the late 1600s, claiming the territory for their country, and the French fur trappers arrived in the early 1700s. With the Louisiana Purchase of 1803, Kansas became part of the United States, except for a small portion in the southwestern part, which belonged to Spain, then Mexico, then Texas. At times Kansas was a part of the Louisiana Territory and the Missouri Territory; finally, in 1854, it became the Kansas Territory. In 1861 it joined the Union as a state.

Kentucky
No one knows the name of the first European to visit what was to become Kentucky, but several expeditions, both French and English, came to the region during the late 1600s and early 1700s. At the time, the territory was populated by Cherokee, Delaware, Iroquois, Shawnee, and other Indian tribes. In 1750 parts of the region were explored by Thomas Walker, a pioneer scout. He was followed by Daniel Boone, who made four trips into the region between 1767 and 1775. During the Revolutionary War, Boone and George Rogers Clark protected settlers against Indian attacks. In 1776 Kentucky became part of Virginia, and in 1792, Kentucky was admitted to the Union.

Louisiana
In a useless search for gold, the Spanish explorer Hernando de Soto led his men into what was to become Louisiana in 1541. At the time, the region was populated by some 30 Indian tribes, among them the Atakapa, Caddo, Chitimacha, and Tunica. De Soto died in Louisiana in 1542, and the Spanish made no other explorations. The French explorer Robert Cavelier, Sieur de la

Salle, and his men came into the area in 1682 and claimed the Mississippi Valley for France. In 1718 New Orleans was established, and in 1762 France turned over much of Louisiana to Spain, only to get it back in 1800. The area became part of the United States in the Louisiana Purchase of 1803; it was called the Territory of Orleans. In 1812 the territory was renamed Louisiana and became a state of the Union.

Maine

Leif Ericson and his Vikings were probably the first Europeans to arrive in what was to become Maine, when they sailed there about A.D. 1000. Beginning in 1524, France sent a series of expeditions to the area. The English arrived in 1605, when George Waymouth and his men began to explore the Maine coast, and the English established many settlements there in the early 1620s. In 1677, after years of squabbling, Maine became a part of the Massachusetts Colony. Several Revolutionary War battles were fought in the region, and in 1819 the territory became separate from Massachusetts. Maine was admitted to the Union as a state in 1820.

Maryland

It was the Spaniards who first arrived in what was to become Maryland in the 1500s. But it was the British who first moved into the area. In 1608 Captain John Smith of Virginia sailed up the Chesapeake Bay, and in 1631 the first English trading post was established. At the time, the region was populated by Indian tribes, including the Choptank, Nanticoke, Patuxent, Portobago, and others. Cecil Calvert, the second Lord Baltimore, was granted a charter to the Maryland region in 1632, and English colonists arrived in 1634. Maryland was to remain in the hands of the Calvert family for most of the time until the Revolutionary War. Delegates from Maryland signed the Declaration of Independence, the Articles of Confederation, and the Constitution. The colony became a member of the Union in 1788.

Massachusetts

The first European to reach what was to become Massachusetts were probably Vikings under the command of Leif Ericson—in

A.D. 1000. In 1602 Bartholomew Gosnold of England landed on Cuttyhunk Island and named Cape Cod. Captain John Smith sailed along the coast in 1614, and his writings guided the Pilgrims to Massachusetts. More than 100 of these refugees from religious persecution landed in what is now Provincetown Harbor in 1620 and settled Plymouth that same year. Within 20 years, there were eight towns in the Plymouth Colony. The Puritans arrived in Salem in 1629, and in 1630 they founded a new settlement near present-day Boston. Trouble with England began in 1675, with the passage of the Stamp Act in England. Massachusetts residents destroyed the lieutenant governor's home. In 1770 came the Boston Massacre, and in 1773 the Boston Tea Party. The battles of Lexington

and Concord in 1775 signaled the outbreak of the Revolutionary War. Delegates from Massachusetts signed the Declaration of Independence, the Articles of Confederation, and the Constitution. The former colony became a state of the Union in 1788.

Michigan

Possibly the first European to visit what was to become Michigan was Étienne Brulé, a French explorer who came to the Upper Peninsula about 1620. At the time, the region was populated by Chippewa, Menominee, Miami, Ottawa, Potawatomi, and Wyandotte Indians. Other Frenchmen followed Brulé, and by 1700, the French had built many forts, missions, and trading posts on both peninsulas. But after the French and Indian Wars, the territory was turned over to the English, and in 1774, it became part of the province of Quebec. Michigan became part of the Union in 1783, with the end of the Revolutionary War. In 1787 it became part of the Northwest Territory, and by 1803 the region was part of the Indiana Territory. The Territory of Michigan was established in 1805, and the state of Michigan was admitted to the Union in 1837.

Minnesota

Two French fur traders, Pierre Esprit Radisson and Médart Chouart, Sieur de Groseilliers, were probably the first Europeans to arrive in what was to become Minnesota—between 1659 and 1661. At the time, the region was populated by Sioux Indians. It was another Frenchman, Daniel Greysolon, Sieur Duluth (or du Lhut), who claimed the territory for France when he arrived about 1679. Western Minnesota was given to Spain in 1762, but the Spaniards did not try to settle the region. After the French and Indian Wars, France turned over its land east of the Mississippi, including eastern Minnesota, to the British. With the end of the Revolutionary War in 1783, eastern Minnesota became part of the United States. In 1800 France regained the region west of the Mississippi from Spain, and after the Louisiana Purchase of 1803, all of Minnesota belonged to the U.S. Over the years, parts of Minnesota belonged to the Territories of Illinois, Indiana, Iowa, Michigan, Missouri, Wisconsin, and Louisiana. The Minnesota Territory was created in 1849, and it became a state in 1858.

Mississippi

The first European to enter the region that was to become Mississippi was the Spanish explorer Hernando de Soto, who discovered the Mississippi River in 1541. At the time, Indian tribes, including the Chickasaw, Choctaw, Natchez, Biloxi, and Pascagoula, lived in the area. The Spaniards found no treasure and made no settlements. Robert Cavelier, Sieur de la Salle, the French explorer, sailed down the Mississippi in 1682 and claimed the whole Mississippi Valley for France. Beginning in 1699, the French started to establish settlements. At the end of the French and Indian Wars, however, the British were given all the land east of the river, and Mississippi became part of the English province of West Florida. In 1781 Spain took over West Florida, and after the Revolutionary War, the Mississippi region became part of the United States; the Mississippi Territory was organized in 1798. Over the next few years it was enlarged, and in 1817, the area was divided into the Territory of Alabama and the state of Mississippi.

Missouri

Two French explorers, Father Jacques Marquette and Louis Joliet, were probably the first Europeans to enter what would become Missouri when they found the mouth of the Missouri River in 1673. At the time, the area was populated by the Missouri, Osage, Fox, and Sauk Indians. It was Robert Cavelier, Sieur de la Salle, who claimed the entire Mississippi Valley for France in 1682. French trappers, fur traders, missionaries, and seekers of gold and silver explored the territory during the years that followed. In 1762 France ceded its land west of the Mississippi to Spain, but Spain was forced to return it in 1800. In the Louisiana Purchase of 1803, Missouri became part of the United States as part of the Upper Louisiana Territory. The Missouri Territory was organized in 1812. In 1821 it was admitted to the Union as a state.

Montana

Many historians believe that French fur traders came to the region that was to become Montana in the 1740s. The Indians who lived there at the time included the Arapahoe, Assiniboine, Blackfoot, Cheyenne, Crow, Bannock, and Shoshone. Sioux, Mandan, and Nez Percé used the territory as a hunting ground. The United States got most of the region in the Louisiana Purchase of 1803. The first real explorers there were Meriwether Lewis and William

Clark, in 1805 and 1806. Fur traders followed, and at various times, parts of Montana were included in the Territories of Louisiana, Missouri, Nebraska, Dakota, Oregon, Washington, and Idaho. The Montana Territory was created in 1864, and Montana became a state in 1889.

Nebraska

Many early explorers passed near present-day Nebraska, beginning in 1541. In 1682 Robert Cavelier, Sieur de la Salle, claimed the Mississippi Valley, including Nebraska, for France, but no known European had visited the region. In 1720 a Spanish expedition led by Pedro de Villasur came into the Nebraska region, but withdrew after a fight with the Pawnee Indians. At the time, Nebraska was populated by many tribes, including the Missouri, Omaha, Pawnee, Arapahoe, Cheyenne, Comanche, and Sioux. With the Louisiana Purchase in 1803, the still-unsettled region became part of the United States. In 1804 American explorers Meriwether Lewis and William Clark explored eastern Nebraska. Over the years, other explorers and trappers came to the territory. Still, it remained Indian country until 1854, when the Nebraska Territory was established. This territory included Nebraska and parts of Montana, North Dakota, South Dakota, Wyoming, and Colorado. In 1863 it was reduced to about the size of today's state. Nebraska finally became a state in 1867.

Nevada

Probably the first European to arrive in what was to become Nevada was a Spanish missionary, Francisco Garcés, in 1775 or 1776. Fur traders and trappers began to explore in 1825. At that time, there were Mojave, Paiute, Shoshone, and Washoe Indians living in Nevada. The Old Spanish Trail opened the region to trade from the southeast in 1830, but Nevada was a part of Mexico until 1848, when the territory passed to the United States as a result of the Mexican War. In 1850 it was made a part of the Utah Territory, and in 1861 the Nevada Territory was created. Nevada was admitted to the Union as a state in 1864.

New Hampshire

No one knows the identity of the first European to arrive in what is now New Hampshire, but in 1603, an English sea captain, Martin Pring, sailed up the Piscataqua River and may have landed near present-day Portsmouth. Indian tribes including the Pequawket, Amoskeag, Nashua, Piscataqua, and Squamscot lived there at that time. The French explorer Samuel de Champlain landed in 1605, and the English captain John Smith arrived in 1614. The first immigrants came from England in 1623, and soon several settlements were established. In 1641 New Hampshire was made a part of Massachusetts, but it became a separate colony again in 1679. In 1776 New Hampshire formed a government independent of the British. Delegates from New Hampshire signed the Declaration of Independence, the Articles of Confederation, and the Constitution. Statehood came in 1788.

New Jersey

The first explorer of the New Jersey coast was probably Giovanni da Verrazano, an Italian navigator in the employ of France, in 1542. The Indians inhabiting the region at that time were the Lenni-Lanape. An English explorer in the service of The Netherlands, Henry Hudson, explored the Sandy Hook area in 1609. The Dutch and the Swedes were the first people to settle in the area, but the Dutch forced out the Swedes in 1655. In 1664 the English won control of all the Dutch colonies in North America, and in 1676, New Jersey was divided into East Jersey and West Jersey. England reunited the two Jerseys into one colony in 1702. Most of the colonists favored independence before the Revolutionary War, and New Jersey became the scene of many battles during that conflict. Delegates from the colony signed the Declaration of Independence, the Articles of Confederation, and the Constitution, and New Jersey became a state in 1787.

New Mexico

The first Europeans to visit what would become New Mexico were Spaniards in search of gold. This began in 1528, when the region was populated by Pueblo, Navaho, and Apache Indians. The territory was claimed for Spain in 1539 by a priest named Marcos de Niza. Colonization began in 1598, but it was slow, and it wasn't until the early 1800s that trappers and traders moved into the territory. In 1821 Mexico won its freedom from Spain, and New Mexico became a part of Mexico.

In 1848 the region became a part of the United States after the Mexican War. When New Mexico became a territory in 1850, it included Arizona and part of Colorado. The present boundaries were established in 1863, and in 1912, statehood was granted.

New York

It was probably in 1524 that the first European sighted what was to become New York. He was Giovanni da Verrazano, the Italian navigator in the employ of France, who may have sailed into New York Bay and discovered the Hudson River. The region's native peoples included the Delaware, Mohican, Montauk, Mohawk, Oneida, Onondaga, and Seneca Indians. Henry Hudson, an English explorer in the service of the Dutch, sailed up the river that bears his name in 1609. This expedition gave The Netherlands a claim to much of what is now New York, New Jersey, Delaware, and part of Connecticut. But that same year, Samuel de Champlain, coming from Quebec to the northern part of the territory, claimed it for France. The Dutch established several settlements, but in 1667, the English took over the southern part of the region. In 1763, after the French and Indian Wars, England also owned the French land to the north. During the Revolutionary War, New York was the scene of many battles between the Americans and the British. Representatives from New York signed the Declaration of Independence, the Articles of Confederation, and the Constitution, and the colony became a state in 1788.

North Carolina

The first known European to sight the North Carolina coast was the Italian navigator working for France, Giovanni da Verrazano, who visited the Cape Fear area in 1524. At that time, the region was populated by Indian tribes including the Cherokee, Hatteras, Catawba, Chowanoc, Tuscarora, and several others. Several Spanish expeditions visited the region over the next 150 years, but neither they nor the French tried to colonize the territory. In 1585 an English colony was founded on Roanoke Island, but the settlers returned home in 1586. In 1587, another group of English settlers arrived at the island, but in 1590, the colony had disappeared. No one knows what happened to the more than 100 settlers of what is known as "the Lost Colony." The province of Carolana (changed to Carolina in 1663) was established by the English crown in 1629 and included what would become North and South Carolina. Theoretically, it extended to the Pacific Ocean. Settlement began about 1650, and the two Carolinas were divided into North and South in 1711. North Carolina delegates signed the Declaration of Independence, the Articles of Confederation, and the Constitution. The colony was admitted to the Union as a state in 1789.

North Dakota

The first explorer to visit what was to become North Dakota was a French Canadian, Pierre Gaultier de Varennes, Sieur de La Vérendrye, in 1738. The Indians populating the region then were the Arikara, Cheyenne, Hidatsa, Mandan, Assiniboine, Chippewa, and Sioux. In 1762 France gave its land west of the Mississippi River (including North Dakota) to Spain, but it was returned in 1800. With the Louisiana Purchase of 1803, most of the area became part of the United States. The American explorers Meriwether Lewis and William Clark traveled through the territory to chart it and report to the government in 1804–1806. The rest of present-day North Dakota became part of the U.S. through a treaty with Great Britain in 1818. The Dakota Territory, created in 1861, contained what is now North and South Dakota, plus much of Montana and Wyoming. In 1889 the boundary between North and South Dakota was established, and North Dakota was admitted to the Union that year.

Ohio

Probably the first European to visit what was to become Ohio was the Frenchman Robert Cavelier, Sieur de la Salle, who arrived in 1670. At the time, the region was populated by the Delaware, Miami, Shawnee, and Wyandot Indians. La Salle claimed the entire region (then called the Northwest) for France, but the British also claimed all the territory inland from their Atlantic colonies. This argument led to the French and Indian Wars, and when the British defeated the French, it was England who owned all the land to the Mississippi River. After the Revolutionary War, Ohio, now a part of the United States, became part of the Northwest Territory in 1787, and Ohio was admitted to the Union as a state in 1803.

Oklahoma

In 1541, the first Europeans appeared in what was to become Oklahoma. That year, the Spanish explorer Francisco Vásquez de Coronado and his men arrived, searching for gold. But in 1682, when Robert Cavelier, Sieur de la Salle, claimed the Mississippi Valley for France, his claim included Oklahoma. At the time, Arapahoe, Caddo, Cheyenne, Comanche, Kiowa, Osage, Pawnee, and Wichita Indians lived in the territory. In 1762 France ceded the land west of the Mississippi River to Spain, but it was given back in 1800. Oklahoma became part of the United States with the Louisiana Purchase of 1803. Oklahoma was first a part of the District of Louisiana, then the Louisiana Territory, then the Missouri Territory, then the Arkansas Territory, then the Indian Territory. The Territory of Oklahoma was established in 1890, and Oklahoma was admitted to the Union in 1907.

Oregon

Some historians think that the British explorer Sir Francis Drake touched Oregon's southern coast in 1579. He was followed by the English captain James Cook in 1778. Americans landed on the coast in 1788, and George Vancouver of England explored the area in 1792. Many Indians lived there at the time, including the Chinook, Multnoma, Bannock, Cayuse, Paiute, Nez Percé, Klamath, and Modoc. American explorers Meriwether Lewis and William Clark arrived in 1805, which gave the United States a claim to the territory, stretching from Alaska to California. But three other countries—Russia, Spain, and England—also claimed part of the region. Russia and Spain withdrew, and in 1846 Great Britain and the U.S. agreed on the present western border between the United States and Canada. The Oregon Territory, established in 1848, included what is now Washington. In 1853 the Washington Territory was created, and Oregon became a state of the Union in 1859.

Pennsylvania

An English explorer in the employ of The Netherlands, Henry Hudson, sailed into Delaware Bay in 1609, and his reports drew other Dutch explorers to the area. At this time, what would become Pennsylvania was populated by Conoy, Delaware, Nanticoke, Shawnee, and Susquehannock Indians. The English captured the area from the Dutch in 1664. King Charles II of England gave the region to William Penn, an English Quaker, in a royal grant of 1681. Penn came to the New World in 1682, set up a constitution, and made friends with the Indians. Pennsylvania was one of the colonies that desired independence from Great Britain, and the First Continental Congress met in Philadelphia in 1774. The Second Continental Congress met there in 1775–1776, adopting the Declaration of Independence. Delegates from Pennsylvania also signed the Articles of Confederation and the Constitution, and the former colony became a state of the Union in 1787.

Rhode Island

It is possible that a Portuguese navigator, Miguel de Cortoreal, was the first to sight what was to become Rhode Island in 1511. But it is certain that Giovanni da Verrazano, an Italian in the service of

France, sailed into Narragansett Bay in 1526. At the time, Narraganset, Niantic, Nipmuck, Pequot, and Wampanoag Indians lived in the area. Roger Williams of Massachusetts and his followers arrived in the territory in 1636, and other groups from Massachusetts followed. The people of Rhode Island were among the first to resist British taxation, beginning in 1769. In 1776 Rhode Island was the first colony to declare its independence from the British Crown. Representatives from Rhode Island signed the Declaration of Independence, the Articles of Confederation, and the Constitution, and the former colony became a state in 1790.

South Carolina

Francisco Gordillo, a Spanish explorer, led an expedition to the Carolina coast in 1521, and he was followed by other Spaniards. The Indians who lived in what would become South Carolina were the Catawba, Cherokee, Yamasee, and several other tribes. In the early 1600s, England claimed all the North American mainland, part of which was a grant by King Charles I of England made in 1629 for a strip of land that included present-day North and South Carolina. The grant, extending to the Pacific Ocean, was named the Province of Carolana (the spelling was changed in 1663). Settlers arrived in 1670, and in 1730 the two Carolinas were created. Most of the people in South Carolina favored independence from Britain, and several battles of the Revolutionary War were fought in the colony. Delegates from South Carolina signed the Declaration of Independence, the Articles of Confederation, and the Constitution, and the former colony became a state in 1788.

South Dakota

When Robert Cavelier, Sieur de La Salle, claimed the Mississippi Valley for France in 1682, what would become South Dakota became French territory. At that time, the Arikara, Cheyenne, and Sioux Indians lived in the region. The first known Europeans to visit there were two French-Canadian explorers, François and Louis-Joseph de La Vérendrye, in 1743. In 1762 France ceded its land west of the Mississippi to Spain, but got it back in 1800. With the Louisiana Purchase of 1803, South Dakota became a part of the United States. American explorers Meriwether Lewis and William Clark explored the area in 1804 and 1806, and later, many fur traders arrived in the territory. Between 1812 and 1834, the land that contained the two Dakotas was part of the Missouri Territory. Later, the eastern section became part of the Michigan, Wisconsin, Iowa, and Minnesota Territories successively. The western section became part of the Nebraska Territory in 1854. Congress created the Dakota Territory in 1861, when it consisted of the two Dakotas plus much of Montana and Wyoming. In 1889 the present boundaries of North and South Dakota were established, and South Dakota entered the Union as a state.

Tennessee

The Spanish explorer Hernando de Soto and his men passed through what was to become Tennessee in 1540 but soon left the region. It wasn't until 1673 that English explorers arrived. At the time, the territory was populated by Cherokee and Chickasaw Indians. When Robert Cavelier, Sieur de la Salle, claimed the entire Mississippi Valley for France in 1682, Tennessee was included, but France, Spain, and England all claimed the area. After the French and Indian Wars, it became exclusively British, as part of the colony of North Carolina. After the Revolutionary War, North Carolina gave Tennessee to the United States, and it was called The Territory of the United States South of the River Ohio. Tennessee joined the Union as a state in 1796.

Texas

The exploration of what was to become Texas began in the 1500s, when Spanish expeditions from Mexico arrived on a search for gold. The Indians living in the region at that time included the Nacogdoches, Attacapa, Karankawa, Coahuiltecan, Lipan Apache, Comanche, and Tonkawa. By 1731 more than 90 Spanish expeditions had entered Texas, building forts and establishing missions. When Mexico won its independence from Spain in 1821, Texas became a part of Mexico. Americans moved into the region in 1820. More soon followed, and, by 1830, Mexico was concerned about the incursion and halted immigration. In 1835 the American colonists revolted, and in the rebellion, called the Texas Revolution, American troops captured San Antonio in 1835. But in 1836, the few Americans in the city were forced to take refuge in the Alamo, the chapel of an old Spanish mission. Mexican dictator-general Santa Anna attacked the Alamo with a huge army, and all the American defenders were killed. A little more than a month later, Santa Anna's army was defeated by Sam Houston at the Battle of San Jacinto, and Texas became independent. For ten years, Texas was a republic, but it was admitted to the Union as a state in 1845.

Utah

Two Spanish missionaries, Silvestre Velez de Escalante and Francisco Atanasio Domínguez, arrived in what was to become Utah in 1776. The Indians who lived in the region were the Gosiute, Paiute, Shoshone, and Ute. Navajo arrived in the 1860s. Spain was not interested in settling the territory, and, over the years, American fur traders and scouts explored the region. By 1830 travelers were crossing central Utah on their way from Santa Fe to Los Angeles. The Mormons were the first permanent settlers in Utah: Brigham Young brought members of the recently founded Church of Jesus Christ of Latter-Day Saints to the Great Salt Lake area in 1847. They instituted irrigation and made farming productive, carving a garden out of the desert. At the time, the territory belonged to Mexico, but after the Mexican War, it became part of the United States. More and more Mormons arrived during the next 40 years, and in 1850, the Utah Territory, which extended far east and west of present-day Utah, was established. For years, Utah wanted to become a state, but Congress hesitated because of the Mormon practice of polygamy (having more than one wife). Finally, the boundaries of Utah were reduced in 1868, polygamy was abolished by the church in 1890, and Utah was admitted as a state of the Union in 1896.

Vermont

Probably the first European to arrive in what was to become Vermont was the French explorer Samuel de Champlain, who discovered what is now Lake Champlain in 1609 and claimed the region for France. The Indians living there at the time were the Abnaki, Mohican, Penacock, and Iroquois. British soldiers arrived in 1690, and the Vermont area became a battleground during the French and Indian Wars, after which Vermont was governed by the English during the late 1700s. But both the New Hampshire and New York Colonies still claimed the Vermont territory. Several Revolutionary War battles were fought in Vermont, and in 1777, Vermont declared its independence from the colonies. It remained an independent nation until 1790, when the arguments with New York and New Hampshire were settled. Vermont joined the Union in 1791.

Virginia

The first Europeans to arrive in what was to become Virginia were
Spanish Jesuit priests, who established a mission in 1570. The area
was then populated by Indian tribes including the Powhatan,
Monacan, Nahyssan, Susquehannock, Cherokee, and Nottoway.
Then, in 1584, Queen Elizabeth I of England gave Sir Walter
Raleigh permission to establish colonies in the New World, and
several expeditions went out. In 1607 settlement began, and by
1619, the House of Burgesses—the first representative legislature
in America—had been established. In 1660 England began to
exercise more control over the colony, and by 1765, there was
much discontent in Virginia. Representatives from Virginia signed
the Declaration of Independence, the Articles of Confederation,
and the Constitution, and the former colony became a state of the
Union in 1788.

Washington

Although the coastline was sighted much earlier, the first Europeans to land in what would become Washington State did not arrive until the late 1700s. At the time, the area was populated by many Indian tribes, including the Cayuse, Colville, Nez Percé, Okanogan, Spokane, Yakima, Chinook, and Puyallup. In 1775 Spaniards led by Bruno Heceta and Juan Francisco de la Bodega y Quadra landed near present-day Point Grenville. Between 1792 and 1794, the English explorer Captain George Vancouver made a survey of Puget Sound and Georgia Gulf, on the basis of which Great Britain claimed the territory. An American, Captain Robert Gray, explored the region in 1792, giving the United States a claim. During the early 1800s, both the British and the Americans arrived and set up fur trading centers. In 1844 the western boundary between Canada and the United States was established, and in 1848, the Oregon Territory of which Washington was a part, was created. The Washington Territory, established in 1853, included Washington, northern Idaho, and western Montana. The territory was expanded in 1859 to include the southern parts of what are now Idaho and Wyoming, and in 1863, the Idaho Territory was created, and Washington got its present boundaries. In 1889 Washington joined the Union as a state.

West Virginia

The area that was to become West Virginia was originally a part of Virginia. The first Europeans to arrive in the area were Germans— the explorer John Lederer and his companions—in 1669. The Indians who lived in the region at the time were the Cherokee, Conoy, Delaware, Shawnee, and Susquehannock. German and Scotch-Irish settlers moved into the territory, and as early as 1776, sought independence from the rest of Virginia, which was controlled by eastern planters and aristocrats. In 1861 the western counties of Virginia formed a new state called Kanawha, seceding from Virginia. West Virginia was admitted to the Union in 1863.

Wisconsin

The first European to set foot in what would become Wisconsin was the French explorer Jean Nicolet, who was seeking a water route to China in 1634. At that time, the Indians living in the region were the Winnebago, Dakota, and Menominee. In the late 1600s, other Indians arrived, among them the Chippewa, Sac, Fox, Ottawa, Kickapoo, Miami, Illinois, and Potawatomie. About 20 years after the Nicolet visit, two other Frenchmen, Pierre Esprit Radisson and Médart Chouart, Sieur de Groseilliers, explored the area seeking furs. Other Frenchmen arrived during the next 100 years. After the French and Indian Wars, Wisconsin became an English possession, as part of the province of Quebec. After the Revolutionary War, the United States owned Wisconsin, which became, in turn, part of the Indiana, Illinois, and Michigan Territories. The Wisconsin Territory was created in 1836 and included Wisconsin and parts of present-day Minnesota, Iowa, North Dakota, and South Dakota. Finally, in 1848, the present boundaries of Wisconsin were established, and it joined the Union as a state.

Wyoming

It is possible that French trappers entered the region that was to become Wyoming in the mid-1700s, but exploration did not really begin until after 1800. Arapahoe, Bannock, Blackfoot, Cheyenne, Crow, Flathead, Nez Percé, Shoshone, Sioux, and Ute Indians lived there at the time. The United States had bought the area from France in 1803, as part of the Louisiana Purchase, and American trappers entered what was then the Louisiana Territory. Over the years, Wyoming became part of six other territories: Missouri, Nebraska, Oregon, Washington, Idaho, and Dakota. Finally, in 1868, the Wyoming Territory was created, and Wyoming joined the Union as a state in 1890.

★ 3 ★
In The Beginning

So here we are, a land of 50 states—all of them different, yet all having much in common. How did we acquire these states, when did they enter the Union, and why are they called by their various names? Some of this has been touched upon in the previous chapter. Here are several different ways of comparing the states directly, beginning with their acquisitions.

Wars, Treaties, Purchases, and Annexations

Unfortunately, most of the states became part of the Union, either directly or indirectly, because of wars that we have fought. It should be pointed out that we did not always acquire all of a state at the same time. For example, Alabama is made up of a section that was acquired as the result of a treaty and a section that was seized during a war.

The Revolutionary War
(1775–1781, 25 states): Connecticut, Delaware, Georgia, Illinois, Indiana, Kentucky, Maine, Maryland, Massachusetts, Michigan, Minnesota, Mississippi, New Hampshire, New Jersey, New York, North Carolina, Ohio, Pennsylvania, Rhode Island, South Carolina, Tennessee, Vermont, Virginia, West Virginia, Wisconsin.

The Louisiana Purchase
(1803, 12 states): Arkansas, Colorado, Iowa, Kansas, Louisiana, Missouri, Montana, Nebraska, North Dakota, Oklahoma, South Dakota, Wyoming.

The War of 1812
(1812–1814, 1 state): Alabama.

The Seminole Wars
(1836, 1 state): Florida.

The Texas Revolution
(1836, 1 state): Texas.

The Mexican War
(1846–1848, 5 states): Arizona, California, Nevada, New Mexico, Utah.

Treaty with England
(1846, 2 states): Oregon, Washington.

American Exploration
(1 state): Idaho.

Alaska Purchase
(1867, 1 state): Alaska.

Hawaiian Annexation
(1898, 1 state): Hawaii.

When Were They Settled?

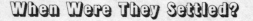

As we have seen in the previous chapter, the various states were first settled by European explorers who came from England, Spain, France, The Netherlands, Sweden, and Russia. Here are the states in the order their first tiny communities were settled.

1. **Florida** (St. Augustine, 1565)—Spain
2. **New Mexico** (Santa Fe, 1610)—Spain
3. **Virginia** (Jamestown, 1607)—England
4. **Massachusetts** (Plymouth, 1620)—England
5. **New Hampshire** (Odiorne's Point, now a part of Rye, 1623)— England

6. **Maine** (near Saco, 1623)—England
7. **New York** (Fort Orange, now Albany, 1624)—The Netherlands
8. **Connecticut** (Windsor, 1633)—England
9. **Maryland** (St. Mary's City, 1634)—England
10. **Rhode Island** (Providence, 1635)—England
11. **Delaware** (Fort Christina, now part of Wilmington, 1638)—Sweden
12. **Pennsylvania** (Tinicum Island, 1643)—England
13. **New Jersey** (Bergen, 1660)—The Netherlands
14. **Wisconsin** (Ashland, 1660)—France
15. **Michigan** (Sault St. Marie, 1668)—France
16. **South Carolina** (Albemarle Point, 1670)—England
17. **Arkansas** (Arkansas Post, 1686)—France
18. **Vermont** (Fort Drummer, now Brattleboro, 1690)—England
19. **Mississippi** (Old Biloxi, now Ocean Springs, 1699)—France
20. **Illinois** (Cahokia, 1699)—France
21. **North Carolina** (Bath, 1705)—England
22. **Alabama** (Mobile, 1711)—France
23. **Louisiana** (Natchitoches, 1714)—France
24. **Texas** (San Antonio, 1718)—Spain
25. **West Virginia** (Shepherdstown, 1727)—England
26. **Indiana** (Vincennes, 1731)—France
27. **Georgia** (Savannah, 1733)—England
28. **Missouri** (Ste. Genevieve, 1735)—France
29. **California** (San Diego, 1769)—Spain
30. **Kentucky** (Harrodsburg, 1774)—England
31. **Arizona** (Tucson, 1776)—Spain
32. **Tennessee** (Fort Nashborough, now Nashville, 1779)—England

33. **Ohio** (Marietta, 1788)—England
34. **Alaska** (New Archangel, now Sitka, 1804)—Russia
35. **Iowa** (Fort Madison, 1808)—U.S.A.
36. **Oregon** (Astoria, 1811)—U.S.A.
37. **North Dakota** (Pembina, 1812)—U.S.A.
38. **South Dakota** (Fort Pierre, 1817)—U.S.A.
39. **Minnesota** (Fort St. Anthony, now Fort Snelling, 1819)—U.S.A.
40. **Hawaii** (Honolulu, 1820)—U.S.A.
41. **Oklahoma** (Fort Towson and Fort Gibson, 1824)—U.S.A.
42. **Washington** (Vancouver, 1825)—England
43. **Kansas** (Fort Leavenworth, 1827)—U.S.A.
44. **Colorado** (Bent's Ford, 1833)—U.S.A.
45. **Wyoming** (Fort Laramie, 1834)—U.S.A.
46. **Utah** (Salt Lake City, 1847)—U.S.A.
47. **Montana** (Fort Benton, 1847)—U.S.A.
48. **Nevada** (Mormon Station, now Genoa, 1851)—U.S.A.
49. **Nebraska** (Omaha, 1854)—U.S.A.
50. **Idaho** (Franklin, 1860)—U.S.A.

When Did They Join the Union?

The original 13 British colonies joined the Union in the order that they ratified the Constitution. Thereafter, states were admitted as their petitions were approved by the Congress. Here they are, in the order of their becoming a part of the United States.
 1. **Delaware**   December 7, 1787
 2. **Pennsylvania**   December 12, 1787
 3. **New Jersey**   December 18, 1787
 4. **Georgia**   January 2, 1788
 5. **Connecticut**   January 9, 1788
 6. **Massachusetts**   February 6, 1788
 7. **Maryland**   April 28, 1888
 8. **South Carolina**   May 23, 1888
 9. **New Hampshire**   June 21, 1788
10. **Virginia**   June 25, 1788
11. **New York**   July 26, 1788

12. **North Carolina**   November 21, 1789
13. **Rhode Island**   May 29, 1790
14. **Vermont**   March 4, 1791
15. **Kentucky**   June 1, 1792
16. **Tennessee**   June 1, 1796
17. **Ohio**   March 1, 1803
18. **Louisiana**   April 30, 1812
19. **Indiana**   December 11, 1816
20. **Mississippi**   December 10, 1817
21. **Illinois**   December 3, 1818
22. **Alabama**   December 14, 1819
23. **Maine**   March 15, 1820
24. **Missouri**   August 10, 1821
25. **Arkansas**   June 15, 1836
26. **Michigan**   January 26, 1837
27. **Florida**   March 3, 1845
28. **Texas**   December 29, 1845
29. **Iowa**   December 26, 1846
30. **Wisconsin**   May 29, 1848
31. **California**   September 9, 1850
32. **Minnesota**   May 11, 1858
33. **Oregon**   February 14, 1859
34. **Kansas**   January 29, 1861
35. **West Virginia**   June 20, 1863
36. **Nevada**   October 31, 1864
37. **Nebraska**   March 1, 1867
38. **Colorado**   August 1, 1876
39. **North Dakota**   November 2, 1889
40. **South Dakota**   November 2, 1889
41. **Montana**   November 8, 1889
42. **Washington**   November 11, 1889
43. **Idaho**   July 3, 1890
44. **Wyoming**   July 10, 1890
45. **Utah**   January 4, 1896
46. **Oklahoma**   November 16, 1907
47. **New Mexico**   January 6, 1912
48. **Arizona**   February 14, 1912
49. **Alaska**   January 3, 1959
50. **Hawaii**   August 21, 1959

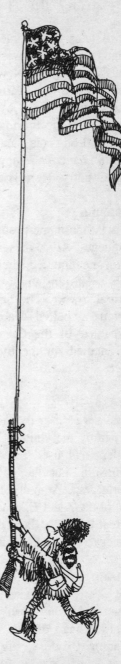

Why Do We Call It What We Call It?

Most states have names that can be traced back to various Indian languages. Others were named by early European settlers. Georgia, New Jersey, New Hampshire, New York, North Carolina, Maryland, South Carolina, Virginia, and West Virginia, among others, were named by the English. The Spanish gave us California, Colorado, Florida, Nevada, and Texas. The French named Maine, Louisiana, and Vermont, and the Dutch came up with Rhode Island. Washington was named for a person—the Father of Our Country. Here is the rundown of state names.

Alabama
This Indian name probably comes from two words in the Choctaw language—*Alba,* meaning vegetation (herbs, plants, or weeds) and *Amo,* meaning a gatherer, picker, or shearer. Taken together, they have been translated as "I open (or I clear) the thicket," or simply "tribal town." The name was first used for a tribe of Indians—variously spelled Alabamas, Alibamons, Alibamu, Limamu, and Alibamo—of the Creek confederacy. Later, the Alabama River was named for the Indians, and the state got its name from the river.

Alaska
Alaska was known as Russian America until it was purchased from Russia by the United States in 1867. Up to that time, the Russian settlers had used the word Alaska to refer only to the Alaskan Peninsula, but the U.S. expanded this reference to include the whole area. Actually, the name represents the Russian pronunciation of the Aleut Eskimo word *Aláxsxaq,* which means "peninsula," "great lands," "land that is not an island," "mainland," or "the object toward which the action of the sea is directed."

Arizona
No one is sure where this name came from, but it may have originated in the Spanish pronunciation of either one or two words in the Papago dialect of the Pima Indians: *Aleh-zon* or *Arizonac,* meaning "little spring place." On the other hand, it may have come from *Arizuma,* which was Aztec for "silver-bearing."

Arkansas

The name of this state comes from the French pronunciation of the name of a Siouan tribe—the Quapaw—meaning "downstream people." In 1881 the state legislature declared that the official pronunciation of the state name should drop the final "s," even though Arkansas is actually another form of "Kansas."

California

The original Spanish settlers referred to the region as Alta (Upper) California to distinguish it from Baja (pronounced Ba-ha) or Lower California, which is now a Mexican state. California was the name of a treasure island filled with gold in a Spanish novel of 1510—*Las Sergas de Esplandian* by Garcia Ordonez de Montalvo. Some have claimed that the name came from the 11th-century *Song of Roland*, which mentioned a capital city called Califerne. But since the Montalvo work was contemporary with the early exploration of California, that is the more likely source.

Colorado

When Colorado became a territory, several names were suggested for the region. Among them were Osage, Idaho, Jefferson, and Colona. But the name Colorado—Spanish for red-colored—had been given to the Colorado River, which flows through canyons of red stone, and the state was named for the river.

Connecticut

This small New England state also took its name from a river. The Connecticut River was so called from the Mohican Indian word *Quinnehtukqut,* meaning "beside the long tidal river," "on the long tidal wave," or "long river place."

Delaware

The state of Delaware and the Delaware Indians (a branch of the Lenni-Lenape) were both named for the Delaware River. The river, in turn, was named by the English for Sir Thomas West, Lord de la Warr, who was the first governor of the Virginia colony.

District of Columbia

The District was named after Christopher Columbus.

Florida

The Spanish explorer Ponce de León discovered the area on Easter Sunday in 1513. He named the new land *La Florida* for *Pascua Florida,* the Spanish feast of flowers at Eastertime.

Georgia

James Oglethorpe had been granted a charter in the New World by King George II of England, and he named the colony after the ruler.

Hawaii

When the English explorer Captain James Cook discovered the Hawaiian Islands in 1778, he named them the Sandwich Islands after his patron, the Earl of Sandwich. But by 1819, they had been renamed the Kingdom of Hawaii by King Kamehameha I. There are diverse explanations about where the name came from. It may have been from Hawaii Loa, the discoverer of the islands in native folklore. It may also have come from two Hawaiian words— *Hawa,* meaning a traditional homeland, and *ii,* meaning small or raging.

Idaho

Some experts believe that the state was named by George M. Willing, when he was running for office in Colorado. He wanted his home territory named Idaho and claimed that it was an old Shoshone word meaning "gem of the mountains," when actually he had invented the word. On the other hand, there is a theory that Idaho might be a Kiowa Apache term for the Comanche Indians.

Illinois

The name Illinois was coined by La Salle, the French explorer. It was his spelling of the Illinois and Peoria Indian word *Ilini* (plural, *Iliniwok*) meaning man or warrior.

Indiana

The name of this state was created by the United States Congress. It means "Land of the Indians."

Iowa

This state was named for the native Iowa Indians, who took their name from the Iowa River. It comes from the Indian word *Ayux-wa*, which means either "one who puts to sleep," or "beautiful land." The French spelled it Ayoua, and Ioway was the British spelling.

Kansas

Kansas is the French spelling of the word "KaNze," which was used by the Kansa (or Kaw), Omaha, Osage, and Dakota Sioux Indians to mean "people of the south wind."

Kentucky

Kentucky's name came from a Cherokee Indian word meaning "land of tomorrow," "meadowland," or "the dark and bloody ground."

Louisiana

When the French explorer La Salle claimed the Mississippi Valley for his homeland, he named it *La Louisianne* after his king, Louis XIV.

Maine

No one is sure where the name of Maine came from. French explorers may have named the region after the ancient French province of Mayne. On the other hand, it may have been christened by the English, using the term of the early explorers for a mainland as opposed to an island.

Maryland

King Charles I of England gave a charter for the colony to Lord Baltimore on condition that the new land be called Maryland for his queen—Henrietta Maria—who was popularly called Queen Mary.

Massachusetts

This name came from the Massachusetts Indians. It meant "near the great hill," or "the place of the great hill." This site was identified by Captain John Smith as the Great Blue Hill, which lies south of present-day Milton.

Michigan

There are at least two theories about how the state got its name. One holds that it was named after Lake Michigan, from the Chippewa Indian words *mici gama,* meaning "great water." Another theory says that it came from an open area on the west side of the Lower Peninsula named *majigan* (for "clearing") by the Chippewa.

Minnesota

The name Minnesota was originally applied to the Minnesota River. *Mnishota* came from the Dakota Sioux language and meant "cloudy water," or "sky-tinted water."

Mississippi

The state was named for the nation's greatest river, but the river itself had various names during the 16th and 17th centuries. Gulf Coast Indians called it *Malabouchia* and Spaniards called it both

Rio del Espiritú Santo and *Rio Grande del Florida.* The French
called it the Colbert River and the St. Louis River. The present
name came either from the Chippewa word *mici zibi,* or the
Algonquian word *messipi,* meaning "great river" or "gathering-in
of all the waters." The theory that the name meant "father of
waters" has been discredited.

Missouri
The state was named for the Missouri River, which, in turn, was
named for the Missouri Indians. In the Algonquian language, the
term meant either "muddy water," or "the town of large canoes."

Montana
Montana was named from the Spanish word for "mountainous,"
which originated in the Latin *montaanus.*

Nebraska
The river that the French called the Platte ("broad river") was
called *Nibôápka,* or *Nebrathka,* by the Omaha, or Oto, Indians.
This name also meant "flat water," or "broad river," and gave
the state its name.

Nevada
In the 17th and 18th centuries, Spanish sailors en route between
the Philippines and Mexico saw the mountain ranges of California
from their ships. They called them the Sierra Nevada, or "snowy
range." When the Territory of Nevada was established, this name
was shortened to Nevada, which means "snow-clad" in Spanish.

New Hampshire
Captain John Mason of the British Royal Navy was given a grant
for what is now New Hampshire in 1629. He named it after
Hampshire, the English county that was his boyhood home.

New Jersey
When Sir John Berkeley and Sir George Carteret of England
received a royal charter for this colony, they named it for the island
of Jersey in the English Channel, where Cartaret had been born
and served as lieutenant governor.

New Mexico
The upper region of the Rio Grande Valley was called *Nuevo México* by the Spanish as early as 1561. *México* came from the Aztec word meaning "Place of Mexìtli (one of the Aztec gods). When New Mexico came under American control, *Neuvo México* was anglicized.

New York
Originally, New York was called New Amsterdam by its Dutch settlers, but when England gained possession of the territory in 1664, the name was changed to New York in honor of King Charles II's brother, the Duke of York and Albany.

North Carolina
North and South Carolina were originally one colony. Carolina was first named for France's King Charles IX and then in honor of England's Kings Charles I and Charles II. *Carolus* is the Latin form of "Charles."

North Dakota
The Sioux Indians in North Dakota called themselves *Dakota,* or *Lakota,* meaning "allies" or "friends."

Ohio
This state was named for the Ohio River, which the Iroquois Indians had called *Ohio*—"large," "fine," or "beautiful river."

Oklahoma
The word "Oklahoma" was coined by the Reverend Allan Wright, an Indian missionary who spoke Choctaw, by combining two Indian words: *'okla,* or "people," and *homá,* "red." Originally, Oklahoma was to be reserved as Indian territory.

Oregon
There are several theories about how Oregon got its name. One holds that it came from the French-Canadian word *ouragan,* meaning "storm" or "hurricane." Another says that the Columbia River was once called "the river of storms" by Canadian fur traders, and the state was named for the river. Another claims that

the name came from the Spanish word *orejon*, or "big-ear," which was applied to a number of Indian tribes in the region. Still another holds that it comes from another Spanish word, *orégano*, or wild sage, a plant that is common in the area.

Pennsylvania

The British Crown owed a great deal of money to Admiral William Penn, and, to pay off the debt, King Charles II of England granted Penn's son, the Quaker William Penn, a tract of land in the New World in 1681. Penn suggested calling it Sylvania—Latin for woods or woodland—but the king insisted on "Pennsylvania," or "Penn's woods."

Rhode Island

The origin of this state's name is uncertain. One theory says that it was named by the explorer Giovanni da Verrazano, who discovered an island in Narragansett Bay in 1542 that he thought comparable in size to the island of Rhodes in the Mediterranean Sea. It is far more likely that it was named by the Dutch explorer Adriaen Block, who called it *Roodt Eylandt,* or "red island," for its red-clay soil. The name was anglicized later.

South Carolina

With North Carolina, South Carolina was once part of the colony of Carolina, named after Charles IX of France and Charles I and II of England. The colony was divided in 1729.

South Dakota

The two Dakotas were named for the Dakota Sioux, whose tribal name meant "friend" or "ally." North and South Dakota were separated in 1889.

Tennessee

The Cherokee Indians called two villages on what is now the Little Tennessee River *Tanasi,* a word whose meaning is unknown. The name was applied to both the river and the region.

Texas

In the language of the Caddo Indians, *Texas,* or *Teysha,* meant "Hello, friend." The word was variously spelled *Texias, Tejas,* and *Teysas.*

Utah

When the Mormons settled the area, they proposed the name Deseret, meaning "the land of the honeybee," for the future state, but it was rejected by Congress. The White Mountain Apache Indians of the region referred to the Navajo Indians as *Yuttahih,* or "one who is higher up." European settlers thought the word referred to the Utes, who lived farther up in the mountains than the Navajo, so the state became known as Utah through a misunderstanding.

Vermont

It was the French explorer Samuel de Champlain who named the area *Vert Mont,* or "Green Mountain," in 1647. The name was combined in 1777.

Virginia

In 1584 Virginia was named by Sir Walter Raleigh in honor of Queen Elizabeth I of England, who was called the "Virgin Queen."

Washington

The Washington Territory was named after George Washington. When the bill creating the Territory of Columbia (named for the Columbia River) was introduced in Congress, the name was changed to Washington because the country already had a District of Columbia.

West Virginia

This state, until 1861, was part of Virginia, named for Queen Elizabeth I of England.

Wisconsin

In early reports, the area was spelled Ouisconsin or Mesconsing, from the Chippewa name for the Wisconsin River. The word has been variously translated as "grassy place," "gathering of the waters," "wild rice country," and "home land."

Wyoming

The name was taken from the Wyoming Valley in Pennsylvania, and came from two words in the Delaware Indian language— *mecheweami-ing,* meaning "at the big flats," "upon the great plain," or "large prairie place."

State Nicknames

Every state has at least one nickname, most of which have obvious roots. Here are the common ones.

Alabama

The state has no official nickname, but it is most commonly called "the Heart of Dixie," because of its prominent role in the Confederacy during the Civil War. It is also called "the Yellowhammer State" after the state bird—the yellowhammer—which was chosen because its colors matched those of the uniforms worn by a company of Alabama Confederate soldiers. Finally, because of the NASA-Marshall Space Flight Center in Huntsville, Alabama has been called "the Pioneer Space Capital of the World."

Alaska

Because of its northern position on the globe, Alaska has been called "the Land of the Midnight Sun." Its vast areas of wilderness have given it the nickname "America's Last Frontier." When William Seward, Abraham Lincoln's Secretary of State, arranged for its purchase from Russia, it was given two derogatory nicknames— "Seward's Folly" and "Seward's Ice Box."

Arizona

The most famous nickname for Arizona is "the Grand Canyon State," for its magnificent national park. It is also called "The Copper State" for its production of that metal, and "the Apache State" for the number of Indians who lived there.

Arkansas

The official nickname of Arkansas is "the Land of Opportunity." When the manufacture of Bowie knives became an important industry, Arkansas became known as "the Bowie State" and "The Toothpick State (a joking reference to the knives)." "The Hot Water State" refers to the region's hot springs.

California

The official nickname of California, adopted in 1968, is "the Golden State." This was selected not only because of the California Gold Rush in 1848–1849, but also for the fields of yellow poppies that are so common in the state.

Colorado

Since Colorado was admitted to the Union 100 years after the signing of the Declaration of Independence, it is called "the Centennial State." Because of its high mountains, it is also called "the Highest State" and "the Switzerland of America."

Connecticut

The legislature made the nickname "the Constitution State" official in 1959, because Connecticut was the first state to have a written constitution. Its other nickname is not so complimentary. The original Yankee Peddlers were from Connecticut, and reportedly, they carried wood carved in the shape of nutmegs (a popular spice) to sell to unsuspecting housewives on the frontier, even though nutmegs were not found in the state. Because of this confidence game, the state has been called "the Nutmeg State."

Delaware
Since Delaware was the first state to ratify the United States Constitution, it is referred to as "the First State." It was Thomas Jefferson who created its other nickname—"the Diamond State" —when he said that Delaware was like a diamond—small, but of great value.

Florida
Because of its climate and other tourist attractions Florida has been nicknamed "the Sunshine State," "the Alligator State," "the Everglades State," and "the Southernmost State" (although Hawaii is farther south). Since it is prominent in the citrus industry, it is also called "the Orange State."

Georgia
The state has no official nickname, but several unofficial ones. Agricultural production has given it the nicknames "the Peach State" and "the Goober [peanut] State." Because of its importance in business and finance, it is called "the Empire State of the South" and "the Yankee-Land of the South." "The Cracker State" refers to the braggarts who moved in from the mountains of Virginia and North Carolina, and "the Buzzard State" refers to the fact that the buzzard was once protected by state law.

Hawaii
In 1959 the state legislature adopted "the Aloha State" as the official nickname, *Aloha* meaning both hello and goodbye in Hawaiian. It is also called "the Pineapple State" for its fruit industry, "the Paradise of the Pacific" for its beauty, and "the Youngest State" because it was the last to join the Union.

Idaho
From the time that most people thought "Idaho" was an Indian word for "gem of the mountains," the state as been referred to as "the Gem State" and "the Gem of the Mountains."

Illinois

In 1955 the state legislature officially adopted the nickname "Land of Lincoln," since Illinois was the state where Abraham Lincoln began his legal and political career. It is also called "the Prairie State," because of its vast grasslands. The importance of its corn crop led to "the Corn State" as another nickname. And it must have been cynical out-of-staters who coined the term "the Sucker State."

Indiana

The state's official nickname was adopted by its general assembly— "the Crossroads of America." But the most common nickname is "the Hoosier State." This is shrouded in mystery, since no one knows where the word came from. However, there are at least four theories. Some say that a contractor named Samuel Hoosier, working on the Ohio Falls Canal at Louisville, Kentucky, in 1826, gave employment preference to men living on the Indiana side of the Ohio River. These men became known as "Hoosier's Men." Others maintain that it stems from the answer that frontiersmen of southern Indiana gave to a knock at the doors of their log cabins late at night: "Who's here?" Still another explanation is that the word is a corruption of "husher," a name given to early riverboat workers who could hush anyone with brute force. Finally, and even more far-fetched, is the story in which an Indiana man, excited about the valor of a certain type of European soldier, beat up a bully and shouted, "I'm a Hoosier"—meaning a Hussar.

Iowa

Although it is unofficial, the most common nickname for Iowa is "the Hawkeye State." This was given as a tribute to the heroic Indian chief Black Hawk, who came to Iowa to die in 1838 after his release from prison for leading an uprising.

Kansas

At one time, the area was known as "Bleeding Kansas," for pre-Civil War strife about the slavery issue. Most commonly, Kansas is known as "the Sunflower State," for the wildflowers that grow on its plains. Kansas weather is called to mind by "the

Cyclone State,'' and "the Squatter State'' refers to the squatters who settled the new territory. Kansas is also known as "the Jayhawk State,'' after the pillagers, called Jayhawks, who first occupied the Kansas borders. As a result, Kansas soldiers became known as "Jayhawkers.''

Kentucky

The most common nickname for Kentucky is "the Bluegrass State,'' for its beautiful native grass. Two crops have been important in the state's history, so it is also called "the Hemp State'' and "the Tobacco State.'' On a more somber note, it has been referred to as "the Dark and Bloody Ground'' (a translation of its Indian name) because of the many battles between Indians and settlers fought there.

Louisiana

Louisiana has several nicknames. It is known as "the Bayou State'' for its many beautiful bayous, and "the Fisherman's Paradise'' for its excellent fishing. Because of its geographical position at the river's mouth, it is nicknamed "the Child of the Mississippi,'' and agriculture has given it the name "the Sugar State.'' "The Pelican State'' is a tribute to its state bird.

Maine

Officially, Maine is known as "the Pine Tree State,'' for its state tree. Because of its lumber industry, it is also called "the Lumber State,'' and because it borders on Canada, "the Border State.'' Finally, it is called "the Old Dirigo State'' after its motto, *Dirigo* (Latin for "I Direct.'')

Maryland

In 1923 Maryland began to be called "the Free State" when it refused to pass an enforcement act for the Prohibition Amendment. Its other nickname, "the Old Line State," supposedly came from George Washington, in praise of Maryland's regular line troops who served well in the Revolutionary War.

Massachusetts

Because of Massachusetts Bay, the state is called "the Bay State" and "the Old Bay State." For the state's early settlers, it is also called "the Pilgrim State" and "the Puritan State." "The Old Colony State" refers to the original Plymouth Colony and the Puritan practice of serving baked beans for Sunday meals gave rise to "the Baked Bean State."

Michigan

At one time, large numbers of wolverines roamed the area, and the state became known as "the Wolverine State." The Great Lakes that surround Michigan account for the nicknames "Great Lakes State," "Lake State," and "Lady of the Lake." Detroit's automobile industry gave rise to "the Auto State."

Minnesota

Minnesota is known as "the North Star State" after its motto. It is also known as "the Land of 10,000 Lakes," although it has many more than that. Other nicknames include "the Gopher State," for the many gophers that once lived on its prairies, and "the Bread and Butter State" for its leadership in wheat and dairy production.

Mississippi

Called "the Magnolia State" for its state flower, Mississippi is also referred to as "the Eagle State" and "the Border-Eagle State" because of the bird on its coat of arms. Like Louisiana, it is called "the Bayou State" for its numerous bayous, and it is also nicknamed "the Mud-Cat State" for the numerous catfish in its streams and swamps.

Missouri
The best-known nickname for Missouri is "the Show Me State," indicating stubbornness combined with common sense. In its early years as a state, the people advocated gold and silver currency, and that led to another nickname—"the Bullion State." The area is filled with caves, so Missouri is called "the Cave State," and, for its mountains, "the Ozark State."

Montana
"The Treasure State" and "the Bonanza State" refer to Montana's mining industry, and the state is also called "the Big Sky Country" for its great mountains and valleys. Another nickname inspired by its mountains is "the Stub Toe State."

Nebraska
The first official nickname for the state, established by the state legislature in 1895, was "the Tree Planters' State." But in deference to Nebraska football, the legislature changed the nickname to "the Cornhusker State" in 1945. Unofficially, it is called "the Antelope State" for the animals that once roamed its prairies, and "the Bug-Eating State" for its many bull bats, which eat insects.

Nevada
The state is nicknamed "the Sage State" and "the Sagebrush State" for the wild sage plants that are so common there. Because of its mining history, it is also called "the Silver State" and "the Mining State." Nevada was admitted to the Union in 1864, while the Civil War was being fought, so it is often called "the Battle Born State."

New Hampshire
Extensive granite deposits in this state gave it the name "the Granite State," and "the White Mountain State" originated in its scenic mountains. They also gave rise to the nickname "the Switzerland of America." The many rivers flowing from the mountains gave New Hampshire the name "Mother of Rivers."

New Jersey

One of the state's most important industries is truck farming, so New Jersey is often called "the Garden State." Shellfishing is another major industry, giving rise to "the Clam State." At one time, a railroad was so influential in the state that it has been called "the Camden and Amboy State." "The Jersey Blue State" refers to the blue uniforms of New Jersey soldiers in the Revolutionary War, and "the Pathway of the Revolution" recalls the many battles fought in New Jersey during that conflict.

New Mexico

New Mexico is commonly called "the Land of Enchantment," "the Cactus State" for the number of cacti that grow there, and "the Spanish State" in honor of its Hispanic heritage.

New York

Because of its wealth and variety of resources, New York is commonly called "the Empire State." It is also nicknamed "the Excelsior State" after its motto, which means "Ever upward." In the early days, the Dutchmen who settled there wore a distinctive type of breeches, so New York is also called "the Knickerbocker State."

North Carolina

Since North Carolina was separated from South Carolina in 1729, it is often called "the Old North State." Another familiar nickname is "the Tar Heel State." This came from a derogatory name applied to North Carolina Civil War soldiers by other Confederate soldiers from Mississippi. The North Carolina troops were chased from their position on a hill by Union soldiers—thus, they had forgotten to "tar their heels" in order to stand fast and maintain their position. Because of an important industry, the state is also called "the Turpentine State."

North Dakota

"The Peace Garden State" refers to a large park called "the Peace Garden" extending into the Canadian province of Manitoba; it symbolizes international accord. The state is also called "the Sioux State" and "the Land of the Dakotas" in honor of its native people. Another nickname is "Flickertail State," for the flickertail squirrel that is so common there.

Ohio

Ohio is nicknamed "the Buckeye State" for a regional tree producing nuts that resemble the eye of a deer when opened. And perhaps from an incident that occurred in 1788, when a very tall man named Colonel Sproat led a group to a fort and was referred to by the local Indians as "Big Buckeye." The state is also referred to as "the Mother of Modern Presidents," since seven American chief executives were born there.

Oklahoma

The two state nicknames for Oklahoma refer to the opening of the Oklahoma Territory for settlement in 1889. "Sooner State" refers to the "Sooners," who illegally crossed into the territory to stake claims before the designated time and date, and "the Boomer State" to the so-called Boomers, who legally entered the territory to settle.

Oregon

The most common nickname for the state is "the Beaver State," after the state animal. Because there is so much rain there, it is also called "the Web-Foot State." Early settlers suffered many privations, so Oregon is also referred to as "the Hard-Case State."

Pennsylvania

Because of William Penn's religious affiliation, Pennsylvania is often called "the Quaker State," but it is more often nicknamed "the Keystone State," probably for its geographical location and importance in the original 13 colonies.

Rhode Island

Since Rhode Island is the smallest state in the Union, it is often called "Little Rhody" or "the Smallest State." It also uses the name "Ocean State" to promote tourism. Another nickname is "the Land of Roger Williams" in honor of its first leader, and, since its official name is The State of Rhode Island and Providence Plantations, it is called "the Plantation State."

South Carolina

"The Palmetto State" is a nickname that refers to the state tree. South Carolina is also called "the Rice State" and "the Swamp State" for its rice production. Because of its shape, it has been nicknamed "the Keystone of the South Atlantic Seaboard," and, because of the iodine content of many of its plants, it is called "the Iodine State."

South Dakota

South Dakota has two official nicknames—"the Sunshine State" to promote tourism, and "the Coyote State" for the many coyotes that live there. It is also referred to as "the Blizzard State" for its weather and "the Artesian State" for its artesian wells.

Tennessee

Because of the valor of Tennessee volunteer troops fighting under Andrew Jackson in the Battle of New Orleans during the War of 1812, Tennessee is called "the Volunteer State." Other nicknames for the state are "the Big Bend State" for the Tennessee River, and "the Mother of Southwestern Statesmen" for the three American presidents who were born there. Tennessee was once called "the Hog State" and "the Hominy State" for its pork and corn-product industries.

Texas

"The Lone Star State" is the nickname that arose from the state flag, which symbolizes the history of Texas as an independent republic fighting alone for its freedom. Texas is also called "the Beef State" for its cattle ranching and "the Banner State" for its prominent place in the Union.

Utah

The state emblem is the beehive, so Utah is most often called "the Beehive State." Because of its Mormon heritage, it is also referred to as "the Mormon State" and "the Land of the Saints"—the Mormon Church's official name is The Church of Jesus Christ of Latter-Day Saints. Finally, because of the Great Salt Lake, it is called "the Salt Lake State."

Vermont
Because of the beautiful mountains there, Vermont is nicknamed "the Green Mountain State."

Virginia
In 1663, King Charles II of England added the arms of Virginia to his shield, along with the arms of his other dominions—France, Ireland, and Scotland. Thus, Virginia is often called "the Old Dominion State" or "the Ancient Dominion State." Early settlers who were loyal to England were called Cavaliers, so Virginia is also called "the Cavalier State." "The Mother of States" signifies that it was the first to be colonized, and "the Mother of Presidents" and "the Mother of Statesmen" refers to the large number of political leaders who were born there.

Washington
The most common nickname for Washington is "the Evergreen State," for its many fir and pine trees. The state was once known as "the Chinook State" for both the salmon industry and the Indian tribe of that name.

West Virginia
Because of the beautiful Allegheny Mountains in West Virginia, it is called "the Mountain State" and "the Switzerland of America." And because of its shape, it has been nicknamed "the Panhandle State."

Wisconsin
The most common nickname for Wisconsin, although it is unofficial, is "the Badger State." This did not originally refer to the animal, but rather to the early lead miners who lived underground in dugout homes and were called badgers. Later, the badger became the state animal of Wisconsin. Because of its copper mines, it is also called "the Copper State."

Wyoming

"The Equality State" was given to Wyoming because it was the first state to give women the right to vote, and "Equality" is the state motto. Wyoming is also called "Big Wyoming" and "the Cowboy State."

The Confederate States of America

The neat accumulation of states from 13 to 50 was not as neat as it might seem. The four years of bloodshed that were the Civil War (1861–1865) left a heritage of grief and bitterness. Several states of the Union seceded to join the Confederate States of America. After the war, which meant little but misery for them, they were put under Federal military occupation and rule; only later were they readmitted to the Union. Here are those states.

	Date of Secession	Date of Readmission
South Carolina	December 20, 1860	June 25, 1868
Mississippi	January 9, 1861	February 23, 1870
Florida	January 10, 1861	June 25, 1868
Alabama	January 11, 1861	June 25, 1868
Georgia	January 19, 1861	July 15, 1870
Louisiana	January 26, 1861	June 25, 1868
Texas	February 1, 1861	March 30, 1870
Virginia	April 17, 1861	January 26, 1870
Arkansas	May 6, 1861	June 22, 1868
Tennessee	May 7, 1861	July 24, 1866
North Carolina	May 21, 1861	June 25, 1868

★ 4 ★
State Capitals

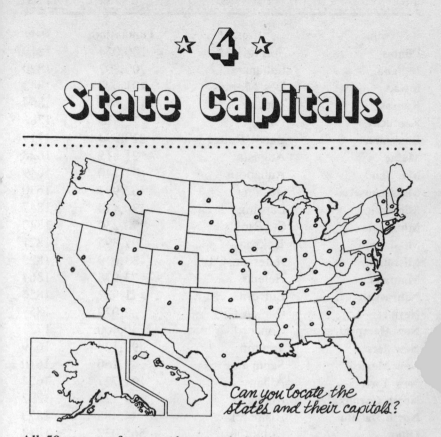

Can you locate the
states and their capitols?

All 50 states, of course, have capital cities, and here they are.

State	Capital	Population	Date
Alabama	Montgomery	177,857	1814
Alaska	Juneau	19,528	1880
Arizona	Phoenix	789,704	1864
Arkansas	Little Rock	159,159	1812
California	Sacramento	275,741	1839
Colorado	Denver	492,686	1858
Connecticut	Hartford	136,392	1623
Delaware	Dover	23,507	1717
Florida	Tallahassee	81,548	1824
Georgia	Atlanta	425,022	1837
Hawaii	Honolulu	365,048	1794
Idaho	Boise	102,249	1862

State	Capital	Population	Date
Illinois	Springfield	100,054	1819
Indiana	Indianapolis	700,807	1820
Iowa	Des Moines	191,003	1843
Kansas	Topeka	118,690	1854
Kentucky	Frankfort	25,973	1786
Louisiana	Baton Rouge	220,394	1719
Maine	Augusta	21,819	1628
Maryland	Annapolis	31,740	1649
Massachusetts	Boston	562,994	1630
Michigan	Lansing	130,414	1847
Minnesota	St. Paul	270,230	1840
Mississippi	Jackson	202,895	1821
Missouri	Jefferson City	33,619	1823
Montana	Helena	23,938	1864
Nebraska	Lincoln	171,932	1856
Nevada	Carson City	32,022	1858
New Hampshire	Concord	30,400	1727
New Jersey	Trenton	92,124	1679
New Mexico	Santa Fe	49,160	1610
New York	Albany	101,727	1624
North Carolina	Raleigh	149,771	1792
North Dakota	Bismarck	44,485	1873
Ohio	Columbus	565,032	1812
Oklahoma	Oklahoma City	404,014	1889
Oregon	Salem	89,091	1840
Pennsylvania	Harrisburg	53,264	1718
Rhode Island	Providence	156,804	1636
South Carolina	Columbia	101,229	1786
South Dakota	Pierre	11,973	1880
Tennessee	Nashville	455,651	1779
Texas	Austin	345,890	1839
Utah	Salt Lake City	163,034	1847
Vermont	Montpelier	8,241	1787
Virginia	Richmond	219,214	1607
Washington	Olympia	27,441	1850
West Virginia	Charleston	63,968	1794
Wisconsin	Madison	170,616	1837
Wyoming	Cheyenne	47,283	1867

State Capitals—One by One

Here, in alphabetical order, are the state capitals, with information about each one.

Albany, New York
Between 1777 and 1797, Kingston, Poughkeepsie, and New York City were temporary capitals of New York. Albany was finally selected as the permanent capital in 1797. Located on the western bank of the Hudson River at a point where Henry Hudson sailed his *Half Moon* in 1609, Albany was settled by Dutch, Norwegians, Danes, Germans, and Scots under the patroonship of Kiliaen Van Rensselaer of The Netherlands. When the British took over in 1664, the city was named in honor of the British Duke of Kent and Albany. It became a fur trading center in 1754.

Annapolis, Maryland
St. Mary's was Maryland's first capital, from 1634 to 1694. Annapolis was named the capital in 1694. Annapolis is truly a colonial town, with its charming narrow streets and old houses. The site of the United States Naval Academy (since 1845), it became the provincial capital in 1695, and was the first peacetime capital of the United States when Congress met there from November 26, 1783, to August 13, 1784.

Atlanta, Georgia
The first capital of Georgia was Savannah, from 1733 to 1786. Savannah was followed by Augusta (1786–1795), Louisville (1796–1806), and Milledgeville (1807–1868). Atlanta became the capital in 1868. In the beginning, what is now Atlanta was an Indian settlement called Standing Peachtree. Atlanta was only 27 years old when 90 percent of its homes and other buildings were destroyed in a 117-day siege by the Union Army. But the people returned to the ruins and began to build what was to become one of the most important cities in the South.

Augusta, Maine

From 1820 to 1832, Portland was the capital of Maine—Augusta was named the capital in 1832. Men from the Plymouth Colony of Massachusetts set up a trading post at an Indian village called Cushnoc in 1628. That was the beginning of Augusta. Then, in 1754, Fort Western was built there to serve as a protection from Indian raids on the settlers. Located 39 miles from the Atlantic Ocean, Augusta is situated at the head of navigation on the Kennebec River.

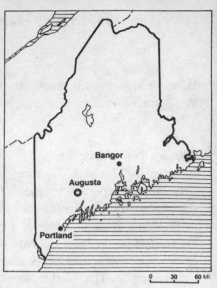

Austin, Texas

Austin has been the capital of Texas since it won its freedom from Mexico. In the beginning, it was simply a pleasant spot on the Colorado River, where Mirabeau B. Lamar, the vice-president of the Republic of Texas, camped in 1838. The following year, Lamar became the president of the republic, and suggested that the site be made the location of the new capital. Named after Stephen F. Austin, the leader of the first American colony in Texas, it is now a city of handsome buildings and beautiful homes.

Baton Rouge, Louisiana

The first capital of Louisiana was New Orleans, from 1812 to 1830. This was followed by Donaldsonville (1831), New Orleans again (1831–1849), Baton Rouge (1850–1861), Opelousas (1862–1863), Shreveport (1864), and New Orleans for the third time (1864–1881). Finally, Baton Rouge was made the permanent capital in 1882. Founded by the French, the city was named after a red post that marked the boundary between the territories of two Indian tribes. Today, this gracious city is a major Mississippi River port.

Bismarck, North Dakota
Bismarck, the former territorial capital, was made the capital of North Dakota in 1889, the year of the state's admission to the Union. Early visitors to the Bismarck area included explorers Meriwether Lewis and William Clark in 1804. They were followed by such luminaries as the scout Jim Bridger; the Indian warrior Sitting Bull; and the future president Theodore Roosevelt. The city began as a frontier town, but today it is the center of vast farming lands—a truly modern city.

Boise, Idaho
The first capital of Idaho was Lewiston (1863–1864); Boise was selected in 1864. Boise was settled by French trappers, who named the area *les bois* (the woods) for its many forests. Today it is a modern manufacturing center.

Boston, Massachusetts
Boston became the capital of Massachusetts in 1632. Boston was first settled by John Winthrop and 800 colonists in 1630, and 200 of the settlers died during the first winter there. The Revolutionary War began there in 1770, with the Boston Massacre, which was followed by the Boston Tea Party in 1773. Today, Boston is a thriving city that has managed to preserve its colonial charm.

Carson City, Nevada
Carson City became the capital of the state in 1861. It was first called Eagle Ranch, and later was renamed for the famous scout Kit Carson. Located near the edge of the forested eastern slope of the Sierra Nevada in Eagle Valley, it is today a modern city that looks to the future as well as the past.

Charleston, West Virginia
The first capital of West Virginia was Wheeling, from 1863 to 1870. This was followed by Charleston (1870–1875), and Wheeling again (1875–1885). Finally, Charleston was made the permanent capital in 1885. It was Daniel Boone who first lived in the area—until 1795. Today, the city is the manufacturing and trade center of the Great Kanawha Valley.

Cheyenne, Wyoming

Cheyenne became the state capital in 1869—when the town was only two years old. It was named for an Algonquian Indian tribe that roamed the area. The town prospered when the railroad came through in 1867, and it became a wild frontier town, nicknamed "Hell-on-Wheels." Today, the city is a wholesale, retail, banking, and ranching center.

Columbia, South Carolina

The first capital of South Carolina was Charleston, from 1670 to 1790. Columbia was selected in 1790. It was a planned town, laid out in a checkerboard pattern in 1786, but in 1865, during the Civil War, Union General William T. Sherman and his men reduced the city to ashes. A new city of stately buildings arose from those ashes. Today, it is a trade, industry, and finance center.

Columbus, Ohio

The first capital of Ohio was Chillicothe, from 1803 to 1810. Then came Zanesville (1810–1812), and Chillicothe again (1812–1816). Finally, Columbus became the capital in 1816, when the city was only four years old. It was created and laid out to be the capital city, and was planned with broad, tree-lined streets and beautiful parks. The city is located along the Scioto and Olentangy Rivers, and has become a center of industry and education.

Concord, New Hampshire

For years, the capital city of New Hampshire was in dispute. First it was Portsmouth (1679–1774), then Exeter (1775–1781), then Concord (1782–1784). Concord did not become the permanent capital until 1819. Today, it is the financial, political, and industrial center of the state.

Denver, Colorado
The first capital of Colorado was Colorado City (now Colorado Springs), in 1862. Golden and Denver alternated as the capital from 1863 to 1867, when Denver was named the capital. "The Mile High City" began as a gold camp in 1858. Denver grew rich on gold and silver lodes, and rapidly became the most important city in the state. Today, it is a transportation, industrial, commercial, cultural, and vacation center.

Des Moines, Iowa
The first capital of Iowa was Burlington (1838–1841), followed by Iowa City (1841–1857). Des Moines was finally named the capital city in 1857. Des Moines began as Fort Des Moines, at a point on the Raccoon and Des Moines Rivers, in 1843. Today it is an insurance and industrial center.

Dover, Delaware
New Castle was the capital of Delaware from 1704 to 1777, when Dover was selected. It was William Penn who laid out the town around a beautiful green, and even today there are fine 18th- and 19th-century homes around that common.

Frankfort, Kentucky
The first capital of Kentucky was Lexington (1792–1793). Frankfort was selected in 1793 as a compromise between Lexington and Louisville. This city, surrounded by fertile farm land, was briefly occupied by the Confederates during the Civil War.

Harrisburg, Pennsylvania
The first capital of Pennsylvania was Chester (1681–1683), then Philadelphia (1683–1799), then Lancaster (1799–1812). Finally, Harrisburg was named the capital in 1812. What is probably the finest state capitol building, with its riverside park and forum, is located in this midstate metropolis. The first person to see the site of Harrisburg was Etienne Brulé, the French explorer, as he traveled down the Susquehanna River in 1615. But it took more than 100 years for the area to be settled, when John Harris opened a trading post there.

Hartford, Connecticut

New Haven and Hartford were the twin capitals of Connecticut from 1662 to 1783, when Hartford became the sole capital. In 1662 King Charles II of England granted Hartford a charter that virtually made the town independent of the governor of New England, Sir Edmund Andros. According to legend, Andros sought to seize the charter, but it was hidden in a hollow oak tree—the Charter Oak. Today, the city on the Connecticut River is an industrial and cultural center and the national hub of the insurance business.

Helena, Montana

The first capital of Montana was Bannack, from 1864 to 1865. Then came Virginia City, from 1865 to 1875. Finally, Helena was selected as the state capital in 1875. The city was originally a mining camp called Last Chance—after gold was discovered in a gulch that is now the town's main street. Then it was renamed Helena after a town in Minnesota. Today, it is a center of agricultural and industrial business.

Honolulu, Hawaii

Honolulu became the capital of Hawaii when King Kamehameha III moved there from Maui in 1845. The town was born when the harbor was discovered by whalers and traders from America and Europe, who began to stop there frequently in their ships. Today, it is an important agricultural, military, and naval center.

Indianapolis, Indiana

The first capital of Indiana was Vincennes (1800–1813). Then came Corydon from 1813 to 1824, when Indianapolis was named the capital. When Indianapolis was picked as the state capital, only scattered Indian villages and two families of settlers were in this area of rolling woodlands. A city was laid out in the wheel pattern of Washington, D.C., in a location chosen because it was in the center of the state. Today, Indianapolis is an agricultural and industrial center and the amateur sports capital of the United States.

Jackson, Mississippi

The first capital of Mississippi was Natchez (1798–1802). Then came Washington (1802–1817), Natchez again (1817–1821), and Columbia (1821–1822). Finally, Jackson was named the state capital in 1822. Jackson began as the trading post of a French-Canadian, Louis LeFleur, but later it was laid out as the state capital in a checkerboard pattern. Named for General Andrew Jackson, it was once the Confederate capital during the Civil War until it was destroyed by General Sherman's army. Nicknamed "Chimneyville," the city was rebuilt and is today the hub of the state.

Jefferson City, Missouri

The first capital of Missouri was St. Louis, in 1820. St. Charles was named the capital in 1821, and Jefferson City was selected in 1826. When the town named after Thomas Jefferson was chosen, it consisted of a foundry, a shop, and a mission. And when the state legislature had its first session in "Jeff City," the town had only 31 families.

Juneau, Alaska

The first capital of Alaska was Sitka (1867–1906); Juneau was selected in 1906. This city at the foot of Mt. Juneau was founded during the gold rush of 1880, and was named after a prospector, Joe Juneau, who discovered gold there. Thus it began as a gold mining camp, but today it is one of Alaska's most prominent ports and supports a large fishing industry. Lumbering is also important.

Lansing, Michigan

Detroit was the first state capital of Michigan (1835–1847), and Lansing was selected in 1847. When Lansing was chosen, the "city" consisted of one log house and a saw mill. Today, Lansing is a major heavy-industry center.

Lincoln, Nebraska
Omaha was the capital of Nebraska from 1855 to 1867, when Lincoln became the new capital. (But Lincoln supporters had to move the state books, documents, and furniture late at night in covered wagons to avoid angry residents of Omaha.) Only 30 people lived in the new capital then. Today, Lincoln is a major grain exchange, as well as a manufacturing, trade, and education center.

Little Rock, Arkansas
Arkansas Post was the state capital of Arkansas from 1819 to 1821, when Little Rock was selected. It is likely that Little Rock got its name from French explorers who called this area on the Arkansas River *La Petite Roche,* and the first shack was probably built on the site in 1812. Today, Little Rock is a modern center of commerce, industry, culture, and education.

Madison, Wisconsin
The first capital of Wisconsin, in 1836, was Belmont. In 1837 it was Burlington, which is now in Iowa. Finally, Madison was named the capital in 1838. Located on an isthmus between Lake Mendota and Lake Monona, Madison was a wilderness when it was named as the site of the capital. But today, it has a wealth of recreational, cultural, manufacturing, and educational facilities.

Montgomery, Alabama
The first capital of Alabama was St. Stephens (1817–1819). This was followed by Huntsville (1819–1820), Cahaba (1820–1826), Tuscaloosa (1826–1846), and, finally, Montgomery in 1846. Before the Civil War, Montgomery was a great cotton center, and in 1861 it became the first capital of the Confederacy. Jefferson Davis was inaugurated president here, and it was from Montgomery that the orders to fire on Fort Sumter came. Today, it is a city of historic homes and buildings.

Montpelier, Vermont
Several towns served as capitals of Vermont from 1777 to 1808, when Montpelier became the capital. Located on the banks of the Winooski River, Montpelier is a life insurance center.

Nashville, Tennessee
The first capital of Tennessee was Knoxville (1794–1806), then Kingston (1807), Knoxville again (1807–1811, 1817), Murfreesboro (1819–1825), and, finally, Nashville in 1826. The city began in 1779, when pioneers built a log stockade on the Cumberland River, naming it Fort Nashborough. It was taken by Union troops during the Civil War. Today, "the Athens of the South" is a busy town, and a leader in education, publishing, music recording, and manufacturing.

Oklahoma City, Oklahoma
The first capital of Oklahoma was Guthrie (1890–1910). Oklahoma City was selected in 1910. When the Oklahoma Territory was officially opened to settlement on the morning of April 22, 1889, what would become Oklahoma City was a barren prairie. By nightfall, 10,000 people had moved in. Oil was discovered there in 1928, and today, the city is a leader in the meat-packing, grain-processing, cotton-processing, and iron and steel industries.

Olympia, Washington
Olympia was named the state capital in 1889. Once known as Smithfield, a customhouse was located there, and the United States Collector of Customs persuaded the citizens to rename the town for the scenic Olympic Mountains. Today, it is a parklike community that functions as a seaport, manufacturing, and governmental center.

Phoenix, Arizona
Fort Whipple was the first capital of Arizona, in 1864. The next was Prescott (1864–1867), followed by Tucson (1867–1877), then Prescott again (1877–1889). Finally, Phoenix became the capital in 1889. The city lies on a flat desert surrounded by mountains and green, irrigated fields of cotton, lettuce, melons, vegetables, and alfalfa, and groves of citrus fruit and olives. It is a vacationers' mecca.

Providence, Rhode Island

From 1663 to 1854, this tiny state had five capitals all at the same time: Newport, East Greenwich, Bristol, South Kingstown, and Providence. The state still has intense regional rivalries. From 1854 to 1900, there were two state capitals—Newport and Providence. Finally, Providence became the sole capital in 1900. The city was named by its founder, Roger Williams, who felt that God's providence had guided him to the spot. Located around the junction of the Woonasquatucket and Moshassuck Rivers, the town served in turn as a farming, shipping, and textile center. Today, the city is a spacious modern community.

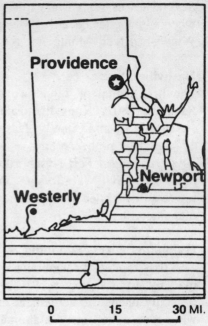

Pierre, South Dakota

The first capital of South Dakota was Yankton (1861–1883). Before the two Dakotas were separated, the next capital was Bismarck (now in North Dakota). In 1889 Pierre was named the capital. The city had long campaigned for this designation and won out because of its central location. Today, it is a cattle, farm, and business center.

Raleigh, North Carolina

The first capital of North Carolina was New Bern (1771–1776); then, from 1776 to 1794, there was no fixed capital. Raleigh was chosen as the capital in 1791, but was not used until 1794. Named for Sir Walter Raleigh, the town was laid out in 1792 as the state capital, after the legislature had ruled that an "unalterable seat of government" should be built within ten miles of Isaac Hunter's tavern, a popular watering hole that also had rooms for legislators. Actually, the site was located within four miles of the tavern. Lots were sold to settlers, and the money used to erect the capitol building and the governor's mansion. The capitol burned down in 1831, and the governor's mansion was destroyed by Union troops during their occupation of the city during the Civil War. But they were rebuilt, and today, Raleigh is a modern city that treasures its past.

Richmond, Virginia

The first capital of Virginia was Jamestown (1607–1699). Then came Williamsburg (1699–1780), followed by Richmond in 1780. The city has had a turbulent history. Indians and settlers warred over the ground where it now stands; Patrick Henry made his "liberty or death" speech there in 1755; British soldiers plundered it during the Revolutionary War; it was the capital of the Confederacy (1861–1865); and it suffered a bad fire as its citizens evacuated the city during the Civil War. Today, Richmond is a modern Southern city that takes pride in its long history.

Sacramento, California

Between 1850 and 1854, California had various capitals—San Jose, Vallejo, and Benicia. Sacramento was selected in 1854. Originally named New Helvetia, the town was established as a settlement for Swiss immigrants by Captain John A. Sutter. But when the California gold rush began, the town collapsed, because so many residents left to seek their fortunes. A new town, Sacramento City, was laid out, and it became the entrance to the gold rush country. Today, "the Camellia Capital of the World" is an important transportation and marketing center for the Sacramento Valley.

St. Paul, Minnesota

St. Paul was selected as the state capital in 1849. Located at the junction of the Mississippi and Minnesota Rivers, the city began in 1807 as Fort Snelling. In 1840 a French-Canadian trader, Pierre Parrant, established a settlement near the fort. His nickname was Pig's Eye, and that is what the town was named. In 1841 a Roman Catholic missionary persuaded the settlers to change the name to St. Paul. The town prospered on river trade, furs, and agriculture, and today it is a city of diversified industry and lovely homes.

Salem, Oregon

The first capital of Oregon was Oregon City (1849–1851), followed by Salem (1851–1855) and Corvallis (1855). Salem was renamed the capital in 1855. Located in the Willamette Valley, Salem is the third largest city in the state, and a center of food processing, light manufacturing, and wood products.

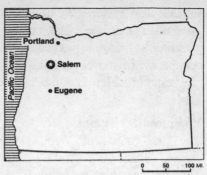

Salt Lake City, Utah

The first capital of Utah was Fillmore (1851–1856); Salt Lake City was selected in 1856. When Brigham Young and his Mormon followers arrived at what was to become Salt Lake City, it was a desert wilderness. The Mormons used irrigation and hard labor to turn it into a garden spot.

Santa Fe, New Mexico

The first capital of New Mexico was San Gabriel (1599–1610). In 1610 Santa Fe was named the capital, making it the oldest state capitol in the nation. That year, Don Pedro de Peralta laid out the Santa Fe plaza and built the Palace of the Governors, but the Spanish were driven out in 1680 during a Pueblo Indian revolt. The Spaniards re-entered the city peacefully in 1692. Then, in 1821, Santa Fe became a Mexican capital, and in 1846, part of the United States. The city was occupied briefly by Confederate troops during the Civil War.

Springfield, Illinois

The first capital of Illinois was Kaskaskia (1818–1820), followed by Vandalia (1820–1839). Finally, Springfield was selected in 1839. The city was settled in 1819 by Elisha Kelly and his four brothers, who came from North Carolina. Named for a nearby spring and the Kelly fields, the town is most famous as the home of Abraham Lincoln from 1837 until he left for Washington, D.C. in 1861 to assume his duties as president.

Tallahassee, Florida

Tallahassee has been the state capital since 1824, the year of its founding. Today, it is a city with the grace of old southern plantation life combined with the memory of frontier days.

Topeka, Kansas

The first capital of Kansas was Fort Leavenworth (1854). Then came Shawnee Mission (1854–1855), Pawnee (1855), and Lecompton (1855–1861). Topeka became the capital in 1861. Topeka was founded in 1854 because a town was needed on the banks of the Kansas (or Kaw) River along the new railroad line. The rail-

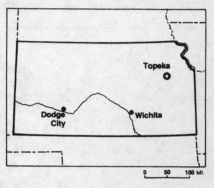

road became the Atchison, Topeka and Santa Fe. Today, Topeka is a modern city, and the site of the world-famous Menninger Foundation, the psychiatric clinic and research center.

Trenton, New Jersey

From 1703 to 1775, New Jersey had twin capitals—Perth Amboy and Burlington. From 1775 to 1790, when Trenton was selected, there was no specific capital. It was in 1776 that the town became famous, when General George Washington and his troops crossed the ice-clogged Delaware River to capture it from the British. The city has long been a leading pottery and rubber manufacturing center, and today it is the site of some 400 manufacturing plants.

★ 5 ★
Odds and Ends

With so many states and such a wide diversity of people, cultures, and history, it is no wonder that many strange and unusual events have occurred in the United States. Here is a sampler.

By Any Other Name

Several states have had other names besides the ones we know them by today.

• When it seceded from the Union at the beginning of the Civil War, Alabama called itself the Republic of Alabama for a short time.

• Before it was purchased by the United States, Alaska was called Russian America.

• After the Mexican War in 1846, and before it was admitted as a state, California was the California Republic.

• For one year, in 1859, Colorado was called the Jefferson Territory.

• Before it became a territory of the United States, Hawaii was the Kingdom of Hawaii from 1842 to 1894, and the Republic of Hawaii from 1894 to 1898.

• From 1784 to 1788, Tennessee was known as either the State of Franklin or the State of Frankland.
• After it won the Texas Revolution, Texas became the Republic of Texas—an independent entity.
• From 1849 to 1850, Utah was the State of Deseret.
• From 1777 to 1790, Vermont, an independent country, called itself New Connecticut. It became Vermont in 1790, but was still an independent state until 1791, when it entered the Union.
• When it broke away from Virginia in 1861, West Virginia called itself Kanawha.

Just Plain Trivia

• Technically, there are only 46 states in the Union, since four of what we call states officially call themselves commonwealths. The four states that are not states are: Kentucky, Massachusetts, Pennsylvania, and Virginia.
• Twenty-four states took their names from an Indian tribe or an Indian language: Alabama, Arizona, Arkansas, Connecticut, Idaho, Illinois, Indiana, Iowa, Kansas, Kentucky, Massachusetts, Michigan, Minnesota, Mississippi, Missouri, Nebraska, North Dakota, Ohio, Oklahoma, South Dakota, Tennessee, Utah, Wisconsin, Wyoming.
• Only two states—Alaska and Hawaii—do not border on another state.
• Four slave states stayed in the Union during the Civil War—Delaware, Kentucky, Maryland, and Missouri.
• Ten states have been named after persons. They are:
Georgia (George II of England)
Louisiana (Louis XIV of France)
Maryland (Henrietta Maria, the queen of Charles I of England)
New York (the Duke of York and Albany of England)
North Carolina (Charles I of England)
Pennsylvania (Sir William Penn, father of William Penn)
South Carolina (Charles I of England)
Virginia (Elizabeth I of England—"The Virgin Queen")
Washington (George Washington)
West Virginia (Elizabeth I of England—"The Virgin Queen")

• A state whose capital was named for a saint: Minnesota (St. Paul).

• Four states whose capitals have been named for presidents:
Mississippi (Jackson)
Missouri (Jefferson City)
Nebraska (Lincoln)
Wisconsin (Madison)

• Four states have capitals whose names end in the word "City":
Missouri (Jefferson City)
Nevada (Carson City)
Oklahoma (Oklahoma City)
Utah (Salt Lake City)

• Only two states border on eight other states: Missouri and Tennessee.

• Four states—Maryland, Massachusetts, Pennsylvania, and Virginia—and the District of Columbia contain the only seven historical places in the country permitted to fly the United States flag 24 hours a day: District of Columbia: The Washington Monument and the White House; Maryland: Ft. McHenry and Flag House Square; Massachusetts: Site of the Battle of Lexington; Pennsylvania: Valley Forge National Historic Park; Virginia: The United States Marine Corps Memorial in Arlington.

• Alaska was purchased from Russia for about two cents an acre, when it was called "Seward's Folly." But gold was discovered there in 1896, and, in 1969, some $900 million were bid for oil leases. It turned out to be a wise investment.

• Connecticut was in at the beginning of telephone service in the United States. The first commercial telephone switchboard was installed in New Haven in 1878, and that city had the first telephone directory—there were 21 phones in New Haven at the time. Hartford had the first pay phone in 1889.

• Connecticut is divided into counties, but they have no political importance. There is a sheriff for each of the eight counties, but his or her job is to assist in courtrooms, serve legal papers, and maintain the county jail—not to maintain the peace. The state has no other elected county governmental officers.

• The Great Seal of Delaware has a mistake on it. Under the seal itself are the dates 1793, 1847, and 1911. The date 1793 marks the year when the original seal was first modified, and 1847 represents the second modification. But the third change occurred in 1907, not 1911.

• The first building to be erected by the government in the District of Columbia was the White House.

• Florida produces 70 percent of the world's grapefruits.

• Georgia, with an area of 58,910 square miles, most closely approaches the average size of the 48 contiguous states.

• The Hawaiian language has only 12 letters—H, K, L, M, N, P, W, and the five vowels. Every word ends with a vowel, and there are no double consonants, since every consonant must be followed by a vowel.

• A large Hawaiian fish is called simply O. A much smaller Hawaiian fish is called *Homomomonukunukuaguk*.

• Idaho is the only state that has never had a foreign flag flying over it.

• The Indiana General Assembly once came close to passing a law making the geometrical value of *pi* three, instead of 3.1459, since three was a simpler number to work with.

• Louisiana does not have counties—it is divided into what are called parishes.

• Maine contains more than 1000 islands within its borders.

• The Pilgrims had intended to land farther south than Plymouth, but they had run out of beer. Aboard the *Mayflower* was John Alden, who was a skilled beer barrelmaker, and one of the first buildings in Plymouth was a brewery.

• Lobsters were once so plentiful in Massachusetts that they were used as fertilizer.

• Nebraska is the only state in the Union with a unicameral state legislature—having only one house, rather than two.

• In building the Hoover Dam in Nevada, concrete had to be poured continually for two years.

• New Hampshire has the largest state legislature of any state—more than 400 members.

• New Hampshire was the site of the signing of the 1905 peace treaty that ended the Russo-Japanese War.

• The first parking meter was installed in Oklahoma City, Oklahoma. The cost was five cents.

• In 1972 two Oklahoma governors had a historic contest. Governor David Hall threw a hand-sized wad of cow dung 68 feet, but was defeated by ex-Governor Dewey Bartlett who tossed one 138 feet.

• Oregon contains the only major city that was named by a coin toss. Amos Lovejoy from Boston and Francis Pettygrove from Portland, Maine, laid out the new city of Portland, Oregon, and each wanted to name it after his home town. So the coin was flipped, and Pettygrove won.

• Rhode Island, the smallest state, has the longest name. Officially, its name is the State of Rhode Island and the Providence Plantations.

• In South Dakota, the huge presidential faces carved into Mount Rushmore National Memorial average 60 feet from the top of the head to the chin. Lincoln's mouth is 22 feet wide.

• In the 1880s, when the western boundary of South Dakota was being drawn, the line was supposed to lie on the 27th meridian west from Washington, D.C. But the boundary surveyed down

from the north missed the one that was being drawn up from the south by about one mile. The two lines were connected anyway, and a slight jog can be seen on the map of the state where it intersects the Montana-Wyoming borderline.

• Texas has had six national flags flying over it—those of Spain, France, Mexico, the Republic of Texas, the Confederate States of America, and the United States of America.

• Texas has the highest number of drive-in theaters of any state.

• Texas is the only state that can legally partition itself—into four states, if it is so desires.

• Utah is the only state that ends with an "h."

• At the beginning of the 1800s, more than 20 percent of the population of all the United States was located in Virginia.

• West Virginia is the only state in the Union to have been carved out of another state—Virginia.
• Wyoming was the first state to give women the vote—in 1869.
• More state names end with the letter "a" than any other letter. There are 21 of them:

Alabama	Iowa	North Dakota
Alaska	Louisiana	Oklahoma
Arizona	Minnesota	Pennsylvania
California	Montana	South Carolina
Florida	Nebraska	South Dakota
Georgia	Nevada	Virginia
Indiana	North Carolina	West Virginia

It's the Law

All states have, or have had, some laws that sound quite strange. Here is an assortment of some of the odder ones. Many of them, of course, have been repealed or replaced, and those that are left are almost never enforced, but somewhere, somehow, they were real laws.

Alabama It was illegal to wear a false moustache in church if it made people laugh.
It was illegal to wear shoes with heels higher than one-half inch.
It was forbidden to put salt on railroad tracks.
It was taboo for a man to beat his wife with a stick larger than his thumb.
Books about outlaws were banned.

Arizona It was illegal to kick a mule. But if a mule kicked a person, it could not be prosecuted.

Arkansas An automobile had to be preceded by a man carrying a red flag.
It was illegal to blindfold cows on public highways.
Filing down a mule's teeth was forbidden.
It was illegal to set up a lunch counter on Memorial Day within a half-mile of a Confederate cemetery.

California It was illegal to shoot any game bird or animal from a car—except a whale.

Peeling an orange in a hotel room was forbidden.

A woman could not go for a drive in a housecoat.

It was taboo to pick feathers from a live goose.

Trapping birds in cemeteries was illegal.

Anyone setting a trap for a mouse had to have a permit.

Colorado It was illegal to watch a dogfight.

Hunting ducks from an airplane was forbidden.

It was not permitted to throw shoes at a bridal couple.

Connecticut Colonial law forbade mothers from kissing their children on Sunday.

It was illegal for a man to write love letters to a girl if her mother had forbidden him to see her.

Anyone flying an American flag that had lost one or more of its stars or stripes was subject to a $7 fine.

Only licensed clergymen were permitted to cross a river on Sunday.

It was illegal to lure bees away from their owner.

Building a dam was legal only if one were a beaver.

It colonial times, children could face the death penalty for disobeying their parents.

District of Columbia All taxicabs had to carry brooms and shovels.

It was illegal to punch a bull in the nose.

Florida All residents had to wear clothing while taking a bath in a bathtub.

A person could be sent to jail for luring his or her neighbor's cook away and then hiring him or her.

It was illegal to remain in an election booth for more than five minutes, and conviction could lead to a fine or a prison sentence.

Georgia Beach lifeguards had to wear bright-red bathing suits and a harness around their necks attached to a 200-foot-long lifeline.

Cruelty by a dentist was only a misdemeanor.

Hawaii It was illegal to insert pennies in one's ears.

Barbers were not permitted to lather their customers with a shaving brush.

Idaho It was illegal to fish for trout from the back of a giraffe.

No one could buy a chicken after dark without the permission of the sheriff.

It was forbidden for a man to give his sweetheart a box of candy weighing less than 50 pounds.

Illinois All healthy males between 21 and 50 years of age had to work in the streets for two days each year.

It was permissible to send an animal to jail.

Catching fish with dynamite was forbidden.

Indiana It was illegal to wear a moustache if the wearer was one who "habitually kisses human beings."

Hotel bed sheets had to be at least 99 inches long and 81 inches wide.

It was illegal for roller-skating instructors to lead their female students astray during a lesson.

Taking a bath during the wintertime was forbidden.

Iowa It was illegal for a woman *not* to wear a corset.

Kansas It was illegal to exhibit the eating of snakes.

Candidates for public office could not give away cigars on election day.

Kentucky A man could not buy a coat unless his wife was along to help in the selection.

It was illegal to sleep on the floor of the Kentucky State House.

No one could sleep in a restaurant legally.

A wife had to receive her husband's permission to rearrange the furniture.

A state law read that "burglary can only be committed in the night-time."

It was illegal for a man to marry his wife's grandmother.

An old law read, "No female shall appear in a bathing suit on any highway within this state unless she is escorted by at least two officers or unless she is armed with a club." The law was later amended to read "The provisions of this statute shall not apply to females weighing less than 90 pounds nor exceeding 200 pounds; nor shall it apply to female horses."

Louisiana By law, any person had the right to grow as tall as he or she liked.

It was illegal for a beauty operator to put cold cream or powder on a customer's feet.

Whistling on Sunday was forbidden.

Maine Buildings made of round logs were exempt from taxes.

All fishermen were required to take off their hats to the game warden.

It was illegal to lead a bear around with a rope.
Walking the streets with one's shoelaces undone was forbidden.
It was illegal to set fire to a mule.

Maryland It was illegal in parts of Maryland to mistreat an oyster.

Massachusetts Women were not permitted to enter beauty shops for the purposes of hair tinting or hair waving.
It was illegal to show movies that lasted more than 20 minutes.
Eating peanuts in church was forbidden.
A dachshund could not be kept as a pet dog.
Digging up the state flower, the mayflower, was punishable by a $50 fine. If the crime were committed in disguise, the fine went up to $100.
It was illegal for a bill collector to dress in "unusual or striking costumes."
Putting tomatoes in clam chowder was forbidden.

Michigan It was illegal to hitch a crocodile to a fire hydrant.
A woman could not lift her skirt more than six inches to avoid a puddle.
By state law, a census of bees had to be made every winter.
If a woman were to leave her husband, he could take possession of all her clothing.
A woman's hair was the property of her husband.
A married couple had to live together or risk imprisonment.

Minnesota It was illegal for a woman to appear on the street dressed as Santa Claus.

Men's and women's underwear could not be hung on the same clothesline at the same time.

Mississippi It was illegal to soap railroad tracks.

When one bought a can of snuff, he or she had to stand at least an arm's length from the seller.

Nebraska It was illegal to picnic in the same place twice within a 30-day period.

A person who sneezed in public could be fined.

A mother could wave her daughter's hair only if she had a state license.

Nevada It was illegal to drive camels onto main highways.

New Jersey No one was permitted to delay or detain a homing pigeon.

New Mexico Bicycle horns had to have a harmonious sound.

It was illegal to climb a building to get a free view of a ball game.

New York It was illegal to pawn an American flag.

A person could be arrested for ringing the doorbell and disturbing the occupant of a house.

A state law once read, "Two vehicles which are passing each other in opposite directions shall have the right of way."

It was a misdemeanor to arrest a dead man for a debt.

Card playing on a train was against the law.

North Carolina Bus companies were permitted to provide free transportation to blind clergymen.

It was illegal to sing out of tune.

Drinking water or milk on a train was not permitted.

North Dakota It was illegal to trap birds in a cemetery.

Railroad engineers could not take their engines home with them unless they carried a full crew.

Oklahoma It was against the law to get a fish drunk.

Even though it is an inland state, it was against the law to catch whales in Oklahoma waters.

A person could be charged with first-degree murder for killing an animal "with malicious intent."

It was illegal to eavesdrop.

A steamboat captain could be held guilty of manslaughter if his boat blew up and killed anyone during a boat race.

Trapping birds in a cemetery was illegal.

Oregon It was illegal for a dead person to serve on a jury.

Pennsylvania There was a 45-cent fine for cursing, but if the name of God were mentioned, the fine went to 67 cents.

It was illegal to talk loudly at picnics.

Every innkeeper had to provide good entertainment for his or her guests.

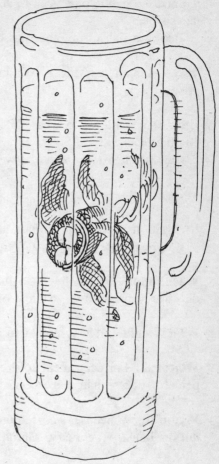

South Carolina It was illegal to file down a mule's teeth.

All citizens were required to carry guns to church.

A person who was attempting suicide and accidentally killed someone else was subject to capital punishment.

It was illegal to "act in an obnoxious manner on the campus of a girls' school without the permission of the principal."

South Dakota An 80-year-old woman could not stop in the street to talk to a young married man.

Tennessee It was illegal for a motorist to drive unless he had warned the public one week in advance by inserting a notice in the newspapers.

Taking a fish off another person's hook was forbidden.

Texas A man carrying a pair of pliers could have been sent to prison.

Utah It was illegal to wear shoes with heels higher than one and one-half inches.

Daylight had to be seen between two dancing partners.

Vermont It was illegal to paint a horse.

Virginia It was illegal to have a bathtub in the house.

Before the Revolutionary War, taxes could be paid in tobacco.

Washington It was illegal to hunt ducks from a rowboat unless one were upright and visible from the waist up.

West Virginia It was illegal to sneeze on a train.

Wisconsin For each meal sold costing 25 cents or more, a small peice of cheese had to be served.

Wyoming A license was required to take a picture of a rabbit during January, February, March, or April.

☆ 6 ☆
A Little Learning

The United States has long been one of the world's strongest supporters of public education—even as high as the university level. Schools are free in every state, and even the state universities are inexpensive. Here is a rundown of education in each state.

Public School Beginnings

Most states began a system of free public education as soon as possible—sometimes even before they were states. Here is when they started, from the first to the last.

State	Date	State	Date
1. Massachusetts	1647	9. Michigan	1809
2. Connecticut	1650	10. Indiana	1816
3. South Carolina	1710	11. New Jersey	1817
4. Louisiana	1772	12. Delaware	1824
5. North Carolina	1776	13. Ohio	1825
6. New York	1784	14. Vermont	1825
7. New Hampshire	1789	15. Maryland	1826
8. Rhode Island	1800	16. Pennsylvania	1834

State	Date	State	Date
17. Kentucky	1838	34. West Virginia	1863
18. Iowa	1839	35. Nevada	1865
19. Missouri	1839	36. Florida	1868
20. Arkansas	1843	37. Maine	1868
21. Hawaii	1843	38. Mississippi	1869
22. Wisconsin	1848	39. Wyoming	1869
23. Minnesota	1849	40. Alaska	c.1860s
24. California	1850	41. Virginia	1870
25. Oregon	1851	42. Arizona	1871
26. Alabama	1854	43. Georgia	1872
27. Texas	1854	44. Tennessee	1873
28. Illinois	1855	45. Idaho	1890
29. Kansas	1855	46. Oklahoma	1890
30. Nebraska	1855	47. Utah	1890
31. Colorado	1859	48. New Mexico	1891
32. North Dakota	1862	49. Montana	1893
33. South Dakota	1862	50. Washington	1895

Public School Enrollment

The states have a wide range of of numbers of pupils attending public schools, but that has to do with their populations. Here are the enrollments, from most to fewest.

State	Enrollment	State	Enrollment
1. California	4,489,322	12. Virginia	979,417
2. Texas	3,236,787	13. Indiana	964,129
3. New York	2,594,070	14. Massachusetts	825,320
4. Illinois	1,811,446	15. Tennessee	823,783
5. Ohio	1,793,411	16. Missouri	802,060
6. Pennsylvania	1,668,542	17. Louisiana	793,093
7. Florida	1,664,774	18. Washington	775,755
8. Michigan	1,606,344	19. Wisconsin	772,363
9. Georgia	1,110,947	20. Alabama	729,234
10. New Jersey	1,092,982	21. Minnesota	721,481
11. North Carolina	1,085,976	22. Maryland	683,797

State	Enrollment	State	Enrollment
23. Kentucky	642,696	38. Idaho	212,444
24. South Carolina	614,921	39. Maine	211,817
25. Oklahoma	584,212	40. Nevada	168,353
26. Arizona	572,421	41. Hawaii	166,160
27. Colorado	560,236	42. New Hampshire	166,045
28. Mississippi	505,550	43. Montana	152,207
29. Iowa	480,826	44. Rhode Island	134,061
30. Connecticut	465,465	45. South Dakota	126,817
31. Oregon	455,895	46. North Dakota	119,004
32. Arkansas	437,036	47. Alaska	105,678
33. Utah	423,386	48. Wyoming	98,455
34. Kansas	421,112	49. Delaware	95,659
35. West Virginia	344,236	50. Vermont	92,755
36. New Mexico	287,229	51. D.C.	86,435
37. Nebraska	268,100		

Private School Enrollment

Many students in every state attend private elementary and secondary schools. Here is the enrollment, state by state, from the greatest number to the smallest.

State	Enrollment	State	Enrollment
1. New York	579,670	4. Illinois	349,463
2. California	513,709	5. Ohio	268,357
3. Pennsylvania	402,058	6. New Jersey	229,878

State	Enrollment	State	Enrollment
7. Michigan	211,871	30. Hawaii	37,147
8. Florida	204,988	31. Colorado	35,250
9. Wisconsin	162,361	32. Kansas	33,889
10. Louisiana	158,921	33. Rhode Island	29,875
11. Texas	148,534	34. Oregon	27,828
12. Massachusetts	138,333	35. Delaware	23,374
13. Missouri	126,319	36. D.C.	21,203
14. Maryland	106,447	37. New Hampshire	20,721
15. Indiana	100,234	38. Arkansas	18,423
16. Minnesota	88,996	39. New Mexico	18,027
17. Connecticut	88,404	40. Maine	17,540
18. Georgia	82,505	41. Oklahoma	16,335
19. Virginia	75,069	42. West Virginia	12,608
20. Tennessee	71,617	43. South Dakota	10,898
21. Kentucky	69,728	44. North Dakota	10,659
22. Alabama	62,669	45. Montana	7,668
23. North Carolina	58,078	46. Vermont	7,555
24. Washington	55,950	47. Nevada	6,599
25. Iowa	55,277	48. Idaho	5,839
26. Mississippi	50,116	49. Utah	5,555
27. South Carolina	49,619	50. Alaska	3,800
28. Arizona	40,261	51. Wyoming	3,036
29. Nebraska	38,574		

High School Graduates

Nationwide, 73.1 percent of all students graduate from high school. But the percentages of high school graduation vary widely from state to state. Here are the graduation percentages from highest to lowest.

State	% Graduated	State	% Graduated
1. Minnesota	88.7	4. Nebraska	86.7
2. North Dakota	88.4	5. Iowa	86.6
3. South Dakota	86.9	6. Montana	84.5

State	% Graduated	State	% Graduated
7. Hawaii	84.5	30. Oklahoma	75.8
8. Kansas	84.1	31. New Hampshire	74.6
9. Wisconsin	83.7	32. Alaska	73.6
10. Vermont	82.7	33. New Mexico	73.2
11. Utah	82.5	34. Rhode Island	72.0
12. Nevada	81.3	35. Michigan	71.4
13. Pennsylvania	81.1	36. Delaware	71.0
14. New Jersey	79.7	37. Oregon	70.8
15. Idaho	79.6	38. Arizona	70.0
16. Wyoming	79.6	39. Alabama	69.5
17. Ohio	79.2	40. North Carolina	69.1
18. Maine	78.8	41. California	68.5
19. Arkansas	78.6	42. Kentucky	67.9
20. Connecticut	78.2	43. South Carolina	67.8
21. Washington	78.1	44. Tennessee	67.2
22. Illinois	77.8	45. New York	66.7
23. West Virginia	77.1	46. Texas	65.9
24. Virginia	76.6	47. Mississippi	65.6
25. Maryland	76.5	48. Georgia	65.0
26. Missouri	76.1	49. Florida	63.5
27. Colorado	76.0	50. Louisiana	61.6
28. Massachusetts	76.0	51. D.C.	59.5
29. Indiana	75.9		

State Universities—Oldest to Youngest

One of the first things that the various states did was to establish state universities. Here they are, from oldest to youngest, with their dates of founding.

State University	Founded
1. The University of Delaware	1743
2. Rutgers (New Jersey)	1766
3. The University of Georgia	1785
4. The University of Vermont	1791
5. The University of Tennessee	1794
6. The University of North Carolina	1795
7. The University of South Carolina	1801
8. The State University of New York	1816
9. The University of Michigan	1817
10. The University of Virginia	1819
11. Indiana University	1820
12. The University of Alabama	1831

State University	Founded
13. The University of Missouri	1839
14. The University of Oklahoma	1842
15. The University of Mississippi	1844
16. The University of Iowa	1847
17. The University of Wisconsin	1848
18. The University of Utah	1850
19. The University of Minnesota	1851
20. The University of Florida	1853
21. Pennsylvania State University	1855
22. The University of Maryland	1856
23. Louisiana State University	1860
24. The University of Washington	1861
25. The University of South Dakota	1862
26. The University of Massachusetts	1863
27. The University of Maine	1865
28. The University of Kentucky	1865
29. The University of Kansas	1866
30. The University of New Hampshire	1866
31. The University of Illinois	1867
32. West Virginia University	1867
33. The University of California	1868
34. The University of Nebraska	1869
35. The Ohio State University	1870
36. The University of Arkansas	1871
37. The University of Nevada	1874
38. The University of Colorado	1876
39. The University of Oregon	1876
40. The University of Connecticut	1881
41. The University of North Dakota	1883
42. The University of Texas	1883
43. The University of Arizona	1885
44. The University of Wyoming	1886
45. The University of Idaho	1889
46. The University of New Mexico	1889
47. The University of Rhode Island	1892
48. The University of Montana	1893
49. The University of Hawaii	1907
50. The University of Alaska	1917

★ 7 ★
LET'S HAVE FUN

Every state seems to have hundreds of places to have fun. Here are some outstanding examples.

State Fairs

Most states have state or regional fairs where there are exhibits, shows, midway rides competition, and just plain fun.

Where?	When?
Alabama, Birmingham	Early October to mid-October
Alaska, Palmer	Late August to early September
Arizona, Phoenix	Late October to early November
Arkansas, Little Rock	Late September to early October
California, Sacramento	Late August to early September
Colorado, Pueblo	Late August to early September
Connecticut, Part of Eastern States Exposition in Springfield, Massachusetts	September

Where?	When?
Delaware, Harrington	End of July
Florida, Tampa	Early to mid-February
Georgia, Macon	Late October
Hawaii, Honolulu	Late May to mid-June
Idaho, 1 Boise	Late August
2 Blackfoot	Early September
Illinois, Springfield	Early August
Indiana, Indianapolis	Mid-August
Iowa, Des Moines	Mid- to late August
Kansas, Hutchinson	Second week in September
Kentucky, Louisville	Mid-August
Louisiana, Shreveport	Late October
Maine, Skowhegan	· Mid-August
Maryland, Timonium	Late August to early September
Massachusetts, Part of the Eastern States Exposition in Springfield, Massachusetts	September
Michigan, Detroit	Late August to early September
Minnesota, St. Paul	Late August to early September
Mississippi, Jackson	Second full week in October
Missouri, Sedalia	Mid- to late August
Montana, Great Falls	Late July to early August
Nebraska, Lincoln	Late August to early September
Nevada, Reno	Late August
New Hampshire, Plymouth	Late August
New Jersey, Cherry Hill	Early August
New Mexico, Albuquerque	Mid-September
New York, Syracuse	Late August to early September
North Carolina, Raleigh	Mid-October
North Dakota, Minot	Third week in July
Ohio, Columbus	Early to late August
Oklahoma, Oklahoma City	Late September to early October
Oregon, Salem	Late August to early September
Pennsylvania, Harrisburg	Mid-January
Rhode Island, East Greenwich	Mid-August
South Carolina, Columbia	Mid-October
South Dakota, Huron	Late August to early September
Tennessee, Nashville	Mid-September

Where?	**When?**
Texas, Dallas	Mid-October
Utah, Salt Lake City	Early September
Vermont, Rutland	Early September
Virginia, Richmond	Late September to early October
Washington, 1 Centralia (Southwest Washington State Fair)	Third week in August
2 Colville (Northeast Washington State Fair)	Mid-September
3 Puyallup (Western Washington Fair)	Mid-September
4 Walla Walla (Southeastern Washington Fair)	Early September
5 Yakima (Central Washington State Fair)	Late September
West Virginia, Fairlea	Late August
Wisconsin, West Allis	Late July to early August
Wyoming, Douglas	Late August

Amusement and Theme Parks

Another great place for family fun is the amusement park or theme park. Here are several of them, grouped by states.

Alaska
Alaskaland (Fairbanks)

Arizona
London Bridge English Village (Lake Havasu City)

Arkansas
Dogpatch, USA (Harrison)
Magic Springs Family Theme Park (Hot Springs)

California
Castle Amusement Park (Riverside)
Children's Fairyland (Oakland)
Disneyland (Anaheim)
Great America (Santa Clara)
Knott's Berry Farm (Buena Park)
Santa's Village (Skyforest)
Six Flags Magic Mountain (Valencia)
Universal Studios (Los Angeles)

Colorado
Flying W Ranch (Colorado Springs)

Florida
Busch Gardens—"The Dark Continent" (Tampa)
Circus Winter Quarters (Venice)
Cypress Gardens (Winter Haven)
Miracle Strip Amusement Park (Panama City)
Old Town (Kissimmee)
Sea World/Florida (Orlando)
Shipwreck Island (Panama City)
Six Flags—Atlantis (Hollywood)
Universal Studios Florida (Orlando)
Walt Disney World (Lake Buena Vista)
Water Mania (Kissimmee)
Weeki Wachee Spring (Brooksville)
Wet 'N Wild (Orlando)

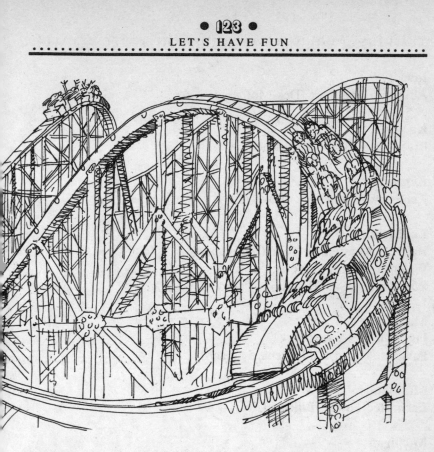

Georgia
Six Flags Over Georgia (Atlanta)
Stone Mountain Park (Atlanta)
White Water (Marietta)

Hawaii
Castle Park—Hawaii's Enchanted Kingdom (Honolulu)

Illinois
Racing Rapids Action Water Park (Dundee)
Santa's Village Theme Park (Dundee)
Seven Acres Antique Village and Museum (Union)

Indiana
Columbian Park (Lafayette)
Holiday World (Santa Claus)
Riverside Park (Logansport)

Iowa
Adventureland Park (Des Moines)

Kansas
Riverside Park (Independence)

Kentucky
Kentucky Action Park (Cave City)

Louisiana
Hamel's Amusement Park (Shreveport)
Water Town (Shreveport)
Waterland, USA (Houma)

Maine
Funtown, USA (Saco)
Palace Playland (Old Orchard Beach)

Maryland
Enchanted Forest (Ellicott City)

Michigan
Boblo Island (Detroit)
Michigan's Adventure Amusement Park (Muskegon)
Pleasure Island Water Fun Park (Muskegon)
Suwanee Park (Dearborn)

Minnesota
Depot Square (Duluth)
Paul Bunyan Amusement Center (Brainerd)

Missouri
Oceans of Fun (Kansas City)
Six Flags Over Mid-America (St. Louis)
Worlds of Fun (Kansas City)

Nevada
Ponderosa Ranch and Western Theme Park (Crystal Bay)

New Hampshire
Clark's Trading Post (Lincoln)
Fantasy Farm and Whale's Tail Water Park (Lincoln)
Santa's Village (Jefferson)
Story Land (Jackson)
Surf Coaster (Laconia)
Water Country (Portsmouth)

New Jersey
Action Park (Vernon)
Land of Make Believe (Hackettstown)
Six Flags Great Adventure (Jackson)
Storybook Land (Atlantic City)

New York
Astroland Amusement Park (Brooklyn)
Carson City (Catskill)
Darien Lake Theme Park (Buffalo)
Enchanted Forest of the Adirondacks (Old Forge)
Fantasy Island (Niagara Falls)
Great Escape (Lake George Village)
Niagara Splash Water Park (Niagara Falls)
Santa's Workshop (Wilmington)
Zoom Flume Aquamusement Park (East Durham)

North Carolina
Carowinds (Charlotte)
Frontier Fort (Wilmington)
Ghost Town in the Sky (Maggie Valley)
Santa's Land (Cherokee)
Tweetsie Railroad (Blowing Rock)

Ohio
Cedar Point (Sandusky)
Erieview Park (Geneva-on-the-Lake)
Geauga Lake (Aurora)
Kings Island (Mason)
Sea World (Aurora)

Oklahoma
Bell's Amusement Park (Tulsa)
Big Splash Water Park (Tulsa)
Frontier City (Oklahoma City)
White Water (Oklahoma City)

Oregon
Enchanted Forest (Salem)
Oaks Amusement Park (Portland)

Pennsylvania
Dutch Wonderland (Lancaster)
Fantasy Forest (Altoona)
Hersheypark (Hershey)
Idlewild Park (Ligonier)
Kennywood Park (Pittsburgh)
Story Book Forest (Ligonier)
Waldameer Park (Erie)

Rhode Island
Rocky Point Amusement Park (Warwick)

South Dakota
Flinstones Bedrock City (Custer)
Story Book Island (Rapid City)

Tennessee
Dollywood (Pigeon Forge)
Libertyland (Memphis)
Magic World (Pigeon Forge)
Ogle's Water Park (Pigeon Forge)
Opryland (Nashville)

Texas
Alamo Village Movie Location (Brackettville)
Rolling Waters (Texarkana)
Six Flags Over Texas (Arlington)
Water Park USA (San Antonio)
Water Wonderland (Odessa)
Wonderland Amusement Park (Amarillo)

Utah
Lagoon Amusement Park and Pioneer Village (Salt Lake City)
Raging Waters (Salt Lake City)

Vermont
Santa's Land (Brattleboro)

Virginia
Busch Gardens—"The Old Country" (Williamsburg)

Washington
Enchanted Village (Tacoma)
Fun Forest Amusement Park (Seattle)
Never Never Land (Tacoma)

Wisconsin
Bay Beach Amusement Park and Wildlife Sanctuary (Green Bay)
Circus World Museum (Baraboo)
Dutchman's Landing Family Fun Park (Green Bay)
Riverview Park and Waterworld (Wisconsin Dells)
Water Thrills (Waupaca)

Historic Attractions

There are many places in the country where visitors can relive the past—historic sites that have been preserved or restored to take us back in time. Here are some of them, with their locations.

Alabama
Burritt Museum and Park (Huntsville)
Museum Village at Constitution Hall Park (Huntsville)
Old North Hull Street Historic District (Montgomery)
Pike Pioneer Museum (Troy)

Arizona
Old Tombstone (Tombstone)
Old Tucson (Tucson)

Rawhide (Scottsdale)
Sharlot Hall Museum (Prescott)

Arkansas
Arkansas Territorial Restoration
  (Little Rock)
Mountain Village 1890
  (Bull Shoals)
Old Washington Historic State Park (Hope)
Ozark Folk Center State Park (Mountain View)
Pioneer Village (Rison)
Robinson Farm Museum and Heritage Center (Valley Springs)

California
Alcatraz Island (San Francisco)
Ardenwood Regional Preserve and Historic Farm (Fremont)
Calico Ghost Town Regional Park (Barstow)
Columbia State Historic Park (Sonora)
El Presidio de Santa Barbara State Historic Park (Santa Barbara)
Fisherman's Village (Marina del Rey)
Historic Ships (San Francisco)
Kern County Museum and Pioneer Village (Bakersfield)
Laws Railroad Museum and Historical Site (Bishop)
Monterey State Historic Park (Monterey)
Old Sacramento Historic District (Sacramento)
Old Town (San Diego)
Old Town San Diego State Historic Park (San Diego)
Outdoor Museum (Yreka)
Seaport Village (San Diego)
Stagecoach Inn Museum Complex (Thousand Oaks)

Colorado
Argo Town, USA (Idaho Springs)
Buckskin Joe (Cañon City)
Centennial Village (Greeley)
Georgetown Loop Historic Mining and Railroad Park (Georgetown)
Old Town (Burlington)
United States Air Force Academy (Colorado Springs)
White Horse Ranch Historic Site (Colorado Springs)

Connecticut
Massacoh Plantation—Simsbury Historic Center (Simsbury)
Mystic Seaport (Mystic)
Nook Farm (Hartford)
United States Coast Guard Academy (New London)

Delaware
John Dickinson Plantation (Dover)
Winterthur Museum and Gardens (Wilmington)

Florida
Kissimmee Cow Camp (Lake Wales)
Manatee Village Historical Park (Bradenton)
Pioneer Florida Museum (Dade City)
Spanish Quarter (St. Augustine)
Tallahassee Junior Museum (Tallahassee)

Georgia
Georgia Agrirama—Agricultural
    Heritage Center (Tifton)
Museum of the Hills and Fantasy
    Kingdom (Helen)
New Echota Historic Site (Calhoun)
Westville (Lumpkin)

Illinois
Bishop Hill State Historic Site
    (Bishop Hill)
Joseph Smith Historic Center
    (Nauvoo)
Lincoln's New Salem State Historic
    Site (Petersburg)
Long Grove Village (Arlington Heights)
Midway Village (Rockford)
Naper Settlement (Naperville)
Nauvoo Restoration (Nauvoo)

Indiana
Amish Acres (Nappanee)
Amishville (Geneva)
Conner Prairie (Noblesville)
Historic Billie Creek Village (Rockville)
Historic Fort Wayne (Fort Wayne)
Historic New Harmony (New Harmony)
Lincoln Living Historical Farm
  (Lincoln Boyhood National Memo-
  rial and Lincoln State Park)

Iowa
Bentonsport-National Historic District (Fairfield)
Fort Dodge Historical Museum (Fort Dodge)
Herbert Hoover National Historic Site (Iowa City)
Heritage Village (Des Moines)
Homestead (Amana Colonies)
Kalona Historical Village (Kalona)
Living History Farms (Des Moines)
Nelson Pioneer Farm and Craft Museum (Oskaloosa)
Pella Historical Village Museum (Pella)
South Amana (Amana Colonies)

Kansas
Barton County Historical Village (Great Bend)
Fort Larned National Historic Site (Larned)
Fort Markley and Indian Village (Seneca)
Fort Scott National Historic Site (Fort Scott)
Historic Front Street (Dodge City)
"Old Abilene Town" (Abilene)
Old Fort Bissell (Phillipsburg)
Old Shawnee Town (Kansas City)

Kentucky
Constitution Square State Shrine (Danville)
Lincoln Homestead State Park (Bardstown)
My Old Kentucky Home State Park (Bardstown)
Old Bardstown Village and Civil War Museum (Bardstown)
Old Fort Harrod State Park (Harrodsburg)

Old Washington (Maysville)
Shaker Village at Pleasant Hill (Harrodsburg)

Louisiana
Fort St. Jean Baptiste State Commemorative Area (Natchitoches)
Heritage Museum and Village (Baton Rouge)
Washington (Opelousas)

Maine
Norlands Living History Center (Auburn)
York Village (York)

Maryland
Chesapeake Bay Maritime Museum (St. Michaels)
Fort McHenry National Monument and Historic Shrine (Baltimore)
Historic St. Mary's City (St. Mary's City)
United States Naval Academy (Annapolis)

Massachusetts
Battleship Cove (Fall River)
Fruitlands Museums (Concord)
Gore Place (Waltham)
Hancock Shaker Village (Pittsfield)
Historic Deerfield (Deerfield)
Old Sturbridge Village (Sturbridge)
Pioneer Village (Salem)
Plimoth Plantation (Plymouth)
Salem Maritime National Historic Site (Salem)
Storrowtown Village (Springfield)

Michigan
Colonial Michilimackinac State Park (Mackinaw City)
Crossroads Village/Huckleberry Railroad (Flint)
Dutch Village (Holland)
Greenfield Village (Dearborn)
Historic Fort Wayne (Detroit)
Mackinac Island State Park (Mackinac Island)
White Pine Village (Ludington)

Minnesota
Freeborn County Historical Museum and Village (Albert Lea)
Lumbertown, USA (Brainerd)
Nobles County Pioneer Village (Worthington)
Pioneer Farms and Village (Roseau)
Rapid River Logging Camp (Park Rapids)
Village of Yesteryear (Owatonna)

Mississippi
Grand Gulf Military Park (Port Gibson)

Missouri
Benjamin Ranch (Kansas City)
Bequette-Ribault Living History Museum (Sainte Genevieve)
Fort Osage (Independence)
Mark Twain Museum and Boyhood Home (Hannibal)
Missouri Town 1855 (Blue Springs)

Montana
Grant-Kohrns Ranch National Historic Site (Deer Lodge)
Nevada City (Virginia City)
St. Mary's Mission (Hamilton)
World Museum of Mining and Hell Roarin' Gulch (Butte)

Nebraska
Brownville (Auburn)
Fort Robinson Museum (Crawford)
Harold Warp Pioneer Village (Minden)
Railroad Town (Grand Island)
Trails and Rails Museum (Kearney)

Nevada
Bonnie Springs Old Nevada (Las Vegas)

New Hampshire
America's Stonehenge (Salem)
Canterbury Shaker Village (Concord)
Six Gun City (Jefferson)

New Jersey
Batsto State Historic Site (Batsto)
Clinton Historical Museum Village (Clinton)
Fosterfields Historical Farm (Morristown)
Historic Allaire Village (Allaire State Park)
Historic Cold Spring Village (Cape May)
Historic Towne of Smithville (Absecon)
Victorian Wheaton Village (Millville)
Waterloo Village Restoration (Stanhope)

New Mexico
Ghost Town of Shakespeare (Lordsburg)
Old Town (Albuquerque)
The Plaza (Santa Fe)

New York
Adirondack Museum (Blue Mountain Lake)
Athens (Catskill)
Bronck Museum (Coxsakie)
Erie Canal Village (Rome)
The Farmer's Museum and Village Crossroads (Cooperstown)
Genesee Country Village and Museum (Avon)
Huguenot Street Old Stone Houses (New Paltz)
Museum Village in Orange County (Monroe)
Old Bethpage Village Restoration (Bethpage)
Old Canal Town (Delevan)
Philipsburg Manor (North Tarrytown)

Rensselaerville (Albany)
Richmondtown Restoration (State Island)
Suffolk Marine Museum (Sayville)
United States Merchant Marine Academy (Kings Point)
United States Military Academy (West Point)

North Carolina
Bath State Historic Site (Washington)
Emerald Village (Little Switzerland)
Historic Bethabara Park (Winston-Salem)
Old Salem (Winston-Salem)
Town Creek Indian Mound State Historic Site (Albemarle)
Village of Yesteryear (Greenville)

North Dakota
Bonanzaville, USA (Fargo)
Frontier Village (Jamestown)

Ohio
Au Glaize Village (Defiance)
Geauga County Historical Society—Century Village (Chardon)
Ghost Town (Findlay)
Historic Lyme Village (Bellevue)
Ohio Village (Columbus)
Olentangy Indian Caverns and Ohio Frontierland (Delaware)
Roscoe Village Restoration (Coshocton)
Sauder Farm and Craft Village (Wauseon)
Schoenbrunn Village State Memorial (New Philadelphia)

Oklahoma
Har-Ber Village (Grand Lake)
Indian City—USA (Anadarko)

Oregon
Mission Hill Village (Salem)

Pennsylvania
Amish Farm and House (Lancaster)
Amish Homestead (Lancaster)

Amish Village (Bird-in-Hand)
Eckley uaners' Village (Hazelton)
Historic Schaefferstown (Cornwall)
Independence National Historical
  Park (Philadelphia)
Meadowcroft Village (Washington)
Memorytown, USA (Mount Pocono)
Mill Bridge Village (Lancaster)
Old Bedford Village (Bedford)
Old Economy Village (Ambridge)
Penn's Landing (Philadelphia)
Quiet Valley Living Historical
  Farm (Stroudsburg)

Rhode Island
Prescott Farm and Windmill House
  (Portsmouth)
Watson Farm (Jamestown)

South Carolina
Historic District (Cheraw)

South Dakota
Prairie Village (Madison)
Rockerville Ghost Town (Rapid City)

Tennessee
Casey Jones Village (Jackson)
Music Village USA (Nashville)

Texas
Buffalo Gap Historic Village (Abilene)
Fort Inglish (Bonham)
Gladys City—Spindletop Boomtown (Beaumont)
Grayson County Frontier Village (Denison)
Heritage Garden Village (Woodville)
La Villita (San Antonio)
Log Cabin Village (Fort Worth)
Pioneer Museum (Fredericksburg)

Pioneer Town (Wimberley)
Pioneer Village (Corsicana)
Pioneer Village (Gonzales)

Utah
Ronald V. Jensen Historical Farm and Man and
   His Bread Museum (Logan)
Wheeler Historic Farm (Salt Lake City)

Vermont
Candle Mill Village (Arlington)
Shelburne Museum (Shelburne)

Virginia
Blue Ridge Farm Museum (Martinsville)
Claude Moore Colonial Farm (Turkey Run)
Colonial Williamsburg (Williamsburg)
Colvin Run Mill Park (McLean)
Jamestown Festival Park (Jamestown)
Kecoughtan Indian Village (Hampton)
Meadow Farm Museum (Richmond)
Museum of American Frontier Culture (Staunton)
"New Towne" (Jamestown)

Washington
Camp Six (Tacoma)
Pioneer Farm (Tacoma)

West Virginia
Harpers Ferry National Historical Park (Harpers Ferry)
West Virginia State Farm Museum (Point Pleasant)

Wisconsin
Galloway House and Village (Fond du Lac)
Heritage Hill State Park (Green Bay)
Historical Society Log Village and Museum (Reedsburg)
Historyland (Hayward)
Old Falls Village (Menomonee Falls)

Old Wade House Historic Site (Elkhart Lake)
Old World Wisconsin (Waukesha)
Paul Bunyan Logging Camp (Eau Claire)
Pendarvis Cornish Restoration (Mineral Point)
Pinecrest Historical Village (Manitowoc)
Swiss Historical Village (New Glarus)
Wild Rose Pioneer Museum (Wautoma)

Wyoming
Riverton Museum (Riverton)
South Pass City (Lander)

National Parks

The United States National Park Service maintains national parks all over the country where enjoyable and educational times can be spent. Here they are, with their years of establishment, size, and nearest town.

National Parks	Established	Acreage	Nearest Town or City
ALASKA			
Denali	1917	1,716,726	Healy
Gates of the Arctic	1978	7,523,888	Big Lake
Glacier Bay	1925	3,225,284	Hoonah
Katmai	1918	3,716,000	King Salmon
Kenai Fjords	1978	669,541	Homer
Kobuc Valley	1978	1,750,421	Kotzebue
Lake Clark	1978	2,636,839	Anchor Point
Wrangell-St. Elias	1978	8,331,604	Cordova
ARIZONA			
Grand Canyon	1908	1,218,375	Grand View
Petrified Forest	1906	93,533	Woodruff
ARKANSAS			
Hot Springs	1921	5,938	Mountain Pine

National Parks	Established	Acreage	Nearest Town or City
CALIFORNIA			
Channel Islands	1938	249,354	Oxnard
Kings Canyon	1890	461,901	Visalia
Lassen Volcanic	1907	106,372	Redding
Redwood	1968	110,178	Orick
Sequoia	1890	402,482	Visalia
Yosemite	1890	761,170	Fresno
COLORADO			
Mesa Verde	1906	52,085	Cortez
Rocky Mountain	1915	265,200	Boulder
FLORIDA			
Biscayne	1968	173,039	Key Biscayne
Everglades	1934	1,398,938	Florida City
HAWAII			
Haleakala	1916	28,655	Kahului
Hawaii Volcanoes	1916	229,177	Hilo
KENTUCKY			
Mammoth Cave	1926	52,428	Bowling Green
MAINE			
Acadia	1916	41,357	Bar Harbor
MICHIGAN			
Isle Royale	1931	571,790	Houghton
MINNESOTA			
Voyageurs	1971	218,059	International Falls
MONTANA			
Glacier	1910	1,013,572	Kalispell
NEVADA			
Great Basin	1922	76,109	Baker

National Parks	Established	Acreage	Nearest Town or City
NEW MEXICO			
Carlsbad Caverns	1923	46,755	Carlsbad
NORTH CAROLINA			
Great Smoky Mountains	1926	76,109	Morganton
NORTH DAKOTA			
Theodore Roosevelt	1947	70,416	Watford City and Belfield
OREGON			
Crater Lake	1902	183,224	Medford
SOUTH DAKOTA			
Badlands	1929	243,302	Rapid City
Wind Cave	1903	28,292	Hot Springs
TEXAS			
Big Bend	1935	735,416	Alpine
Guadalupe Mountains	1966	76,293	El Paso
UTAH			
Arches	1929	41,357	Moab
Bryce Canyon	1923	35,835	Panguitch
Canyonlands	1964	337,570	Moab and Monticello
Capitol Reef	1937	241,904	Richfield
Zion	1909	146,598	St. George
VIRGINIA			
Shenandoah	1926	195,382	Front Royal
WASHINGTON			
Mount Rainier	1899	235,404	Enumclaw

National Parks	Established	Acreage	Nearest Town or City
North Cascades	1968	504,781	Bellingham
Olympic	1909	921,935	Port Angeles
WYOMING			
Grand Teton	1929	310,521	Jackson
Yellowstone	1872	2,219,785	Cody

Halls of Fame

Most people have heard of the professional sports halls of fame, but there are many more halls in all parts of the country. Here are some of them.

Alabama
Alabama Sports Hall of Fame (Birmingham)

California
San Diego Hall of Champions (San Diego)

Colorado
Figure Skating Hall of Fame (Colorado Springs)
Pro Rodeo Hall of Champions (Colorado Springs)

Florida
International Swimming Hall of Fame (Fort Lauderdale)
PGA Hall of Fame (Palm Beach Gardens)

Idaho
Fiddlers Hall of Fame (Weiser)

Indiana
Auto Racing Hall of Fame (Indianapolis)
Indiana Football Hall of Fame (Richmond)
International Palace of Sports Hall of Fame (Warsaw)
US Track and Field Hall of Fame (Angola)

Kansas
Agricultural Hall of Fame (Kansas City)
Greyhound Racing Hall of Fame (Abilene)

Maryland
Lacrosse Hall of Fame (Baltimore)

Massachusetts
Basketball Hall of Fame (Springfield)
Volleyball Hall of Fame (Holyoke)

Michigan
Afro-American Sports Hall of Fame (Detroit)
National Ski Hall of Fame (Ishpeming)

Minnesota
US Hockey Hall of Fame (Eveleth)

Missouri
National Bowling Hall of Fame (St. Louis)
St. Louis Sports Hall of Fame (St. Louis)

New Mexico
International Space Hall of Fame (Alamagordo)

New York
Boxing Hall of Fame (Canastota)
The Hall of Fame for Great Americans (The Bronx)
National Baseball Hall of Fame (Cooperstown)
National Women's Hall of Fame (Seneca Falls)
Soccer Hall of Fame (Oneonta)
Speed Skating Hall of Fame (Newburg)
Trotting Hall of Fame (Goshen)

North Carolina
PGA/World Golf Hall of Fame (Pinehurst)

Ohio
College Football Hall of Fame (Mason)
National Aviation Hall of Fame (Dayton)
Rock-and-Roll Hall of Fame (Cleveland)
Trapshooting Hall of Fame (Vandalia)

Oklahoma
International Photography Hall of Fame (Oklahoma City)
National Cowboy Hall of Fame (Oklahoma City)
National Hall of Fame for Famous American Indians (Anadarko)
National Softball Hall of Fame (Oklahoma City)
National Wrestling Hall of Fame (Stillwater)
Rodeo Cowboy Hall of Fame (Oklahoma City)

Pennsylvania
Little League Hall of Fame (Williamsport)

Rhode Island
International Tennis Hall of Fame (Newport)

South Carolina
NMPA Stock Car Hall of Fame (Darlington)

Tennessee
Country Music Hall of Fame (Nashville)

Texas
National Cowgirl Hall of Fame (Hereford)
Texas Rangers Hall of Fame (Waco)

Utah
Hollywood Stuntmen's Hall of Fame (Moab)

Wisconsin
Green Bay Packers Hall of Fame (Green Bay)

Unusual Festivals

Odd and even strange annual events are held all over the country.
Here are some of them, with cities and dates.

Alabama
Joe Wheeler Civil War Re-enactment (Decatur, September)
National Peanut Festival (Dothan, Mid-October)
National Shrimp Festival (Gulf Shores, Mid-October)
Tale Telling Festival (Selma, Mid-October)

Alaska
Ice Climbing Festival (Valdez, February)

Arizona
Chili Cook-Off (Kingman, May)
"Helldorado" Historical Re-enactment (Tombstone, Late October)
La Vuelta de Bisbee Bicycle Races (Bisbee, Late April)
Sawdust Festival Loggers' Competition (Payson, Late July)

Arkansas
Confederate Air Force Air Show (Pine Bluff, Late August)
Lum and Abner Days (Mena, June)
Saunders Memorial Muzzleloading and Frontier Gun Shoot (Berryville, Late September)
Toad Suck Daze Toad Jumping Competitions (Conway, Late April)

California
Antique Airplane Fly-In (Watsonville, Memorial Day Weekend)
Calico Hullabaloo (Barstow, Palm Sunday Weekend)
Cross-Country Kinetic Sculpture Race (Eureka, Memorial Day Weekend)
Fabulous Feather Fiesta Days (Oroville, May)
Fandango Celebration (Alturas, Early June)
Festival of Whales (San Juan Capistrano, February)
Gilroy Garlic Festival (Gilroy, Late July)
Graffiti Night (Modesto, June)
Huck Finn Jubilee (Victorville, Mid-June)
Jumping Frog Jamboree (Del Mar, Late April)
Liar's Contest (Borrego Springs, Early April)
National Date Festival (Indio, February)
Stockton Asparagus Festival (Stockton, Late April)
West Coast Antique Fly-In (Merced, Early June)
World Championship Crab Races and Crab Feed (Crescent City, Presidents' Day Weekend)
World Wrist Wrestling Championships (Petaluma, Mid-October)

Colorado
Alferd Packer (The Donner Pass Cannibal) Day (Lake City, September)

Boom Days and Burro Race (Leadville, Early August)
Donkey Derby Days (Cripple Creek, Late June)
Flauschink Ski Events (Crested Butte, Early April)
Kinetic Conveyance Challenge (Boulder, Early May)
Sugar Beet Days (Sterling, Late September)
Will Overhead (Fictitious Indy 500 winner) Day (Walsenburg, Late May)
World Footbag Association National Footbag Championship (Golden, Late July)
World's Championship Pack Burro Race (Fairplay, Late July)

Connecticut
Balloons Over Bristol (Bristol, Memorial Day Weekend)
Barnum Festival (Bridgeport, Late June-Early July)
Powder House Day (New Haven, Late April or Early May)
Shad Derby Festival (Windsor, Mid-May)
Taste of Hartford (Hartford, May)

Delaware
Separation Day (New Castle, Late June)

District of Columbia
Easter Egg Roll (Washington, Easter)

Florida
Animal Day (Gainesville, February)
Billy Bowlegs Festival (Fort Walton Beach, Early June)
Cracker Day (Deerfield Beach, Early April)
Gasparilla Pirate Invasion (Tampa, Early February)
Swamp Buggy Days (Naples, Late February)
Turtle Crawl (Melbourne, June-September)
Turtle Watch (Jensen Beach, June-July)
Watermelon Festival (Chiefland, Late June)

Georgia
Appalachian Wagon Train (Chatsworth, Early July)
Bite of the 'Boro (Statesboro, Mid-May)
Okefenokee Spring Fling (Waycross, Late March)
"Tybee Jubilee" (Tybee Island, Mid-September)

Hawaii
Hula Festival (Honolulu, August)

Idaho
Gem Dandy Days (Jerome, Mid-August)
Idaho State Championship Cutter and Chariot Races (Pocatello, February)

Illinois
Autumn on Parade (Oregon, Early October)
Bishop Hill Jordbruksdagarna Agricultural Celebration (Bishop Hill, Late September)
Burgoo (Pioneer Stew) Festival (Peru, October)
Grand Prix of Karting (Quincy, Early June)
Grundy County Corn Festival (Morris, Mid-September)
Jaycees Deutschfest (Belleville, Late June)
Joe Naper Day (Naperville, June)
Pet Parade (La Grange, June)
Scarecrow Festival (St. Charles, Mid-October)
Steamboat Days (Peoria, Father's Day)
Taste of Chicago (Chicago, Summer)
Warren County Prime Beef Festival (Monmouth, Early September)
Waterway Daze (Joliet, July)
"World's Largest Garage Sale" (Evanston, Late July)

Indiana
Circus City Festival (Peru, Mid-July)
Gaslight Festival (Anderson, Early June)
Germania Maennerchor (German Festival) Volkfest (Evansville, Mid-August)
Iron Horse Festival (Logansport, Late July)
Jail "Breakout" (Crawfordsville, Labor Day)
James Whitcomb Riley Festival (Greenfield, Early October)
Johnny Appleseed Festival (Fort Wayne, Late September)
Little 500 Bicycle Race (Bloomington, Late April)
Orange County Pumpkin Festival (French Lick, Late September-Early October)
Popcorn Festival (Valparaiso, Early September)
Round Barn Festival (Rochester, Early July)

Iowa

Houby Days Czech Festival
(Cedar Rapids, Weekend After
Mother's Day)
Old Capitol Criterium Bicycle
Race (Iowa City, April)
Pufferbilly Days (Boone,
Early September)

Kansas

Buffalo Bill Cody Days
(Leavenworth, Late September)
Gool Ol' Days Celebration (Fort Scott, Early June)
International Pancake Race (Liberal, Shrove Tuesday)
"Neewollah" Halloween Festival (Independence, Late October)

Kentucky

Corn Island Storytelling Festival (Louisville, Mid-September)
International Banana Festival (Fulton, Late September)
International Barbecue Festival (Owensboro, Mid-May)

Louisiana

Contraband Days (Lake Charles, Late April-Early May)
International Rice Festival (Lafayette, Late October)
Louisiana Shrimp and Petroleum Festival and Fair (Morgan City,
Labor Day Weekend)
Louisiana Yambilee Yam Celebration (Opelousas, Late October)
Mudbug Madness Crawfish Celebration (Shreveport, May)
Praline Festival (Houma, Early May)
Tamale Fiesta (Many, Mid-October)

Maine

Houlton Potato Feast (Houlton, Late August)
Kenduskeag Steam Canoe Race (Bangor, Mid-April)
Whatever Week (Augusta, July)

Maryland

John Hanson Patriots Fife and Drum Corps Muster (Waldorf,
Mid-April)

Jousting Tournament (Easton, Early August)
Maryland Kite Festival (Baltimore, April)
National Hard Crab Derby and Fair (Crisfield, Labor Day Weekend)

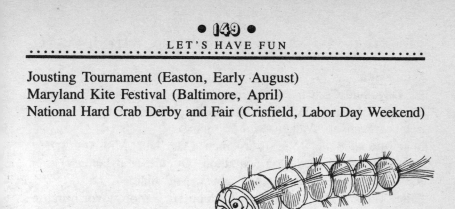

Massachusetts
Apple Squeeze Festival (Lenox, Late September)
Haunted Happenings (Salem, Late October)
Salmagundi Fair (Newburyport, Memorial Day Weekend)
Sand Castle Contest (Nantucket Island, August)
Sheep Shearing Festival (North Andover, Late May)
Summerthing (Boston, Summer)

Michigan
Cereal City Festival (Battle Creek, Early June)
Ice Sculpture Spectacular (Plymouth, January)
Mint Festival (St. Johns, Mid-August)
MuzzleLoaders Festival (Dearborn, Mid-June)
Potato Festival (Bay City, Late July)
Red Earth Loppet Ski Races (Marquette, Early March)
Tip-Up-Town USA Ice Festival (Houghton Lake, Late January)

Minnesota

Ag Days and Corn Feed (Spring Valley, Late August)
Defeat of Jesse James Days (Northfield, Mid-September)
Eelpout Festival (Walker, Mid-February)
International Rolle Bolle Tournament (Marshall, Mid-August)
John Beargrease Sled Dog Marathon (Duluth, Mid-January)
Judy Garland Festival (Grand Rapids, Mid-June)
King Turkey Days and Great Gobbler Gallop (Worthington, Mid-September)
Korn and Klover Karnival (Hinckley, Mid-July)
Last Chance Curling Bonspeil (Hibbing, Early April)
Laura Ingalls Wilder Pageant (Tracy, Early July)
Operation Jumpfest Skydiving Competition (Albert Lea, Early July)
Sinclair Lewis Days (Sauk Centre, Mid-June)

Mississippi

Anniversary of the Landing of d'Iberville (Ocean Springs, Late April)

Missouri

Baldknobbers Hillbilly Jamboree (Branson, May-October)
Bennett Spring Hillbilly Days (Lebanon, Father's Day Weekend)
Bushwhacker Days (Nevada, Late June)
Grape Stomping Festival (Hermann, Mid-August)
Tom Sawyer Days (Hannibal, Early July)
Truman Week Celebration (Independence, Early May)

Montana

Corn Cob Days (Chinook, August)
Milk River Wagon Train (Malta, Labor Day)
Peter Paddlefish Day (Sidney, May 1)
Sweet Pea Festival (Bozeman, Early August)

Nebraska

Applejack Festival (Nebraska City, Late September)
Chicken Show (Wayne, Early July)
LaVitsef Celebration (Norfolk, Late September)

Nevada
Boulder Damboree (Boulder City, July 4)
Bristlecone Chariot Races (Ely, Early March)
Camel Races (Virginia City, Early September)
Cowboy Poetry Gathering (Elko, Late January)
Wells Pony Express Race (Wells, Mid-May)
Whistle-Off (Carson City, August)

New Hampshire
Mud Bowl Football Game (North Conway, September)
SummerStreet (Littleton, June)

New Jersey
Hermit Crab Race and Miss Crustacean Contest (Ocean City, August)
Miscellaneous Suntanning Tournament (Ocean City, Late August)
National Bocce Tournament (Asbury Park, Late June)

New Mexico
Dairy Day Picnic and Great Milk Carton Boat Race (Roswell, Early June)
International Balloon Fiesta (Albuquerque, Early October)
Overland Wind Sail Race (Lordsburg, March)
Piñata Festival (Tucumcari, Late June)
Smokey Bear Stampede (Ruidoso, Early June)
Whole Enchilada Fiesta (Las Cruces, Early October)

New York
Alpo International Dog Sled Races (Saranac Lake, Late January)
Annual Return of the Sacandaga Swifts (Gloversville, Early May)
Fort Ticonderoga Muzzle Loading Rifle Shoot (Ticonderoga, Early May and Mid-September)
The Hill Cumora Scottish Pageant (Palmyra, Late July-Early August)
Inner Tube Regatta (Wellsville, Memorial Day Weekend)
Toy Festival (East Aurora, Late August)
World Series of Bocce (Rome, Mid-July)

North Carolina
Leaf Lookers Bluegrass and Clogging Show (Franklin, Mid-October)
National Whistlers' Convention (Raleigh, Late April)
Shooting in the New Year (Cherryville, New Year's Eve)
Waldensian Celebration of the Glorious Return (Morganton, Mid-August)
World Gee Haw Whimmy Diddle Competition (Asheville, Mid-May)

North Dakota
Potato Bowl Weekend (Grand Forks, Mid-September)
Steam Threshers Show (Carrington, Late September)

Ohio
International Chicken Flying Meet (Gallipolis, May)
Johnny Appleseed Festival (Lisbon, Early September)
National Jigsaw Puzzle Championship (Athens, Late August)
Roy Rogers Convention and Western Festival (Portsmouth, Early June)
Woolly Bear Festival (Vermillion, Late September-Early October)

Oklahoma
Chocolate Festival (Norman, Early February)
Kiamichi Owa Chito Festival (Broken Bow, Late June)
Pelican Festival (Grand Lake, Late September)

Oregon
Annual Moon Tree Run (Cave Junction, Early June)
Barbershop Quartet Cabaret (Seaside, January)

Concours D'Elegance Auto Show (Forest Grove, Late July)
Crab Feed and Seafood Festival (Astoria, Early April)
Miner's Jubilee (Baker, Late July)
Return of the Stern-Wheeler Days (Hood River, June)
Sandcastle Contest (Cannon Beach, May or June)
"62" Day Celebration (John Day, Early June)

Pennsylvania
Chocolate Festival (Hershey, February)
Das Awkscht Fescht Ethnic Festival (Allentown, Early August)
Mifflin County Goose Day Celebration (Lewiston, Late September)
St. Ubaldo Day (Scranton, Memorial Day Weekend)

Rhode Island
Hot-Air Balloon Festival (Kingston, Late July or Early August)

South Carolina
"Come See Me" (Rock Hill, Mid-April)
Freedom Weekend Aloft (Greenville, July 4 Weekend)
Palmetto Balloon Classic (Camden, Early May)

South Dakota
Laura Ingalls Wilder Pageant (Huron, Late July)
Oahe Days (Pierre, Early August)
Snow Queen Festival (Aberdeen, Early January)
Steam Threshing Jamboree (Madison, Late August)

Tennessee
Covered Bridge Celebration (Elizabethton, Early June)
Mule Day (Columbia, Early April)
National Storytelling Festival (Johnson City, Early October)
Spring Fun Show (Shelbyville, Late May)
Walking Horse Show (Clarksville, Early July)
World's Biggest Fish Fry (Paris, April)

Texas
Big Bend Bash (Alpine, Late February)
CavOILcade (Port Arthur, Early October)
Come and Take It Celebration (Gonzales, Early October)

Goat Cook-Off and Goat Roping (Sonora, Mid-May)
Great Mosquito Festival (Brazosport, Late July)
Rattlesnake Roundup (Big Spring, Late March)
Republic of Texas Chilympiad (San Marcos, Late September)
Rose Bowl Chili Cook-Off (Tyler, Late March)
Superbull (Del Rio, Early May)
White Buffalo Days (Snyder, Mid-October)
World's Largest Fish Fry (Fritch, Early June)

Utah
Deseret Vagabond Days (Kanab, Mid-June)
Golden Onion Days (Payson, Labor Day Weekend)
Ride and Tie (Park City, Mid-July)

Vermont
Bay Day (St. Albans, July 4 Weekend)
Wurstfest (Stratton Mountain, Labor Day Weekend)

Virginia
Chili Cookoff (Roanoke, May)
Happy Birthday USA (Staunton, July)
Pony Penning (Chincoteauge, July)
Pork, Peanut and Pine Festival (Surry, July)
Richmond Newspapers Marathon (Richmond, Late October)
Virginia Poultry Festival (Harrisonburg, Mid-May)

Washington
Barbershop Concert and Salmon Barbeque (Anacortes, Late July)
Chokes and Spokes Old Car Nostalgia Days (Colville, Memorial Day Weekend)
Ezra Meeker Days (Puyallup, Early June)
Farmer Consumer Awareness Day (Quincy, Early September)
Krazy Days (Chehalis, Early July)
Loggerodeo (Sedro Woolley, Early July)
Lummi Stommish Water Carnival (Bellingham, Mid-June)

West Virginia
Apple Butter Festival (Berkeley Springs, Columbus Day Weekend)
Webster Springs Woodchopping Festival (Webster Springs, Late May)

Wisconsin

Bratwurst Day (Sheboygan, Early August)
Chocolate Festival (Burlington, May)
Flambeau Rama (Park Falls, Early August)
Fyr-Bal Fest Scandinavian Festival (Ephriam, June)
Hodag Country Festival (Rhinelander, Mid-July)
Julehelgen Norwegian Christmas Celebration (Cable, Late November
  or Early December)
Port Fish Day (Port Washington, Late July)
Salmon-A-Rama (Racine, Early July)
Wannigan Days (St. Croix Falls, Mid-June)
Wilhelm Tell Festival (New Glarus, Labor Day Weekend)

Wyoming

Buffalo Barbeque (Dubois, Mid-August)
Buffalo Bill Birthday Celebration (Cody, Late February)
Invitational Chariot Races (Torrington, Mid-March)
Mountain Man Rendezvous (Evanston, Labor Day Weekend)
Pack Horse Race (Pinedale, Mid-June)

At the Movies

Over the years, many motion pictures have contained the name of
a state in their titles, even though it was unlikely that the film had
actually been shot in that state. Indeed, it is possible that the name
of the state had nothing to do with the plot. Here are some of
them.

Alaska
North to Alaska (1960)

Arizona
Arizona (1940)
Arizona Bushwhackers (1968)
Arizona Raiders (1965)
Arizona to Broadway (1933)
The Baron of Arizona (1950)
Raising Arizona (1987)
Thunder Over Arizona (1956)

Arkansas
The Arkansas Traveler (1938)

California
California (1946)
California Conquest (1952)
California Dreaming (1979)
California Girls (1985)
California Gold Rush (1981)
The California Kid (1974)
California Split (1974)
California Straight Ahead (1937)
California Suite (1978)
A Death in California (1985)
In Old California (1942)
Raiders of Old California (1957)

Colorado
Colorado Territory (1949)
The Man from Colorado (1948)

Connecticut
Christmas in Connecticut (1945)
*A Connecticut Yankee in King
   Arthur's Court* (1949)

Florida
Florida Special (1936)
Florida Straits (1986)

Georgia
Georgia, Georgia (1972)
The Georgia Peaches (1980)

Hawaii
Blue Hawaii (1961)
Hawaii (1966)
The Hawaiians (1970)
Hawaii Five-0 (1968)
M Station: Hawaii (1980)
Paradise, Hawaiian Style
   (1966)

Idaho
Duchess of Idaho (1950)

Illinois
Abe Lincoln in Illinois (1940)

Indiana
The Boy from Indiana (1950)
Home in Indiana (1944)
*Indiana Jones and the Last
   Crusade* (1989)
*Indiana Jones and the Temple
   of Doom* (1984)

Kansas
Kansas Pacific (1953)
Kansas Raiders (1950)
The Kid from Kansas (1941)
Masterson of Kansas (1954)

Kentucky
Blue Grass of Kentucky (1950)
In Old Kentucky (1935)

The Kentuckian (1955)
Kentucky (1938)
Kentucky Fried Movie (1977)
Kentucky Kernels (1934)
Kentucky Moonshine (1938)
Kentucky Woman (1983)
The Lady's From Kentucky
  (1939)

Louisiana
Lady From Louisiana (1941)

Louisiana (1984)
Louisiana Hayride (1944)
Louisiana Purchase (1941)
Louisiana Story (1948)

Michigan
Michigan Kid (1947)

Minnesota
The Great Northfield,
  Minnesota Raid (1972)
Minnesota Clay (1965)
Off the Minnesota Strip (1980)

Mississippi
Lacy and the Mississippi Queen
  (1978)
Mississippi (1935)
Mississippi Blues (1983)
Mississippi Gambler (1953)
Mississippi Mermaid (1969)

Missouri
The Girl From Missouri (1934)
The Great Missouri Raid (1950)
I'm From Missouri (1939)
The Missouri Breaks (1976)
The Missouri Traveler (1958)

Montana
Badlands of Montana (1957)
Montana (1950)
Montana Belle (1952)
Montana Mike (1947)
Montana Territory (1952)
Red Skies of Montana (1952)

Nebraska
The Nebraskan (1953)

Nevada
Nevada (1944)
The Nevadan (1950)
Nevada Smith (1966)
Nevada Smith (1975)
Wanda Nevada (1979)

New Hampshire
The Hotel New Hampshire (1984)

New Mexico
New Mexico (1951)

North and South Carolina
Thunder in Carolina (1960)

North and South Dakota
Badlands of Dakota (1941)
The Black Dakotas (1954)
Dakota (1945)
Dakota Incident (1956)
Dakota Lil (1950)
The Man From Dakota (1940)

Oklahoma
Al Jennings of Oklahoma (1951)
Baja Oklahoma (1988)
The Boy From Oklahoma (1954)
The Doolins of Oklahoma (1949)
In Old Oklahoma (1943)
Oklahoma! (1955)
Oklahoma Annie (1952)
Oklahoma Crude (1973)
The Oklahoma Kid (1939)
The Oklahoman (1957)
Oklahoma Territory (1960)
The Oklahoma Woman (1956)

Oregon
Oregon Passage (1957)
The Oregon Trail (1959)
The Oregon Trail (1976)

South Carolina
(See North and South Carolina)

South Dakota
(See North and South Dakota)

Tennessee
Tennessee Champ (1954)
Tennessee Johnson (1942)
Tennessee's Partner (1955)

Texas
Africa—Texas Style! (1967)
An Angel From Texas (1940)
The Kid From Texas (1950)
The Lady From Texas (1951)
Lone Texan (1959)
Murder in Texas (1981)
Once Upon a Texas Train (1988)
Paris, Texas (1984)
Return of the Texan (1952)
A Small Town in Texas (1976)
The Tall Texan (1953)
The Texan Meets Calamity Jane (1950)
The Texans (1938)
Texas (1941)
Texas Across the River (1966)
Texas, Brooklyn and Heaven (1948)
Texas Carnival (1951)

The Texas Chainsaw Massacre
  (1974)
The Texas Chainsaw
  Massacre 2 (1986)
Texas Detour (1978)
Texas Lady (1955)
The Texas Rangers (1936)
The Texas Rangers (1951)
Texas Rangers Ride Again
  (1940)
Three Guns for Texas (1968)
Three Young Texans (1954)
Two Guys From Texas (1948)

Virginia (1941)
The Virginian (1929)
The Virginian (1946)

Wyoming
Green Grass of Wyoming
  (1948)
Wyoming (1940)
Wyoming (1947)
The Wyoming Kid (1947)
Wyoming Mail (1950)
Wyoming Renegades (1955)

Virginia
The Howards of Virginia (1940)

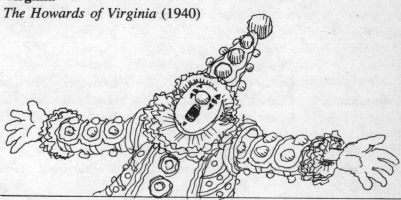

Great Music

Symphonic music, opera, and ballet are presented all over the country. Here are some of the more prominent performing groups, state by state.

State	Company	City
Alabama	Alabama Symphony	Birmingham
	Huntsville Symphony	Huntsville
Alaska	Anchorage Opera	Anchorage

State	Company	City
Arizona	Arizona Opera Company	Phoenix and Tucson
	Ballet Arizona	Phoenix
	Phoenix Symphony	Phoenix
	Tucson Symphony	Tucson
Arkansas	Arkansas Symphony	Little Rock
California	Los Angeles Music Center Opera Association	Los Angeles
	Los Angeles Philharmonic	Los Angeles
	Oakland Ballet	Oakland
	Opera San Jose	San Jose
	San Diego Opera	San Diego
	San Francisco Ballet	San Francisco
	San Francisco Opera	San Francisco
	San Francisco Symphony	San Francisco
Colorado	Ballet/Aspen	Aspen
	Central City Opera	Denver
	Denver Symphony	Denver
	Opera Colorado	Denver
Connecticut	Connecticut Ballet	Hartford
	Connecticut Grand Opera	Hartford
	Hartford Symphony	Hartford
	Stamford State Opera	Stamford
District of Columbia	National Symphony	Washington
Florida	The Florida Orchestra	Clearwater and Tampa
	Greater Miami Opera Association	Miami
	Jacksonville Symphony	Jacksonville
	Miami City Ballet	Miami
	Orlando Opera Company	Orlando
Georgia	Atlanta Ballet	Atlanta
	Atlanta Opera	Atlanta
	Atlanta Symphony	Atlanta
Hawaii	Hawaii Opera Theatre	Honolulu
	Honolulu Symphony	Honolulu
Idaho	Boise Philharmonic	Boise

State	Company	City
Illinois	Ballet Chicago	Chicago
	Civic Opera	Chicago
	Chicago Symphony	Chicago
	Grant Park Symphony	Chicago
	Lyric Opera of Chicago	Chicago
Indiana	Fort Wayne Philharmonic	Fort Wayne
	Indianapolis Opera	Indianapolis
	Indianapolis Symphony	Indianapolis
	South Bend Symphony	South Bend
Iowa	Des Moines Metro Opera	Des Moines
	Des Moines Symphony	Des Moines
Kansas	Wichita Symphony	Wichita
Kentucky	Kentucky Opera	Louisville
	Lexington Philharmonic	Lexington
	Louisville Ballet	Louisville
	Louisville Orchestra	Louisville
Louisiana	New Orleans Opera Association	New Orleans
	New Orleans Symphony	New Orleans
Maine	Bangor Symphony	Bangor
Maryland	Baltimore Symphony	Baltimore
Massachusetts	Boston Pops	Boston
	Boston Symphony	Boston
	Opera Company of Boston	Boston
Michigan	Detroit Symphony	Detroit
	Grand Rapids Symphony	Grand Rapids
	Michigan Opera Theatre	Detroit
Minnesota	Minnesota Opera Company	St. Paul
	Minnesota Symphony	Minneapolis
Mississippi	Jackson Symphony	Jackson
Missouri	Kansas City Symphony	Kansas City
	Lyric Opera of Kansas City	Kansas City
	Muny Opera	St. Louis
	St. Louis Opera Theatre	St. Louis
	St. Louis Symphony	St. Louis
	State Ballet of Missouri	St. Louis
Nebraska	Opera/Omaha	Omaha
	Omaha Symphony	Omaha

State	Company	City
Nevada	Nevada Opera	Reno
New Jersey	New Jersey State Opera	Newark
	New Jersey Symphony	Newark
New Mexico	Albuquerque Opera Theater	Albuquerque
	New Mexico Symphony	Albuquerque
	Orchestra of Santa Fe	Santa Fe
	Santa Fe Opera	Santa Fe
	Southwest Ballet Company	Albuquerque
New York	Alvin Ailey American Dance Theater	New York City
	American Ballet Theatre	New York City
	Buffalo Philharmonic	Buffalo
	Dance Theatre of Harlem	New York City
	Glimmerglass Opera	Cooperstown
	Metropolitan Opera Association	New York City
	New York City Ballet	New York City
	New York City Opera	New York City
	New York Philharmonic	New York City
	Rochester Philharmonic	Rochester
	Syracuse Symphony	Syracuse
North Carolina	Charlotte Symphony	Charlotte
	North Carolina Dance Theater	Winston-Salem
	North Carolina Symphony	Raleigh
	Opera Carolina	Charlotte
Ohio	Ballet Metropolitan	Columbus
	Cincinnati Ballet Company	Cincinnati
	Cincinnati Opera Association	Cincinnati

State	Company	City
	Cincinnati Symphony	Cincinnati
	Cleveland Ballet	Cleveland
	Cleveland Opera	Cleveland
	Cleveland Orchestra	Cleveland
	Columbus Symphony	Columbus
	Opera/Columbus	Columbus
Oklahoma	Ballet Oklahoma	Oklahoma City
	Oklahoma Symphony	Oklahoma City
	Tulsa Ballet Theatre	Tulsa
	Tulsa Opera	Tulsa
	Tulsa Philharmonic	Tulsa
Oregon	Eugene Symphony	Eugene
	Oregon Symphony	Portland
	Portland Opera Association	Portland
Pennsylvania	Opera Company of Philadelphia	Philadelphia
	Pennsylvania Ballet	Philadelphia
	Philadelphia Orchestra	Philadelphia
	Pittsburgh Opera	Pittsburgh
	Pittsburgh Symphony	Pittsburgh
Rhode Island	Rhode Island Philharmonic	Providence
South Carolina	Charleston Symphony	Charleston
South Dakota	South Dakota Symphony	Sioux Falls
Tennessee	Chattanooga Opera Association	Chattanooga
	Chattanooga Symphony	Chattanooga
	Knoxville Symphony	Knoxville
	Memphis Symphony	Memphis
	Nashville Symphony	Nashville
	Opera Memphis	Memphis

State	Company	City
Texas	Dallas Ballet	Dallas
	Dallas Opera	Dallas
	Dallas Symphony	Dallas
	Fort Worth Opera	Fort Worth
	Fort Worth Symphony	Fort Worth
	Houston Ballet	Houston
	Houston Grand Opera Association	Houston
	Houston Symphony	Houston
	Lyric Opera of Dallas	Dallas
	San Antonio Symphony	San Antonio
Utah	Utah Opera	Salt Lake City
	Utah Symphony	Salt Lake City
Virginia	Virginia Opera	Norfolk
	Virginia Symphony	Norfolk
Washington	Pacific Northwest Ballet	Seattle
	Seattle Opera Association	Seattle
	Seattle Symphony	Seattle
	Spokane Symphony	Spokane
	Tacoma Symphony	Tacoma
Wisconsin	Milwaukee Ballet	Milwaukee
	Milwaukee Symphony	Milwaukee

Sports

The United States is sports mad, and games, matches, and meets are held all over the country.

Alabama

Alabama is one of the premier football states in the Union. Several collegiate bowl games are played there each year—the All-American Bowl in Birmingham, the Senior Bowl in Mobile, and the Blue-Gray Football Classic in Montgomery. The University of Alabama Crimson Tide has been named the national college football champions six times (1961, 1964, 1965, 1973, 1978, 1979), and the Auburn University Tigers once (1957).

Alaska
In collegiate basketball, Anchorage is host to the annual Great Alaska Shootout. The Iditarod Trail Race of sled dog teams is run from Anchorage to Nome each year.

Arizona
The Annual Fiesta Bowl collegiate football game is held in Tempe. The Arizona State Sun Devils have won the NCAA baseball championship (1965, 1967, 1969, 1977, 1981), as have the University of Arizona Wildcats (1976, 1980, 1986).

On the professional level, there are the Phoenix Cardinals of the National Football League, and the Phoenix Suns of the National Basketball Association.

Arkansas
Arkansas is primarily a football state. The University of Arkansas Razorbacks have won many bowl games. Their best-known cheer is an old-fashioned hog call!

California
It can be argued that California is our most sport-conscious state. The University of Southern California Trojans were named national collegiate football champions four times (1962, 1967, 1972, 1978). In basketball, the University of California, Los Angeles, Bruins have won the NCAA championship repeatedly (1964, 1965, 1967, 1968, 1969, 1970, 1971, 1972, 1973, 1975). The Universi-

ty of California Golden Bears have won it twice (1942, 1959). Also, the Fresno State Bulldogs won the NIT (1985). In collegiate baseball, the NCAA national championship was won by the University of California (1947, 1957), the University of Southern California (1948, 1958, 1961, 1963, 1968, 1970, 1971, 1972, 1973, 1974, 1978), the Stanford Cardinals (1987, 1988), and the University of California, Fullerton, Titans (1979, 1964). Each year, California is host to the collegiate Freedom Bowl in Anaheim, the California Bowl in Fresno, the Rose Bowl in Pasadena, and the Holiday Bowl in San Diego.

On the professional level, there are many teams. In baseball, it is home to the California Angels (Anaheim), Los Angeles Dodgers, Oakland A's, San Diego Padres, and San Francisco Giants, and in football, the Los Angeles Raiders, Los Angeles Rams, San Diego Chargers, and San Francisco 49ers. In basketball, there are the Golden State Warriors (Oakland), Los Angeles Clippers, Los Angeles Lakers, and Sacramento Kings, and in hockey, the Los Angeles Kings.

Colorado
The University of Colorado Buffalos won the collegiate NIT basketball championship in 1940. The NCAA national hockey championship was won by the Colorado College Tigers (1950, 1957) and the University of Denver Pioneers (1958, 1960, 1961, 1968, 1969).

On the professional level, there are the Denver Broncos of the National Football League and the Denver Nuggets of the National Basketball Association.

Connecticut
The University of Connecticut Huskies won the NIT basketball championship (1988).

On the professional level, Hartford is home to the Whalers of the National Hockey League.

District of Columbia
The University of Georgetown Hoyas won the NCAA national basketball championship in 1984. On the professional level, there are the Washington Redskins of the National Football League.

Florida
Each year, Florida hosts the collegiate post-season games of the Gator Bowl in Jacksonville, the Orange Bowl in Miami, the Florida Citrus Bowl in Orlando, and the Hall of Fame Bowl in Tampa. In football, the University of Miami Hurricanes were named national champions (1983, 1987, 1989). They also won the NCAA national baseball championship (1982, 1985, 1990).

On the professional level, the Miami Dolphins and the Tampa Bay Buccaneers play in the National Football League and the Miami Heat and the Orlando Magic in the National Basketball Association.

Georgia
The Peach Bowl collegiate football game is held annually in Atlanta. The University of Georgia Bulldogs were chosen as national football champions in 1980.

On the professional level, the state boasts the Atlanta Braves of the National League in baseball, the Atlanta Falcons of the National Football League, and the Atlanta Hawks of the National Basketball Association.

Hawaii
Every year, Hawaii is the site of the Hula Bowl, the Aloha Bowl, and the National Football League Pro Bowl—all in Honolulu.

Illinois
In basketball, the Loyola University Ramblers won the NCAA national championship (1963), and the De Paul Blue Devils won the NIT basketball championship (1945), as did the Bradley Braves (1957, 1960, 1964, 1982) and the Southern Illinois Salukis (1967).

On the professional level, baseball is played by the Chicago Cubs of the National League and the Chicago White Sox of the American League. Other teams are the Chicago Bears of the National Football League, the Chicago Bulls of the National Basketball Association, and the Chicago Blackhawks of the National Hockey League.

Indiana

The sport that most people associate with Indiana is auto racing, because of the Indianapolis 500 race. But Indiana's true sport is basketball—called "Hoosier Hysteria." The NCAA basketball championship was won by the Indiana University Hoosiers (1940, 1953, 1976, 1981, 1987), who also won the NIT basketball championship (1979), as did the Purdue University Boilermakers (1974). In football, the University of Notre Dame Fighting Irish have been named national champions eight times (1943, 1946, 1947, 1949, 1966, 1973, 1977, 1988).

On the professional level are the Indianapolis Colts of the National Football League and the Indiana Pacers (Indianapolis) of the National Basketball Association.

Iowa

Iowa is unique in that on the high-school level, girls' games occasionally outdraw boys' games. Iowa is also a hotbed of wrestling enthusiasm.

Kansas

Each year, Kansas is host to the National Junior College Basketball Tournament in Hutchinson and the National Championship Baseball Tournament in Wichita. The University of Kansas Jayhawks won the NCAA basketball championship (1952, 1988), and the Wichita State University Shockers won the NCAA baseball championship (1989).

Kentucky

The University of Kentucky Wildcats have won the NCAA basketball championship (1948, 1949, 1951, 1958, 1978), and the University of Louisville Cardinals were also champions (1980, 1986). The NIT basketball championship went to Kentucky (1946, 1976) and Louisville (1956).

Louisiana

Every year, two college-football bowl games are played in Louisiana— the Sugar Bowl in New Orleans and the Independence Bowl in Shreveport. The Louisiana State University Fighting Tigers were named the national football champions in 1958.

On the professional level, there are the New Orleans Saints of the National Football League.

Maryland

The University of Maryland Terrapins were named national football champions in 1953. The NCAA lacrosse championship has been won by Maryland (1973, 1975) and the Johns Hopkins University Blue Jays (1974, 1978, 1979, 1980, 1984, 1985, 1987).

On the professional level, the Baltimore Orioles play baseball in the American League. The Washington Bullets of the National Basketball Association, and the Washington Capitals of the National Hockey League, both play in Landover.

Massachusetts

Each year the Tipoff Classic college basketball game is held in Springfield. The NCAA basketball championship was won in 1947 by the Holy Cross Crusaders, who also won the NIT championship (1954), and the NCAA baseball championship (1952). The NCAA hockey championship was won by the Boston College Eagles (1949), the Boston University Terriers (1971, 1972, 1978), and the Harvard Crimson (1989).

On the professional level, the Boston Red Sox play in the American League, the New England Patriots (Foxboro) in the National Football League, the Boston Celtics in the National Basketball Association, and the Boston Bruins in the National Hockey League.

Michigan

The University of Michigan Wolverines were named national football champions in 1948, as were the Michigan State University Spartans in 1952 and 1965. In basketball, Michigan won the NCAA national championship in 1989, while Michigan State took it in 1979. Michigan also won the NIT championship in 1984.

Michigan won the NCAA hockey championship (1948, 1951, 1952, 1953, 1964), as did the Michigan Tech Huskies (1962, 1965, 1975), the Lake Superior State University Lakers (1988), and Michigan State (1966, 1986). Michigan also won the NCAA baseball championship in 1953 and 1962.

On the professional level, Michigan has the Detroit Tigers of the American League, the Detroit Lions of the National Football League, the Detroit Pistons of the National Basketball Association, and the Detroit Red Wings of the National Hockey League.

Minnesota

The University of Minnesota Golden Gophers were named national football champions in 1936, 1940, 1941, and 1960. They have also been the NCAA hockey champions (1974, 1976, 1979), and the NCAA baseball champions (1956, 1960, 1964).

Professional teams include the Minnesota Twins of the American League, the Minnesota Vikings of the National Football League, the Minnesota Timberwolves of the National Basketball Association, and the Minnesota North Stars of the National Hockey League, all of whom play in Minneapolis.

Mississippi

The NIT basketball championship was won by the University of Southern Mississippi Golden Eagles in 1987.

Missouri

In basketball, the NIT championship was won by the St. Louis University Billikins in 1948, and the University of Missouri Tigers have won the NCAA baseball championship (1954).

On the professional level, the St. Louis Cardinals play baseball in the National League and the Kansas City Royals in the American League; the Kansas City Chiefs play in the National Football League; and the St. Louis Blues in the National Hockey League.

Nebraska
The NCAA College Baseball World Series is held every year in Omaha. On the collegiate football scene, the University of Nebraska Cornhuskers were named national champions in 1970 and 1971.

Nevada
The NCAA basketball championship was won by the University of Nevada, Las Vegas, Runnin' Rebels (1990).

New Jersey
The NIT championship was won by the Seton Hall Pirates (1953) and the Princeton Tigers (1975).

On the professional level, the Giants and Jets play in the National Football League, the New Jersey Nets in the National Basketball

Association, and the New Jersey Devils in the National Hockey League. All four teams play in East Rutherford.

New York
The Syracuse University Orangemen were named football champions in 1959, as were the Army Cadets in 1944 and 1945. The NIT championship has been won by the Long Island University Black-

birds (1939, 1941), the St. John's Redmen (1943, 1944, 1959, 1965, 1989), the City College of New York Beavers (1950), and the St. Bonaventure Bonnies (1977). The NCAA Hockey Championship was won by the Rensselaer Polytechnic Institute Engineers (1954, 1985) and the Cornell Big Red (1967, 1970). In lacrosse, Cornell won the NCAA national championship in 1971, as did Syracuse in 1983, 1988, 1989.

Professional teams include the New York Mets of the National League, the New York Yankees of the American League, the Buffalo Bills of the National Football League, the New York Knicks of the National Basketball Association, and the New York Rangers, New York Islanders, and Buffalo Sabres of the National Hockey League.

North Carolina
North Carolina is another basketball state. The University of North Carolina Tarheels have won the NCAA national championship twice (1957, 1982), as have the North Carolina State University Wolfpack (1974, 1983). North Carolina won the NIT basketball championship in 1971. In lacrosse, North Carolina won the NCAA championship in 1981, 1982 and 1986, and in baseball, the Wake Forest Demon Deacons won the NCAA national championship in 1955.

On the professional scene, the Charlotte Hornets play in the National Basketball Association.

North Dakota
The University of North Dakota Fighting Sioux won the NCAA national hockey championship in 1959, 1963, 1980, 1982, and 1987.

Ohio
Every year, the All-American Soap Box Derby is held in Akron. The Ohio State University Buckeyes were named national football champions in 1942, 1954, 1957 and 1968.

In basketball, the University of Cincinnati Bearcats won the NCAA national championship in 1961 and 1962, and Ohio State won it in 1960, as well as the NIT championship in 1986. The NIT was also won by the University of Dayton Flyers in 1962 and 1968 and Xavier University's Musketeers (1958). Ohio State was the NCAA baseball champion in 1966.

On the professional level, there are five teams. The Cincinnati Reds play baseball in the National League and the Cleveland Indians in the American League. The Cincinnati Bengals and Cleveland Browns play in the National Football League, and the Cleveland Cavaliers in the National Basketball Association.

Oklahoma

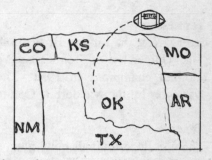

Oklahoma is a football state. The University of Oklahoma Sooners were named national champions in 1950, 1955, 1956, 1974, 1975, and 1985. In basketball, the Oklahoma State Cowboys won the NCAA championship in 1945 and 1946, when they were called Oklahoma A&M. The University of Tulsa Golden Hurricane won the NIT in 1981. Oklahoma won the NCAA baseball championship in 1951, as did Oklahoma State in 1959.

Oregon

The University of Oregon Killer Ducks won the first NCAA basketball championship in 1939.

The professional level is represented by the Portland Trail Blazers of the National Basketball Association.

Pennsylvania

Every year, the Little League World Series is played in Williamsport. In football, the Pennsylvania State University Nittany Lions were named national champions in 1982 and 1986, as were the University of Pittsburgh Panthers, in 1937 and 1976. In basketball, the NCAA national championship has been won by the La Salle Explorers (1954) and the Villanova Wildcats (1985), while the NIT championship was won by the Temple University Owls in 1938 and 1969, La Salle in 1953, and the Duquesne Dukes in 1955.

On the professional level, the state is home to the Pittsburgh Pirates and Philadelphia Phillies of the National League, the

Pittsburgh Steelers and Philadelphia Eagles of the National Football League, the Philadelphia 76ers of the American Basketball Association, and the Philadelphia Flyers and the Pittsburgh Penguins of the National Hockey League.

Rhode Island
In basketball, the NIT championship was won by the Providence College Friars in 1961 and 1963.

Tennessee
Every year, the Liberty Bowl football game is played in Memphis. The University of Tennessee Volunteers were named national football champions in 1951. The NIT basketball championship was won by the Vanderbilt Commodores (1990).

Texas
Three college football bowl games are played annually in Texas—the Cotton Bowl in Dallas, the Sun Bowl in El Paso, and the Bluebonnet Bowl in Houston. In football, the University of Texas Longhorns have been named national champions three times (1963, 1969, 1970). The Texas Christian Horned Frogs took the championship in 1938 and the Texas A&M Aggies in 1939. The University of Texas won the NIT basketball championship in 1978.

In baseball, Texas won the NCAA national championship in 1949, 1950, and 1983.

Professional teams include the Houston Astros of the National League and the Texas Rangers of the American League; the Dallas Cowboys and Houston Oilers of the National Football League; and the Dallas Mavericks, Houston Rockets, and San Antonio Spurs of the National Basketball Association.

Utah
The Brigham Young University Cougars were named national football champions in 1984. In basketball, the University of Utah Utes won the NCAA championship in 1944 and the NIT championship in 1947. Brigham Young has also won the NIT (1951, 1966).

On the professional level, the Utah Jazz (Salt Lake City) play in the National Basketball Association.

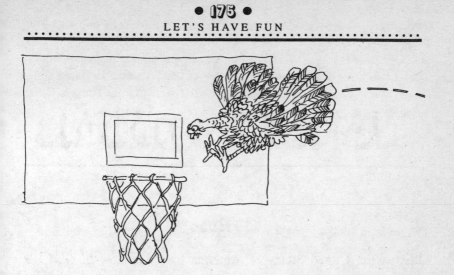

Virginia

The Virginia Tech Gobblers won the NIT basketball championship in 1973, and the University of Virginia Cavaliers won in 1980. Virginia also won the NCAA lacrosse championship in 1972.

Washington

On the professional level, there are the Seattle Mariners of the American League, the Seattle Seahawks of the National Football League, and the Seattle SuperSonics of the National Basketball Association.

West Virginia

The West Virginia University Mountaineers won the NIT basketball championship in 1942.

Wisconsin

The University of Wisconsin Badgers have won the NCAA basketball championship (1941), as have the Marquette University Warriors (1977). Marquette has also won the NIT championship (1970). In hockey, Wisconsin won the NCAA championship in 1973, 1977, 1981, and 1983.

On the professional level, there are the Milwaukee Brewers of the American League, the Green Bay Packers of the National Football League, and the Milwaukee Bucks of the National Basketball Association.

☆ 8 ☆
Written Symbols

....

Mottoes

Just as the United States of America has a motto—*In God We Trust*—every state has a motto that reflects some of its history or ethnic heritage.

Alabama: *Audemus Jura Nostra Defendere*, Latin for *We Dare Maintain Our Rights*.

This motto was adopted in 1923 to replace the previous motto *Here We Rest,* which had been selected by unpopular out-of-staters during the Reconstruction period after the Civil War; it was considered too negative.

Alaska: *North to the Future.*

The year 1963 marked the 100th anniversary of the Alaska Purchase, and the Centennial Commission held a competition to select a state motto. It was won by a Juneau newspaperman, Richard Peter, and the motto was adopted in 1967.

Arizona: *Ditat Deus*, Latin for *God Enriches*.
This motto was suggested by Richard Cunningham McCormick in 1864.

Arkansas: *Regnat Populus*, Latin for *The People Rule*.
This motto was adopted in 1907.

California: *Eureka*, Greek for *I Have Found It*.
The motto came from the Great Seal of California, adopted in 1849, but it is not known whether it referred to the admission of California as a state or to the discovery of gold there.

Colorado: *Nil Sine Numine*, Latin for *Nothing Without Providence*.
Although this Motto is reminiscent of a line from the Roman poet Virgil's *Aeneid*, it was suggested by the first territorial governor of Colorado, William Gilpin.

Connecticut: *Qui Transtulit Sustinet*, Latin for *He Who Transplanted Still Sustains*.
This motto dates back to colonial times, and is an adaptation of the Biblical passage in Psalms 79:3.

Delaware: *Liberty and Independence*.
This motto was added to the state's Great Seal in 1847.

District of Columbia: *Justitia Omnibus*, Latin for *Justice for All*.

Florida: *In God We Trust*.
The motto was adopted in 1868, and was taken from the motto used on the American silver dollar.

Georgia: *Agriculture and Commerce, 1776* and *Wisdom, Justice, Moderation*.
Georgia's two mottoes appear on opposite sides of the Great Seal.

Hawaii: *Ua Mau ke Ea o ka Aina i ka Pono*, Hawaiian for *The Life of the Land is Perpetuated in Righteousness*.
This motto was adopted in 1843 by King Kamehameha III; it had appeared on the coat of arms of the Kingdom of Hawaii.

Idaho: *Esto Perpetua*, Latin for *It Is Forever*.
Originally, this motto was used by the Republic of Venice, Italy; it was adopted by Idaho in 1891.

Illinois: *State Sovereignty, National Union*.
In 1818 this motto appeared on the original state seal.

Indiana: *The Crossroads of America*.
The motto was adopted in 1937, and refers to the fact that at that time the population center of the United States was in Indiana.

Iowa: *Our Liberties We Prize, and Our Rights We Will Maintain*.

This motto was placed on the state seal in 1847, one year after Iowa's entry into the Union.

Kansas: *Ad Astra per Aspera,* Latin for *To the Stars Through Difficulties.*

John J. Ingalls, secretary of the state senate in 1861, added this motto to the Great Seal. He had come across it in his readings with the lawyer under whom he had studied law.

Kentucky: *United We Stand, Divided We Fall.*

This motto was an adaptation of a line from "Liberty Song of 1768" by John Dickinson.

Louisiana: *Union, Justice and Confidence.*

The motto was adopted in 1864 as a rewording of the former motto, *Justice, Union, and Confidence..*

Maine: *Dirigo,* Latin for *I Direct.*

Found on the state seal, it refers to the idea that the state should be a guiding light.

Maryland: *Fatti Maschii Parole Femine* and *Scuto Bonae Voluntatis Tuae Coronasti Nos,* Latin for *Manly Deeds, Womanly Words* and *With Favor Wilt Thou Compass Us As with a Shield.*

The first motto was that of the founding Calvert family, and the second comes from the 12th verse of the Fifth Psalm.

Massachusetts: *Ense Petit Placidam Sub Libertate Quietem,* Latin for *By the Sword We Seek Peace, but Peace Only Under Liberty.*

The motto was first used on the state seal of 1775, and was probably written by Algernon Sydney in 1659.

Michigan: *Si Quaeris Peninsulam Amoenam Circumspice,* Latin for *If You Seek a Pleasant Peninsula, Look About You.*

This motto originally appeared on the Great Seal of 1835; it was selected by Lewis Cass.

Minnesota: *L'Etoile du Nord,* French for *Star of the North.*

Selected in 1861, the motto refers to the fact that Minnesota was known as the North Star State.

Mississippi: *Virtute et Armis,* Latin for *By Valor and Arms.*

In 1894, the state superintendent of education, James Rhea Preston, suggested this motto.

Missouri: *Salus Populi Suprema Lex Esto,* Latin for *The Welfare of the People Shall be the Supreme Law.*

This quotation from the Roman orator, Cicero, in his book *De Legibus*, was adopted as a motto in 1822.

Montana: *Oro y Plata*, Spanish for *Gold and Silver*.
The motto first appeared on the territorial seal in 1865, but no one knows why it was rendered in Spanish.

Nebraska: *Equality Before the Law*.
The motto was adopted in 1867.

Nevada: *All for Our Country*.
This patriotic motto was selected in 1866.

New Hampshire: *Live Free or Die*.
General John Stark first used these words in a toast for a veterans' reunion in 1809, and it was adopted in 1945.

New Jersey: *Liberty and Prosperity*.
This motto was unofficially used by the state for at least a century before it was formally adopted in 1928.

New Mexico: *Crescit Eundo*, Latin for *It Grows As It Goes*.
This has been the motto of New Mexico since territorial times in 1851.

New York: *Excelsior*, Latin for *Ever Upward*.
The motto dates to 1778.

North Carolina: *Esse Quam Videri*, Latin for *To Be Rather Than to Seem*.
The Roman orator Cicero wrote this line, which was adopted as the state motto in 1893.

North Dakota: *Liberty and Union Now and Forever, One and Inseparable*.
Adopted in 1889, this motto is a quote from Daniel Webster's *Reply to Hayne*.

Ohio: *With God, All Things Are Possible*.
Selected in 1959, this motto comes from the Bible—Matthew 19:26.

Oklahoma: *Labor Omnia Vincit*, Latin for *Labor Conquers All Things*.
The Roman poet Virgil wrote the line that was adopted as the state motto in 1906.

Oregon: *The Union*.
The motto was recommended by the legislature in 1857 and adopted in 1859, but an 1849 state seal carried the motto *Alis Volat*

Propriis, Latin for *She Flies with Her Own Wings.* The matter wasn't settled until 1957.

Pennsylvania: *Virtue, Liberty, and Independence.*
Adopted in 1875, this motto first appeared in 1778 in the state coat of arms.

Rhode Island: *Hope.*
This motto goes back to old colonial times—1644.

South Carolina: *Animis Opibusque Parati* and *Dum Spiro Spero,* Latin for *Prepared in Mind and Resources* and *While I Breathe, I Hope.*
These two mottoes were adopted in 1776 after the colony had declared itself independent.

South Dakota: *Under God the People Rule.*
The motto was adopted in both the 1885 and 1889 state constitutions.

Tennessee: *Agriculture and Commerce.*
This motto, taken from the state seal, is still unofficial.

Texas: *Friendship.*
Adopted in 1930, this motto reflects the fact that the name of the state comes from an Indian word, *tejas,* which means friendship.

Utah: *Industry.*
The motto was selected in 1896.

Vermont: *Freedom and Unity.*
This motto comes from the 1778 state seal; it was adopted the following year.

Virginia: *Sic Semper Tyrannis,* Latin for *Thus Ever to Tyrants.*
This motto dates back to the outbreak of the Revolutionary War in 1776.

Washington: *Alki,* Indian for *By and By.*
This motto originated in territorial times. It refers to the feeling among the settlers who landed at Alki Point—what is now Seattle—when they named their settlement "New York-Alki," meaning that they hoped it would someday be the New York of the West Coast.

West Virginia: *Montani Semper Liberi,* Latin for *Mountaineers Are Always Free.*
The motto was adopted in 1863, two years after the state broke away from Virginia.

Wisconsin: *Forward.*

This motto dates back to 1851, the year that railroads came to the state.

Wyoming: *Equal Rights.*

Originally used on the state seal, the motto was adopted in 1955. It refers to the fact that the women of Wyoming were granted the right to vote in 1869, long before they were given the national right to vote by the Nineteenth Amendment to the Constitution in 1920.

Pledges to the Flag

The Pledge of Allegiance to the Flag of the United States of America is of fairly recent vintage. In 1892 *The Youth's Companion,* a popular magazine for boys, ran a contest for the best patriotic-sounding loyalty oath. From this came the pledge that we all know. The only change in it was the addition of the two words "under God," during the Eisenhower administration of the 1950s. Some states have also adopted pledges to their state flags:

Arkansas (1913) "I salute the Arkansas Flag with its diamonds and stars. We pledge our loyalty to thee."

Georgia (1956) "I pledge allegiance to the Georgia flag and to the principles for which it stands: Wisdom, Justice, and Moderation."

Louisiana (1981) "I pledge allegiance to the flag of the state of Louisiana and to the motto for which it stands: A state, under God, united in purpose and ideals, confident that justice shall prevail for all of those abiding here."

Mississippi (1894) "I salute the flag of Mississippi and the sovereign state for which it stands, with pride in her history and achievements and with confidence in her future under the guidance of Almighty God."

New Mexico (1953) New Mexico has both an English and a Spanish version of its pledge to the flag. The English version reads, "I salute the flag of the state of New Mexico, the Zia Indian symbol of perfect friendship among united cultures." The Spanish version reads *"Saludo la bandera del estado de Nueva Méjico, el símbolo zía de amistad perfecta, entre culturas unidas."*

South Carolina (1966) "I salute the flag of South Carolina and pledge to the Palmetto State love, loyalty and faith."

Texas (1876) "Honor the Texas Flag; I pledge allegiance to thee, Texas, one and indivisible."

★ 9 ★
Living Symbols

Almost every state has an official bird, tree, and flower that have special significance for its citizens. Sometimes these emblems have been the subjects of heated debate, as in the case of the bald eagle, our national bird!

Birds

Not everyone was pleased by the bald eagle's selection as a national symbol early in our history. Founding father Benjamin Franklin expressed his opinion strongly in 1784: "I wish the Bald Eagle had not been chosen as the Representative of our Country; he is a Bird of bad moral Character; like those among Men who live by Sharping and Robbing, he is generally poor, and often very lousy. The Turkey is a much more respectable Bird, and withall a true original native of America. He is (though a little vain and silly, it is true, but not the worst emblem for that) a Bird of Courage, and would not hesitate to attack a grenadier of the British Guards who should presume to invade his farmyard with a red coat on."

The eagle was selected early, but it wasn't until 1926 that one of the states got around to naming a state bird—Kentucky, which chose the cardinal. Today, the cardinal is the most popular state bird, shared by seven of our states. Following it in popularity are the western meadowlark (six states), the mockingbird (five), the robin (three), the bluebird (two), the chickadee (two), the eastern goldfinch (two), and the mountain bluebird (two). Only Pennsylvania has no state bird, but the commonwealth does have a state game bird.

Alabama: Yellowhammer (also called the yellow-shafted woodpecker or the flicker)
Alaska: Willow Ptarmigan
Arizona: Cactus Wren (also called Coues' Cactus Wren)
Arkansas: Mockingbird
California: California Valley Quail
Colorado: Lark Bunting
Connecticut: Robin (also called the American Robin)
Delaware: Blue Hen Chicken
District of Columbia: Wood Thrush
Florida: Mockingbird
Georgia: Brown Thrasher
Hawaii: Nene (also called the Hawaiian Goose)
Idaho: Mountain Bluebird
Illinois: Cardinal (also called the Red Bird or Kentucky Cardinal)
Indiana: Cardinal (also called the Red Bird or Kentucky Cardinal)
Iowa: Eastern Goldfinch

Kansas: Western Meadowlark
Kentucky: Cardinal (also called the Red Bird or Kentucky Cardinal)
Louisiana: Brown Pelican (also called the Eastern Brown Pelican)
Maine: Chickadee (also called the Black-Capped Chickadee)
Maryland: Northern Oriole (formerly called the Baltimore Oriole)
Massachusetts: Chickadee (also called the Black-Capped Chickadee)
Michigan: Robin (also called the American Robin)
Minnesota: Loon
Mississippi: Mockingbird
Missouri: Bluebird (also called the Eastern Bluebird and the Blue Robin)
Montana: Western Meadowlark
Nebraska: Western Meadowlark
Nevada: Mountain Bluebird
New Hampshire: Purple Finch
New Jersey: Eastern Goldfinch
New Mexico: Roadrunner (also called the Chaparral Bird)
New York: Bluebird (also called the Eastern Bluebird and the Blue Robin)
North Carolina: Cardinal (also called the Red Bird or Kentucky Cardinal)
North Dakota: Western Meadowlark
Ohio: Cardinal (also called the Red Bird or Kentucky Cardinal)
Oklahoma: Scissor-Tailed Flycatcher
Oregon: Western Meadowlark
Pennsylvania: Ruffed Grouse
Rhode Island: Rhode Island Red

South Carolina: Carolina Wren

South Dakota: Ring-Necked Pheasant (also called the Chinese Pheasant)

Tennessee: Mockingbird

Texas: Mockingbird

Utah: Seagull

Vermont: Hermit Thrush

Virginia: Cardinal (also called the Red Bird or Kentucky Cardinal)

Washington: Willow Goldfinch

West Virginia: Cardinal (also called the Red Bird or Kentucky Cardinal)

Wisconsin: Robin (also called the American Robin)

Wyoming: Western Meadowlark

Trees

It was Texas that chose the first state tree—the pecan—in 1919. Since then, every state has chosen a state tree, and New Jersey has chosen two. Today, the white oak and sugar maple are the most popular state tree; each is shared by four states. Following them in popularity are the southern pine and dogwood (three states each), the palmetto (two), the blue spruce (two), and the tulip poplar (two).

Alabama: Southern Pine

Alaska: Sitka Spruce (also called the Yellow, Tideland, Western, Coast, or Menzies' Spruce)

Arizona: Paloverde (also called the Green-Barked Acacia)

Arkansas: Southern Pine

California: California Redwood (also called the Coast Redwood, the Redwood, the Giant Sequoia, the Sierra Redwood, or the Mammoth Tree)

Colorado: Blue Spruce (also called the Colorado Blue Spruce, the Balsam, the Colorado Spruce, and the Prickly, White, Silver, or Parry's Spruce)

Connecticut: White Oak

Delaware: American Holly (also called the Holly, the White Holly, the Evergreen Holly, and the Boxwood)

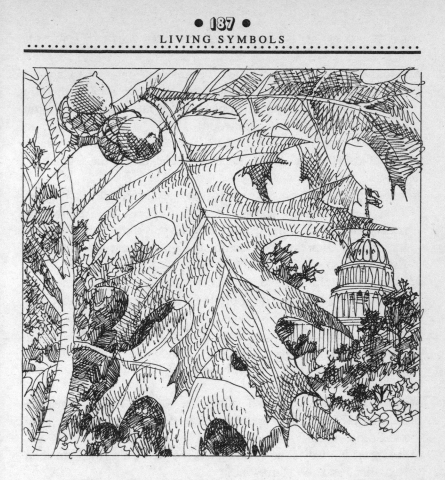

District of Columbia: Scarlet Oak

Florida: Palmetto (also called the Sabal Palmetto, the Cabbage Palm, the Cabbage Palmetto, the Tree Palmetto, or Bank's Palmetto)

Georgia: Live Oak

Hawaii: Kukui

Idaho: Western White Pine (also called the white pine, the Idaho White Pine, the Finger-Cone Pine, the Mountain Pine, the Little Sugar Pine, or the Mountain Weymouth Pine)

Illinois: White Oak

Indiana: Tulip Poplar (also called the Tulip Tree, the Yellow Poplar, the Blue Poplar, the Hickory Poplar, the Basswood, the Cucumber Tree, the Tulipwood, the White Poplar, the Poplar, and the Old-Wive's-Shirt-Tree)

Iowa: Oak (all varieties)

Kansas: Cottonwood (also called the Eastern Poplar, the Carolina Poplar, the Eastern Cottonwood, the Necklace Poplar, the Big Cottonwood, the Vermont Poplar, the Whitewood, the Cotton Tree, and the Yellow Cottonwood)

Kentucky: Coffee Tree (also called the Kentucky Tree, the Coffeebean Tree, the Coffeenut, the Mahogany, the Nickertree, the Stumptree, and the Virgilia)

Louisiana: Bald Cypress (also called the Cypress, the Cypress Tree, the Southern Cypress, the Red Cypress, the Yellow Cypress, the Black Cypress, the White Cypress, the Gulf Cypress, the Swamp Cypress, the Deciduous Cypress, and the Tidewater Red Cypress)

Maine: White Pine (also called the Eastern White Pine, the Northern White Pine, the Soft Pine, the Weymouth Pine, and the Spruce Pine)

Maryland: White Oak

Massachusetts: American Elm (also called the White Elm, the Water Elm, the Gray Elm, the Swamp Elm, the Rock Elm, and the Orme Maigre)

Michigan: White Pine (also called the Eastern White Pine, the Northern White Pine, the Soft Pine, the Weymouth Pine, and the Spruce Pine)

Minnesota: Norway Pine (also called the Red Pine, the Canadian Red Pine, and the Hard Pine)

Mississippi: Magnolia (also called the Evergreen Magnolia, the Big Laurel, the Bull Bay, the Great Laurel Magnolia, the Bat-Tree, the Laurel-Leaved Magnolia, the Large-Flowered Magnolia, and the Laurel Bay)

Missouri: Dogwood (also called the Flowering Dogwood, the Boxwood, the False Box-Dogwood, the New England Boxwood, the Flowering Cornel, and the Cornel)

Montana: Ponderosa Pine (also called the Western Yellow Pine, the Western Soft Pine, the Western Soft Pine, the Yellow Pine, the Bull Pine, the Foothills Yellow Pine, the Red Pine, the Big Pine, the Long-Leaved Pine, the Pitch Pine, the Heavy Wooded Pine, the Heavy Pine, the Sierra Brownbark Pine, or the Montana Black Pine)

Nebraska: Cottonwood (also called the Eastern Poplar, the Carolina Poplar, the Eastern Cottonwood, the Necklace Poplar, the Big

Cottonwood, the Vermont Poplar, the Whitewood, the Cotton
Tree, or the Yellow Cottonwood)

Nevada: Single-Leaf Piñon (also called the Nut Pine, the Pinyon,
the Gray Pine, the Nevada Nut Pine, or the Singleleaf Pinyon
Pine)

New Hampshire: White Birch (also called the Canoe Birch, the
Silver Birch, the Paper Birch, or the Large White Birch)

New Jersey: Red Oak (also called the Northern Red Oak, the Black
Oak, or the Spanish Oak) and Dogwood (also called the Flower-
ing Dogwood, the Boxwood, the False Box-Dogwood, the New
England Boxwood, the Flowering Cornel, and the Cornel)

New Mexico: Nut Pine (also called the Piñon, the Pinyon Pine, the
Colorado Pinyon Pine, or the New Mexico Piñon)

New York: Sugar Maple (also called the Hard Maple, the Rock
Maple, or the Black Maple)

North Carolina: Southern Pine (also called the Longleaf Yellow
Pine, the Pitch Pine, the Hard Pine, the Heart Pine, the
Turpentine Pine, the Rosemary Pine, the Brown Pine, the Fat
Pine, the Longstraw Pine, or the Long-Leaf Pitch Pine)

North Dakota: American Elm (also called the White Elm, the
Water Elm, the Gray Elm, the Swamp Elm, the Rock Elm, or
the Orme Maigre)

Ohio: Buckeye (also called the Ohio Buckeye, the Fetid Buckeye,
the Stinking Buckeye, or the American Horse Chestnut)

Oklahoma: Redbud (also called the Judas Tree, the Red Judas
Tree, the Salad-Tree, or the Canadian Judas Tree)

Oregon: Douglas Fir (also called the Douglas Spruce, the Red Fir,
the Yellow Fir, the Oregon Pine, the Red Pine, the Puget Sound
Pine, the Spruce, the Fir, the Douglas Tree, or the Cork-Barked
Douglas Spruce)

Pennsylvania: Hemlock (also called the Eastern Hemlock, the
Canadian Hemlock, the Hemlock Spruce, the Spruce Pine, the
New England Hemlock, or the Spruce)

Rhode Island: Red Maple (also called the Soft Maple, the Water
Maple, the Scarlet Maple, the White Maple, the Swamp Maple,
the Shoe-Peg Maple, or the Erable)

South Carolina: Palmetto (also called the Sabal Palmetto, the
Cabbage Palm, the Cabbage Palmetto, the Tree Palmetto, or the
Bank's Palmetto)

South Dakota: Black Hills Spruce (also called the White Spruce, the Single Spruce, the Bog Spruce, the Skunk Spruce, the Cat Spruce, the Spruce, the Pine, or the Double Spruce)

Tennessee: Tulip Poplar (also called the Tulip Tree, the Yellow Poplar, the Blue Poplar, the Hickory Poplar, the Basswood, the Cucumber Tree, the Tulipwood, the Whitewood, the White Poplar, the Poplar, or the Old-Wife's-Shirt-Tree)

Texas: Pecan (also called the Pecan Nut, the Pecanier, or the Pecan Hickory)

Utah: Blue Spruce (also called the Colorado Blue Spruce, the Balsam, the Colorado Spruce, the Prickly Spruce, the White Spruce, the Silver Spruce, or the Parry's Spruce)

Vermont: Sugar Maple (also called the Hard Maple, the Rock Maple, or the Black Maple)

Virginia: Dogwood (also called the Flowering Dogwood, the Boxwood, the False Box-Dogwood, the New England Boxwood, the Flowering Cornel, or the Cornel)

Washington: Western Hemlock (also called the West Coast Hemlock, the Pacific Hemlock, the Hemlock Spruce, the California Hemlock Spruce, the Western Hemlock Fir, the Prince Albert's Fir, or the Alaskan Pine)

West Virginia: Sugar Maple (also called the Hard Maple, the Rock Maple, or the Bald Maple)

Wisconsin: Sugar Maple (also called the Hard Maple, the

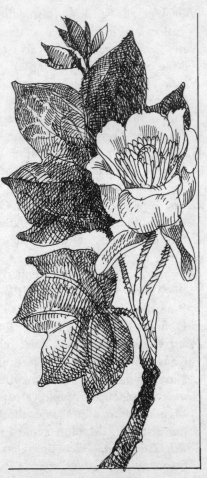

Rock Maple, or the Black
Maple)
Wyoming: Plains Cotton-
wood (also called the
Cottonwood or the
Plains Poplar)

Flowers

Unlike the state birds and trees, hardly any state flower is shared
by even two states. And the state flower can generate almost as
much controversy as the "bald eagle versus turkey" debate about
the national bird in colonial times! For example, the Iowa state
legislature took a dim view of the sunflower, which grows wild in
the Midwest, and passed a bill that called it a "noxious weed."
Since the sunflower is the state flower of Kansas, the Kansas state
legislature showed its displeasure by passing a bill that called the
eastern goldfinch, Iowa's state bird, "a public nuisance."

Some states, on the other hand, are quite fickle about their state
flower. Indiana has changed its mind several times, going from the
carnation to the flower of the tulip tree, to the zinnia, to the peony
(which is not even native to Indiana!).

Alabama: Camellia
Alaska: Wild Forget-Me-Not
Arizona: Saguaro Flower
Arkansas: Apple Blossom
California: Golden Poppy
Colorado: White and Lavender Columbine
Connecticut: Mountain Laurel
Delaware: Peach Blossom
District of Columbia: American Beauty Rose

Florida: Orange Blossom
Georgia: Cherokee Rose
Hawaii: Hibiscus
Idaho: Syringia
Illinois: Violet
Indiana: Peony
Iowa: Wild Rose
Kansas: Sunflower
Kentucky: Goldenrod
Louisiana: Magnolia
Maine: Pine Cone and Tassel
Maryland: Black-eyed Susan
Massachusetts: Mayflower
Michigan: Apple Blossom
Minnesota: Pink and White Lady Slipper
Mississippi: Magnolia
Missouri: Red Haw or Wild Haw
Montana: Bitterroot
Nebraska: Late Goldenrod
Nevada: Sagebrush
New Hampshire: Purple Lilac
New Jersey: Meadow Violet

New Mexico: Yucca Flower
New York: Rose
North Carolina: Dogwood Flower
North Dakota: Wild Prairie Rose
Ohio: Scarlet Carnation
Oklahoma: Mistletoe
Oregon: Oregon Grape
Pennsylvania: Mountain Laurel
Rhode Island: Violet
South Carolina: Yellow Jessamine
South Dakota: American Pasque Flower
Tennessee: State flower: Iris
          State wild flower: Passion Flower
Texas: Bluebonnet
Utah: Sego Lily
Vermont: Red Clover
Virginia: Dogwood
Washington: Pink Rhododendron
West Virginia: Big Laurel
Wisconsin: Wood Violet
Wyoming: Indian Paintbrush

☆ 10 ☆
Some Unusual Symbols

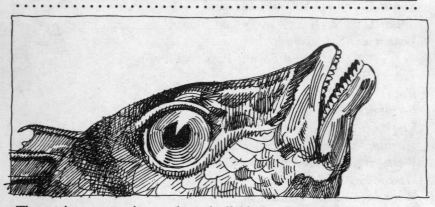

The various states have adopted all kinds of symbols besides the familiar ones like birds, trees, and flowers. They range from the commonplace to the far-out, from state fish to state fossils. Here's a sampling.

State Air Fair
  Florida: Central Florida Air Fair
State American Folk Art Symbol
  Rhode Island: Charles I. D. Looff Carousel
State Animal
  California: California Grizzly Bear
  Colorado: Rocky Mountain Bighorn Sheep
  Connecticut: Sperm Whale
  Florida: Florida Panther
  Illinois: White-Tailed Deer
  Kansas: American Buffalo
  Maine: Moose
  Montana: Grizzly Bear

Nevada: Desert Bighorn Sheep
New Hampshire: White-Tailed Deer
New Jersey: Horse
New Mexico: New Mexico Black Bear
New York: American Beaver
Oklahoma: American Buffalo
Oregon: American Beaver
Pennsylvania: White-Tailed Deer
South Carolina: White-Tailed Deer
South Dakota: Coyote
Utah: Elk
Vermont: Morgan Horse
West Virginia: Black Bear
Wisconsin: Badger
State Art Gallery
North Dakota: University of
    North Dakota Art Gallery,
    Grand Forks
State Atlas
Georgia: The Atlas of Georgia
State Baked Goods
New York: Apple Muffin
State Beautification and Conservation Plant
Pennsylvania: Penngift crownvetch
State Beverage/Drink
Arkansas: Milk
Delaware: Milk
Florida: Orange Juice
Louisiana: Milk
Massachusetts: Cranberry Juice
Minnesota: Milk
Mississippi: Milk
New York: Milk
North Dakota: Milk
Ohio: Tomato Juice
Pennsylvania: Milk
South Carolina: Milk
Vermont: Milk
Virginia: Milk

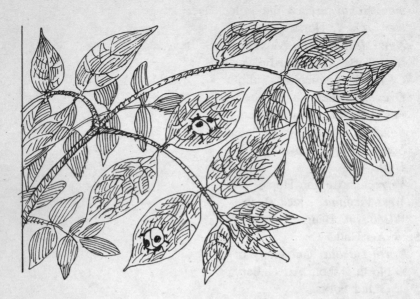

State Bug
  Delaware: Ladybug
State Building and Monument Stone
  Massachusetts: Granite
State Cat
  Maine: Maine Coon Cat
State Colors
  Hawaii: Each inhabited island has its own color: Hawaii, Red;
    Maui, Pink; Molokai, Green; Kahoolawe, Gray; Lanai, Yel-
    low; Oahu, Yellow; Kauai, Purple; Nihau, White
  Nevada: Silver and Blue
  North Carolina: Red and Blue
  Oklahoma: Green and White
State Crustacean
  Louisiana: Crawfish
State Dance
  Alabama: Square Dance
  South Carolina: The Shag
  Washington: Square Dance

State Dog
  Louisiana: Louisiana Catahoula Leopard Dog
  Maryland: Chesapeake Bay Retriever
  Massachusetts: Boston Terrier
  Pennsylvania: Great Dane
  Virginia: American Foxhound
State Domestic Animal
  Wisconsin: Dairy Cow
State Emblem
  Utah: Beehive
State Explorer Rock
  Massachusetts: Dighton Rock
State Festival
  Florida: "Calle Ocho-Open House 8"
State Fine Art
  Tennessee: Porcelain Painting
State Fish
  Alaska: King Salmon
  California: Golden Trout
  Delaware: Weakfish
  Georgia: Largemouth Bass
  Maine: Landlocked Salmon
  Maryland: Striped Bass
  Massachusetts: Cod
  Michigan: Trout
  Minnesota: Walleye
  Mississippi: Largemouth Bass
  Montana: Blackspotted Cutthroat Trout
  Nevada: Lohonton Cutthroat Trout
  New York: Brook Trout or Speckled Trout
  Oklahoma: White Bass
  Oregon: Chinook Salmon
  Pennsylvania: Brook Trout
  South Carolina: Striped Bass
  South Dakota: Walleye
  Utah: Rainbow Trout
  Washington: Steelhead Trout
  West Virginia: Brook Trout
  Wisconsin: Muskellunge or Muskie

State Fossil
  Alabama: Basilosaurus cetoides
  California: Saber-Toothed Cat
  Georgia: Shark Tooth
  Louisiana: Petrified Palmwood
  Maine: Pertica quadrifaria
  Massachusetts: Dinosaur Track
  Mississippi: Prehistoric Whale
  Nebraska: Mammoth
  Nevada: Ichthyosaur
  New Mexico: Coelophysis
  New York: Eurypterus remipes
  North Dakota: Teredo Petrified Wood
State Fossil Shell
  Maryland: Ecphora quadricosata
State Folk Dance
  Tennessee: Square Dance
State Freshwater Fish
  Alabama: Largemouth Bass
  Florida: Florida Largemouth Bass
State Fruit
  Louisiana: Changes annually
  New York: Apple
  South Carolina: Peach
  West Virginia: Apple
State Gem
  Alaska: Jade
  Arizona: Turquoise
  Arkansas: Diamond
  Colorado: Aquamarine
  Florida: Moonstone
  Georgia: Quartz
  Idaho: Star Garnet
  Louisiana: Agate
  Massachusetts: Rhodonite
  Michigan: Chlorastrolite or Greenstone
  Minnesota: Lake Superior Agate
  Montana: Sapphire and Montana Agate

Nebraska: Blue Agate
New Mexico: Turquoise
New York: Garnet
Ohio: Ohio Flint
South Carolina: Amethyst
South Dakota: Fairburn Agate
Tennessee: Tennessee Pearl
Utah: Topaz
Washington: Petrified Wood
Wyoming: Jade

State Grain
Minnesota: Wild Rice

State Grass
Montana: Bluebunch Grass
Nebraska: Little Blue Stem Grass
Nevada: Indian Rice Grass
New Mexico: Blue Grama Grass
North Dakota: Western Wheat Grass
Oklahoma: Indian Grass
South Dakota: Western Wheat Grass

State Heroine
Massachusetts: Deborah Samson

State Historical Rock
Massachusetts: Plymouth Rock

State Horse
  Alabama: Racking Horse
  Idaho: Appaloosa
  Massachusetts: Morgan Horse
State Hostess
  Oregon: Miss Oregon

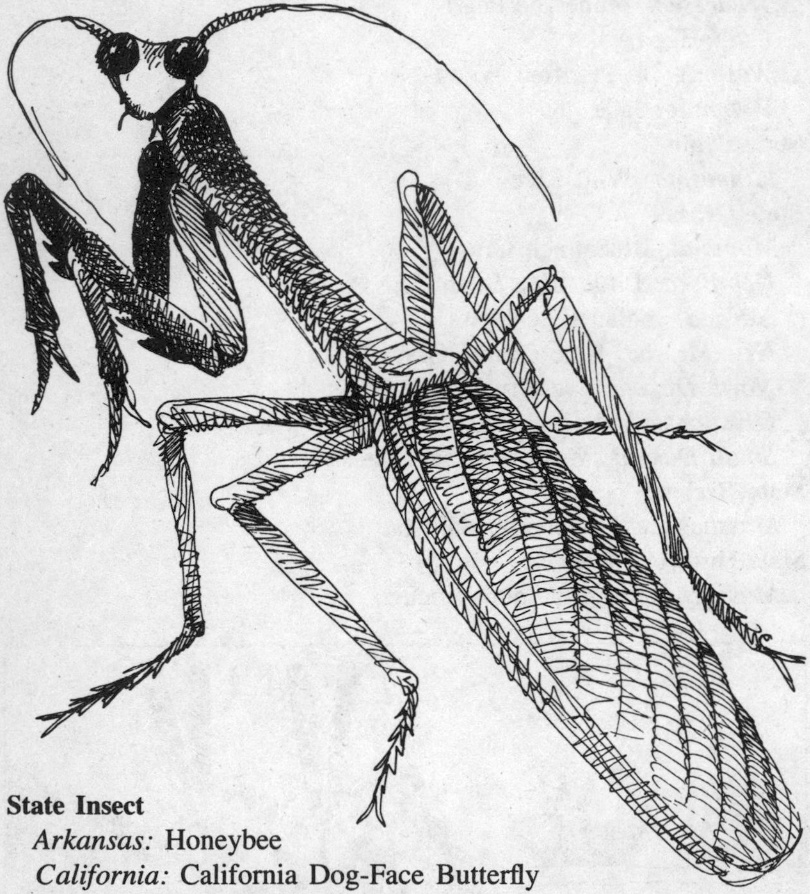

State Insect
  Arkansas: Honeybee
  California: California Dog-Face Butterfly
  Connecticut: Praying Mantis
  Georgia: Honeybee
  Illinois: Monarch Butterfly
  Kansas: Honeybee
  Louisiana: Honeybee
  Maine: Honeybee
  Maryland: Baltimore Checkerspot Butterfly

Massachusetts: Ladybug
Mississippi: Honeybee
Nebraska: Honeybee
New Hampshire: Ladybug
New Jersey: Honeybee
New York: Ladybug
North Carolina: Honeybee
Oregon: Swallowtail Butterfly
Pennsylvania: Firefly
South Dakota: Honeybee
Tennessee: Firefly and
    Ladybug
Utah: Honeybee
Vermont: Honeybee
Wisconsin: Honeybee

State Language
Fifteen states have enacted laws making English the official state language: Arkansas, California, Colorado, Florida, Georgia, Illinois, Indiana, Kentucky, Mississippi, Nebraska, North Carolina, North Dakota, South Carolina, Tennessee, and Virginia. (Arizona also had such a law, but it was declared unconstitutional by a federal judge in 1990.) Hawaii has two official languages: English and Hawaiian.

State Land Mammal
Mississippi: White-Tailed Deer

State Litter Control Symbol
Florida: "Glenn Glitter"

State Mammal
Nebraska: White-Tailed Deer
North Carolina: Gray Squirrel

State Marine Mammal
Alaska: Bowhead Whale
California: California Gray Whale
Florida: Manatee
Georgia: Right Whale
Massachusetts: Right Whale

State Metal
Nevada: Silver

State Mineral
 Alabama: Hematite
 Alaska: Gold
 Arkansas: Quartz Crystal
 California: Native Gold
 Connecticut: Garnet
 Delaware: Sillimanite
 Georgia: Staurolite
 Illinois: Fluorite
 Maine: Tourmaline
 Massachusetts: Babingtonite
 Missouri: Galena
 Rhode Island: Bowenite
 South Dakota: Rose Quartz
 Wisconsin: Galena
State Mushroom
 Minnesota: Morel
State Musical Instrument
 Arkansas: Fiddle
State Neckwear
 Arizona: Bola Tie
State Pageant
 Florida: "Indian River"
State Play
 Florida: Crown and Sword
 Texas: The Lone Star, Texas, Beyond the Sundown, and *Fandangle*
State Poem
 Indiana: "Indiana," by Arthur Franklyn Mapes
 Massachusetts: "Blue Hills of Massachusetts," by Katherine E. Mullen
 Oklahoma: "Howdy Folks," by David Randolph Milsten
 Tennessee: "Oh Tennessee, My Tennessee," by Admiral William Lawrence
State Railroad Museum
 Tennessee: Tennessee Valley Railroad Museum
State Reptile
 California: California Desert Tortoise

Louisiana: Alligator
North Carolina: Eastern Box Turtle
Oklahoma: Collared Lizard

State Rock
Alabama: Marble
Arkansas: Bauxite
California: Serpentine
Iowa: Geode
Massachusetts: Roxbury Pudding Stone
Missouri: Mozarkite
Nebraska: Prairie Agate
North Carolina: Granite
Oklahoma: Barite Rose
Oregon: Thunderegg
Rhode Island: Cumberlandite
Tennessee: Limestone
Wisconsin: Red Granite

State Saltwater Fish
Alabama: Tarpon
Florida: Atlantic Sailfish
North Carolina: Channel Bass or Red Drum

State Saltwater Mammal
Florida: Porpoise

State Shakespeare Festival
Kentucky: Shakespeare in Central Park in Louisville

State Shell
Florida: Horse Conch
Mississippi: Oyster Shell
North Carolina: Scotch Bonnet
South Carolina: Lettered Olive
Virginia: Oyster Shell

State Ship
Connecticut: U.S.S. *Nautilus*
Maryland: Skipjack

State Soil
Vermont: Tunbridge Soil Series
Wisconsin: Antigo Silt Loam

State Sport
  Alaska: Dog Mushing
  Maryland: Jousting
State Stone
  Florida: Agatized Coral
  Indiana: Limestone
  Michigan: Petoskey Stone
  North Carolina: Emerald
  South Carolina: Blue Granite
State Summer Theater
  Maryland: Olney Theatre
State Symbol of Peace
  Wisconsin: Mourning Dove
State Theater
  Maryland: Center Stage in Baltimore
State Tug-of-War Championship
  Kentucky: Nelson County Fair
State Vegetable
  New Mexico: Pinto Bean and Chili
State Water Mammal
  Mississippi: Bottlenosed Dolphin
State Wild Animal
  Tennessee: Raccoon
State Wild Animal Game Species
  Kentucky: Gray Squirrel
State Wildlife Animal
  Wisconsin: White-Tailed Deer

Songs

"The Star Spangled Banner," of course, is the national anthem of the United States. But most of the states have at least one state song. Some oddities can be found on the list. For example, Rogers and Hammerstein, Hoagy Carmichael, and Stephen Foster were all composers of state songs for states in which they never lived. The only states that do *not* have a song are New Jersey and Pennsylvania.

State	Songs
Alabama	"Alabama," with words by Julia S. Tutwiler and music by Edna Glockel Gussen.
Alaska	"Alaska's Flag," with words by Marie Drake and music by Elinor Dusenbury.
Arizona	"Arizona March Song," with words by Margaret Rowe Cliffords and music by Maurice Blumenthal.
Arkansas	"Arkansas," with words and music by Eva Ware Barnett.
California	"I Love You, California," with words by F. B. Silverwood and music by A. F. Frankenstein.
Colorado	"Where the Columbines Grow," with words and music by A. J. Flynn.

Connecticut	"Yankee Doodle," an old folk song of unknown origin.
Delaware	"Our Delaware," with words by George B. Hynson and music by Will M. S. Brown.
Florida	"Old Folks at Home," also known as "The Swanee River," with words and music by Stephen Foster.
Georgia	"Georgia on My Mind," with words by Stuart

State	Songs
	Gorrell and music by Hoagy Carmichael. Originally, "Georgia," with words by Lottie Bell Wylie and music by Robert Loveman, was the official state song; the change was made in 1979. Georgia also has a state waltz, "Our Georgia," with words and music by James B. Burch.
Hawaii	"Hawaii Ponoi," a folk song of unknown origin.
Idaho	"Here We Have Idaho," with words by McKinley Helm and Albert J. Tompkins and music by Sallie Hume Douglas.
Illinois	"Illinois," with words by C. H. Chamberlain and music by Archibald Johnston.
Indiana	"On the Banks of the Wabash, Far Away," with words and music by Paul Dresser.
Iowa	"The Song of Iowa," with words by S. H. M. Byers set to the old Christmas carol "O Tannenbaum." Iowa also has an unofficial state song—the "Iowa Corn Song," by George Hamilton.
Kansas	"Home on the Range," with words by Dr. Brewster Higley and music by Dan Kelly. Kansas also has a state march, "The Kansas March," by Duff E. Middleton.

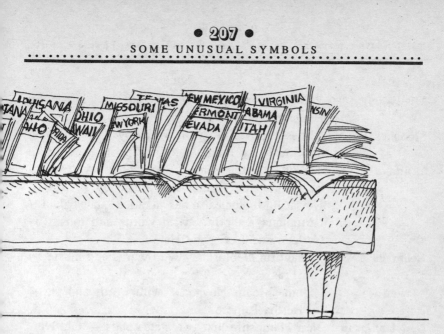

State	Songs
Kentucky	"My Old Kentucky Home," with words and music by Stephen Foster.
Louisiana	Louisiana has two state songs—"Give Me Louisiana," with words and music by Doralice Fontane, and "You Are My Sunshine," with words and music by Jimmy H. Davis and Charles Mitchell.
Maine	"State of Maine Song," with words and music by Roger Vinton Snow.
Maryland	"Maryland! My Maryland!," with words by James Ryder Randall set to the old tune *"Lauriger Horatius."*
Massachusetts	The official commonwealth song is "All Hail to Massachusetts," with words and music by Arthur J. Marsh. Massachusetts also has an official folk song—"Massachusetts," with words and music by Arlo Guthrie.
Michigan	"My Michigan," with words by Giles Kavanagh and music by H. O'Reilly Clint.
Minnesota	"Hail! Minnesota," with words by Truman E. Rickard and Arthur E. Upson, and music by Truman E. Rickard.

State	Songs
Mississippi	"Go, Mississippi," with words and music by Houston Davis.
Missouri	"Missouri Waltz," with words by J. R. Shannon and music by John Valentine Eppel.
Montana	The official state song is "Montana," with words by Charles C. Cohan and music by Joseph E. Howard. Montana also has an official state ballad— "Montana Melody," with words and music by Carleen and LeGrande Harvey.
Nebraska	"Beautiful Nebraska," with words and music by Jim Fras.
Nevada	"Home Means Nevada," with words and music by Bertha Raffeto.
New Hampshire	New Hampshire has two state songs—"Old New Hampshire," with words by John F. Holmes and music by Maurice Hoffmann, and "New Hampshire, My New Hampshire," with words by Julius Richelson and music by Walter P. Smith.
New Mexico	New Mexico has two state songs—one in English and one in Spanish. The English song is "O, Fair New Mexico," with words and music by Elizabeth Garrett. The Spanish Song is "*Asi Es Nuevo Méjico*," with words and music by Almadeo Lucero.
New York	"I Love New York," with words and music by Steve Karmen.
North Carolina	An old song, "The Old North State," is the official state song. North Carolina also has a state musical toast, "A Toast to North Carolina."
North Dakota	"North Dakota Hymn," with words by James W. Foley and music by C. S. Putnam. North Dakota also has a state march—"Spirit of the Land," by James D. Ployhar.
Ohio	"Beautiful Ohio," with words by Ballard Mac-Donald and music by Mary Earl.
Oklahoma	"Oklahoma," with words by Oscar Hammerstein II and music by Richard Rodgers, replaced

State	Songs
	"Oklahoma (A Toast)," by Harriet Parker Camden, in 1953.
Oregon	"Oregon, My Oregon," with words by J. A. Buchanan and music by Henry B. Murtagh.
Rhode Island	"Rhode Island," with words and music by T. Clarke Brown.
South Carolina	South Carolina has two state songs—"Carolina," with words by Henry Timrod and music by Anne Custis Burgess, and "Carolina on My Mind."
South Dakota	"Hail! South Dakota," with words and music by Deecort Hammitt.
Tennessee	The state legislature of Tennessee seems to have a memory problem. It keeps designating new state songs without repealing the act that created the previous one. Currently, there are five state songs: "My Homeland, Tennessee," with words and music by Nell Grayson Taylor and Roy Lamont; "When It's Iris Time in Tennessee," with words and music by Willa Mae Waid; "My Tennessee," with words and music by Francis Hannah Tranum; "The Tennessee Waltz," with words and music by Redd Stewart and Pee Wee King; and "Rocky Top," with words and music by Boudleaux and Felice Bryant.
Texas	"Texas, Our Texas," with words and music by William J. Marsh and Gladys Yoakum Wright. Texas also has a state-flower song—"Bluebonnets," with words by Julia D. Booth and music by Lora C. Crockett.
Utah	"Utah, We Love Thee," with words and music by Evan Stephens.
Vermont	"Hail, Vermont!" with words and music by Josephine Hovey Perry.
Virginia	"Carry Me Back to Old Virginia," with words and music by James B. Bland.
Washington	"Washington, My Home," with words and music by Helen Davis.

State	Songs
West Virginia	West Virginia has three state songs: "This Is My West Virginia," with words and music by Iris Bell; "West Virginia, My Home Sweet Home," with words and music by Julian G. Hearne; and "The West Virginia Hills," with words by David King and music by H. E. Engle.
Wisconsin	"On, Wisconsin," by William T. Purdy.
Wyoming	"Wyoming," with words by Charles E. Winter and music by George E. Knapp.

☆ 11 ☆
People, People, People

Every time we turn around, it seems, the population of the United States increases. On July 1, 1988, it was estimated to be 245,807,000—a far cry from the 2,780,400 who lived here in 1780. But, of course, this population is not evenly distributed among the states. For example, if the total population of the ten states west of the Rocky Mountains, excluding California—Oregon, Washington, Idaho, Montana, Nevada, Wyoming, Colorado, Utah, Arizona, and New Mexico—were totaled, their combined population would be less than that of California. The difference is 20,743,000 for the ten states versus 28,314,000 for California.

State Population

Here are the states, ranked in order of their populations, from the most people to the least, as of July 1, 1988. If the District of Columbia were a state, it would rank 48th, with 617,000 people.

1. California	28,314,000	26. Colorado	3,301,000
2. New York	17,909,000	27. Oklahoma	3,242,000
3. Texas	16,841,000	28. Connecticut	3,233,000
4. Florida	12,335,000	29. Iowa	2,834,000
5. Pennsylvania	12,001,000	30. Oregon	2,767,000
6. Illinois	11,614,000	31. Mississippi	2,620,000
7. Ohio	10,855,000	32. Kansas	2,495,000
8. Michigan	9,240,000	33. Arkansas	2,395,000
9. New Jersey	7,721,000	34. West Virginia	1,876,000
10. North Carolina	6,489,000	35. Utah	1,690,000
11. Georgia	6,342,000	36. Nebraska	1,602,000
12. Virginia	6,015,000	37. New Mexico	1,507,000
13. Massachusetts	5,889,000	38. Maine	1,205,000
14. Indiana	5,556,000	39. Hawaii	1,098,000
15. Missouri	5,141,000	40. New Hampshire	1,085,000
16. Tennessee	4,895,000	41. Nevada	1,054,000
17. Wisconsin	4,855,000	42. Idaho	1,003,000
18. Washington	4,648,000	43. Rhode Island	993,000
19. Maryland	4,622,000	44. Montana	805,000
20. Louisiana	4,408,000	45. South Dakota	713,000
21. Minnesota	4,307,000	46. North Dakota	667,000
22. Alabama	4,102,000	47. Delaware	660,000
23. Kentucky	3,727,000	48. Vermont	557,000
24. Arizona	3,489,000	49. Alaska	524,000
25. South Carolina	3,470,000	50. Wyoming	479,000

State Urban Population

The percentage of people who live in towns and cities varies greatly from state to state. If the District of Columbia were a state, it would rank in first place, since everyone there lives within the city limits of Washington. Here are the states and their percentages of urban population, from highest to lowest.

1.	California	91.3	26.	Minnesota	66.9
2.	New Jersey	89.0	27.	Kansas	66.7
3.	Rhode Island	87.0	28.	Virginia	66.0
4.	Hawaii	86.5	29.	Alaska	64.3
5.	Nevada	85.3	30.	Indiana	64.2
6.	New York	84.6	31.	Wisconsin	64.2
7.	Utah	84.4	32.	Nebraska	62.9
8.	Florida	84.3	33.	Wyoming	62.7
9.	Massachusetts	83.8	34.	Georgia	62.4
10.	Arizona	83.8	35.	Tennessee	60.4
11.	Illinois	83.3	36.	Alabama	60.0
12.	Colorado	80.6	37.	Iowa	58.6
13.	Maryland	80.3	38.	South Carolina	54.1
14.	Texas	79.6	39.	Idaho	54.0
15.	Connecticut	78.8	40.	Montana	52.9
16.	Washington	73.5	41.	New Hampshire	52.2
17.	Ohio	73.3	42.	Arkansas	51.5
18.	New Mexico	72.1	43.	Kentucky	50.9
19.	Michigan	70.7	44.	North Dakota	48.8
20.	Delaware	70.6	45.	Maine	47.5
21.	Pennsylvania	69.3	46.	Mississippi	47.3
22.	Louisiana	68.7	47.	South Dakota	46.4
23.	Missouri	68.1	48.	North Carolina	42.9
24.	Oregon	67.9	49.	West Virginia	36.2
25.	Oklahoma	67.3	50.	Vermont	33.8

Famous People

The many famous, distinguished, and talented people who have been born in the United States have come from all parts of the country. Here are some highly selective lists.

Presidents

Here are our presidents, arranged by the states in which they were born, with their towns of birth, their dates of birth and death, and the years in which they served.

	Birthplace	Born/ Died	In Office
California			
Richard Milhouse Nixon	Yorba Linda	b. 1913	1969–1974
Georgia			
James Earl Carter	Plains	b. 1924	1977–1981
Illinois			
Ronald Wilson Reagan	Tampico	b. 1911	1981–1989
Iowa			
Herbert Clark Hoover	West Branch	1874–1962	1929–1933
Kentucky			
Abraham Lincoln	Hardin County [now Larue County]	1809–1865	1861–1865
Massachusetts			
John Adams	Braintree [now Quincy]	1735–1826	1797–1801

	Birthplace	Born/ Died	In Office
John Quincy Adams	Braintree [now Quincy]	1767–1848	1825–1829
John Fitzgerald Kennedy	Brookline	1917–1963	1961–1963
George Herbert Walker Bush	Milton	b. 1924	1989–
Missouri			
Harry S. Truman	Lamar	1884–1972	1945–1953
Nebraska			
Gerald Rudolph Ford	Omaha	b. 1913	1974–1977
New Hampshire			
Franklin Pierce	Hillboro	1804–1869	1853–1857
New Jersey			
Grover Cleveland	Caldwell	1837–1908	1885–1889 1893–1897
New York			
Martin Van Buren	Kinderhook	1782–1862	1837–1841
Millard Fillmore	Cayuga County	1800–1874	1850–1853
Theodore Roosevelt	New York City	1858–1919	1901–1909
Franklin Delano Roosevelt	near Hyde Park	1882–1945	1933–1945
North Carolina			
James Knox Polk	Mecklenburg County	1795–1849	1845–1849
Andrew Johnson	Raleigh	1808–1875	1865–1869
Ohio			
Ulysses Simpson Grant	Point Pleasant	1822–1885	1869–1877
Rutherford Burchard Hayes	Delaware	1822–1893	1877–1881
James Abram Garfield	Orange	1831–1881	1881
Benjamin Harrison	North Bend	1833–1901	1889–1893
William McKinley	Niles	1843–1901	1897–1901
William Howard Taft	Cincinnati	1857–1930	1909–1913
Warren Gamaliel Harding	near Corsica [now Blooming Grove]	1865–1923	1921–1923

	Birthplace	Born/ Died	In Office
Pennsylvania			
James Buchanan	near Mercers- burg	1791–1868	1857–1861
South Carolina			
Andrew Jackson	Waxhaws District, New Lancaster County	1767–1845	1829–1837
Texas			
Dwight David Eisenhower	Denison	1890–1969	1953–1961
Lyndon Baines Johnson	near Stonewall	1908–1973	1963–1969
Vermont			
Chester Alan Arthur	Fairfield	1829–1886	1881–1885
Calvin Coolidge	Plymouth	1872–1933	1923–1929
Virginia			
George Washington	Westmoreland County	1732–1799	1789–1797
Thomas Jefferson	Shadwell	1743–1826	1801–1809
James Madison	Port Conway	1751–1836	1809–1817
James Monroe	Westmoreland County	1758–1831	1817–1825
William Henry Harrison	Charles City County	1773–1841	1841
John Tyler	Charles City County	1790–1862	1841–1845
Zachary Taylor	Orange County	1784–1850	1849–1850
Woodrow Wilson	Staunton	1856–1924	1913–1921

First Ladies

Here are our presidents' wives—the first ladies—with their states of birth, dates of birth and death, and the years in which they were married.

	Born/ Died	Married
Connecticut		
Edith Kermit Carow Roosevelt	1861–1948	1886
Georgia		
Ellen Louise Axson Wilson	1860–1914	1885
Rosalynn Smith Carter	b. 1927	1946
Illinois		
Elizabeth Bloomer Warren Ford	b. 1918	1948
Iowa		
Lou Henry Hoover	1875–1944	1899
Mamie Geneva Dowd Eisenhower	1896–1979	1916
Kentucky		
Mary Todd Lincoln	1818–1882	1842
Maryland		
Louise Catherine Johnson Adams	1775–1852	1797
Margaret Smith Taylor	1788–1852	1810
Massachusetts		
Abigail Smith Adams	1744–1818	1764
Alice Hathaway Lee Roosevelt	1861–1884	1880

	Born/Died	Married
Missouri		
Julia Dent Grant	1826–1902	1848
Bess Wallace Truman	1885–1982	1919
Nevada		
Thelma Catherine Patricia Ryan Nixon	b. 1912	1940
New Hampshire		
Jane Means Appleton Pierce	1806–1863	1834
New Jersey		
Anna Symmes Harrison	1775–1864	1795
Caroline Carmichael McIntosh Fillmore	1813–1881	1858
New York		
Elizabeth Kortright Monroe	1768–1830	1786
Hannah Hoes Van Buren	1783–1819	1807
Julia Gardiner Tyler	1820–1889	1844
Abigail Powers Fillmore	1798–1853	1826
Frances Folsom Cleveland	1864–1947	1886
Anna Eleanor Roosevelt Roosevelt	1884–1962	1905
Jacqueline Lee Bouvier Kennedy	b. 1929	1953
Anne Frances "Nancy" Robbins Davis Reagan	b. 1923	1952
Barbara Pierce Bush	b. 1925	1945
North Carolina		
Dorothea "Dolley" Payne Todd Madison	1768–1849	1794
Ohio		
Lucy Ware Webb Hayes	1831–1889	1852
Lucretia Rudolph Garfield	1832–1918	1858
Caroline Lavinia Scott Harrison	1832–1892	1853
Ida Saxton McKinley	1847–1907	1871
Helen Herron Taft	1861–1943	1886
Florence Kling De Wolfe Harding	1860–1924	1891
Pennsylvania		
Mary Scott Lord Dimmick Harrison	1858–1948	1896
Tennessee		
Sarah Childress Polk	1803–1891	1824
Eliza McCardle Johnson	1810–1876	1827

	Born/Died	Married
Texas		
Claudia "Lady Bird" Alta Taylor Johnson	b. 1912	1934
Vermont		
Grace Anna Goodhue Coolidge	1879–1957	1905
Virginia		
Martha Dandridge Custis Washington	1732–1802	1759
Martha Wayles Skelton Jefferson	1748–1782	1772
Rachel Donelson Robards Jackson	1767–1828	1791
Letitia Christian Tyler	1790–1842	1813
Ellen Lewis Herndon Arthur	1837–1880	1859
Edith Bolling Galt Wilson	1872–1961	1915

Miss America

Here are the winners of the annual Miss America pageant and the states they have represented.

Alabama: Yolande Betbeze (1951)

Arizona: Jacque Mercer (1949); Vonda Kay Van Dyke (1965)

Arkansas: Donna Axum (1964); Elizabeth Ward (1982)

California: Fay Lamphier (1925); Rosemary LaPlanche (1941); Jean Bartel (1943); Marilyn Buferd (1946); Lee Meriwether (1955); Debra Maffett (1983)

Colorado: Sharon Ritchie (1956); Marilyn Van Derbur (1958); Rebecca Ann King (1974)

Connecticut: Marion Bergeron (1933)

District of Columbia: Margaret Gorman (1921); Venus Ramey (1944)

Georgia: Neva Jane Langley (1953)

Illinois: Lois Delaner (1927); Judith Anne Ford (1969)

Kansas: Deborah Irene Bryant (1966); Debra Dene Barnes (1968)

Michigan: Patricia Donnelly (1939); Nancy Fleming (1961); Pamela Anne Eldred (1970); Kaye Lani Rae Rafko (1988)

Minnesota: BeBe Shopp (1948); Dorothy Kathleen Benham (1977); Gretchen Carlson (1989)

Mississippi: Mary Ann Mobley (1959); Lynda Lee Mead (1960); Cheryl Prewitt (1980); Susan Akin (1986)

Missouri: Debbye Turner (1990)

New Jersey: Bette Cooper (1937); Suzette Charles (1984)

New York: Bess Myerson (1945); Tawney Elaine Godin (1976)

North Carolina: Maria Fletcher (1962)

Ohio: Mary Campbell (1922–1923); Marilyn Meseke (1938); Jacqueline Mayer (1963); Laurie Lea Schaefer (1972); Susan Perkins (1978)

Oklahoma: Norma Smallwood (1926); Jane Anne Jayroe (1967); Susan Powell (1981)

Pennsylvania: Ruth Malcolmson (1924); Henrietta Leaver (1935); Rose Coyle (1936); Frances Marie Burke (1940); Evelyn Margaret Ay (1954)

South Carolina: Marian McKnight (1957)

Tennessee: Barbara Walker (1947); Kellye Cash (1987)

Texas: Jo-Caroll Dennison (1942); Phyllis Ann George (1971); Shirley Cothran (1975)

Utah: Coleen Kay Hutchins (1952); Sharlene Wells (1985)

Virginia: Kylene Barker (1979)

Wisconsin: Terry Anne Meeuwsen (1973)

Academy Award Winners

Oscar-winning Americans come from many different parts of the country. Here are those men and women who have been honored by the Academy of Motion Picture Arts and Sciences for their acting abilities, along with their places of birth, dates of birth and death, the year in which the award was won, and the movie for which it was given.

Alabama

Louise Fletcher, Birmingham, b. 1934 (1975, *One Flew Over the Cuckoo's Nest*)

Arizona

Mary Steenburgen, Newport, b. 1953 (1980, *Melvin & Howard*)

California

Fay Bainter, Los Angeles, b. 1892, d. 1968 (1938, *Jezebel*)

Gloria Grahame, Los Angeles, b. 1925, d. 1981 (1952, *The Bad and the Beautiful*)

Jo Van Fleet, Oakland, b. 1919 (1955, *East of Eden*)

Gregory Peck, La Jolla, b. 1916 (1962, *To Kill a Mockingbird*)

Cliff Robertson, La Jolla, b. 1925 (1968, *Charly*)

Gene Hackman, San Bernardino, b. 1930 (1971, *The French Connection*)

Liza Minnelli, Los Angeles, b. 1946 (1972, *Cabaret*)

Tatum O'Neal, Los Angeles, b. 1963 (1973, *Paper Moon*)

Diane Keaton, Los Angeles, b. 1949 (1977, *Annie Hall*)

Dustin Hoffman, Los Angeles, b. 1937 (1979, *Kramer vs. Kramer;* 1988, *Rain Man*)

Sally Field, Pasadena, b. 1946 (1979, *Norma Rae;* 1984, *Places in the Heart*)

Timothy Hutton, Malibu, b. 1960 (1980, *Ordinary People*)

Robert Duvall, San Diego, b. 1931 (1983, *Tender Mercies*)

Cher, El Centro, b. 1946 (1987, *Moonstruck*)

Connecticut

Katharine Hepburn, Hartford, b. 1907 (1932–1933, *Morning Glory*; 1967, *Guess Who's Coming to Dinner;* 1968, *The Lion in Winter;* 1981, *On Golden Pond*)

Ernest Borgnine, Hamden, b. 1917 (1955, *Marty*)

Ed Begley, Hartford, b. 1901, d. 1970 (1962, *Sweet Bird of Youth*)

District of Columbia

Helen Hayes, Washington, b. 1900 (1931–1932, *The Sin of Madelon Claudet;* 1970, *Airport*)

Goldie Hawn, Washington, b. 1945 (1969, *Cactus Flower*)

William Hurt, Washington, b. 1950 (1985, *Kiss of the Spider Woman*)

Florida

Sidney Poitier, Miami, b. 1927 (1963, *Lilies of the Field*)

Faye Dunaway, Bascom, b. 1941 (1976, *Network*)

Georgia

Charles Coburn, Savannah, b. 1877, d. 1961 (1943, *The More the Merrier*)

Joanne Woodward, Thomasville, b. 1930 (1957, *The Three Faces of Eve*)

Melvyn Douglas, Macon, b. 1901, d. 1983 (1963, *Hud;* 1979, *Being There*)

Illinois

Mary Astor, Quincy, b. 1906 (1941, *The Great Lie*)

Mercedes McCambridge, Joliet, b. 1918 (1949, *All the King's Men*)

William Holden, O'Fallon, b. 1918, d. 1981 (1953, *Stalag 17*)

Dorothy Malone, Chicago, b. 1925 (1956, *Written on the Wind*)

Burl Ives, Hunt Township, b. 1909 (1958, *The Big Country*)

Charlton Heston, Evanston, 1923 (1959, *Ben Hur*)

Jason Robards, Jr., Chicago, b. 1922 (1976, *All the President's Men;* 1977, *Julia*)

Indiana

Karl Malden, Gary, b. 1913 (1951, *A Streetcar Named Desire*)

Iowa

Donna Reed, Denison, b. 1921, d. 1986 (1953, *From Here to Eternity*)

John Wayne, Winterset, b. 1907, d. 1979 (1969, *True Grit*)

Cloris Leachman, Des Moines, b. 1926 (1971, *The Last Picture Show*)

Kansas

Hattie McDaniel, Wichita, b. 1895, d. 1952 (1939, *Gone with the Wind*)

Kentucky

Patricia Neal, Packard, b. 1926 (1963, *Hud*)

Massachusetts

Bette Davis, Lowell, b. 1908, d. 1990 (1935, *Dangerous;* 1938, *Jezebel*)

Walter Brennan, Swampscott, b. 1894, d. 1974 (1936, *Come and Get It;* 1938, *Kentucky;* 1940, *The Westerner*)

Josephine Hull, Newton, b. 1884, d. 1957 (1950, *Harvey*)

Jack Lemmon, Boston, b. 1925 (1955, *Mister Roberts;* 1973, *Save the Tiger*)

Estelle Parsons, Lynn, b. 1927 (1967, *Bonnie and Clyde*)

Jack Albertson, Lynn, b. 1907, d. 1981 (1968, *The Subject Was Roses*)

Ruth Gordon, Wollaston, b. 1896, d. 1985 (1968, *Rosemary's Baby*)

Olympia Dukakis, Boston, b. 1932 (1987, *Moonstruck*)

Geena Davis, Ware, b. 1957 (1988, *The Accidental Tourist*)

Michigan

Kim Hunter, Detroit, b. 1922 (1951, *A Streetcar Named Desire*)

Ellen Burstyn, Detroit, b. 1932 (1974, *Alice Doesn't Live Here Anymore*)

Minnesota

Gale Sondergaard, Litchfield, b. 1899, d. 1985 (1936, *Anthony Adverse*)

Gig Young, St. Cloud, b. 1913, d. 1978 (1969, *They Shoot Horses, Don't They?*)

Jessica Lange, Cloquet, b. 1949 (1982, *Tootsie*)

Missouri

Wallace Beery, Kansas City, b. 1889, d. 1949 (1931–1932, *The Champ*)

Ginger Rogers, Independence, b. 1911 (1940, *Kitty Foyle*)

Jane Darwell, Palmyra, b. 1880, d. 1967 (1940, *The Grapes of Wrath*)

Jane Wyman, St. Joseph, b. 1914 (1948, *Johnny Belinda*)

Shelley Winters, St. Louis, b. 1922 (1959, *The Diary of Anne Frank;* 1965, *A Patch of Blue*)

Geraldine Page, Kirksville, b. 1924, d. 1987 (1985, *The Trip to Bountiful*)

Dianne Wiest, Kansas City, b. 1955 (1986, *Hannah and Her Sisters*)

Kevin Kline, St. Louis, b. 1947 (1988, *A Fish Called Wanda*)

Montana

Gary Cooper, Helena, b. 1901, d. 1961 (1941, *Sergeant York;* 1952, *High Noon*)

Nebraska

Marlon Brando, Omaha, b. 1924 (1954, *On the Waterfront;* 1972, *The Godfather*)

Sandy Dennis, Hastings, b. 1937 (1966, *Who's Afraid of Virginia Woolf?*)

Henry Fonda, Grand Island, b. 1905, d. 1983 (1981, *On Golden Pond*)

New Jersey

Thomas Mitchell, Elizabeth, b. 1892, d. 1962 (1939, *Stagecoach*)

Frank Sinatra, Hoboken, b. 1915 (1953, *From Here to Eternity*)

Eva Marie Saint, Newark, b. 1924 (1954, *On the Waterfront*)

Jack Nicholson, Neptune, b. 1937 (1975, *One Flew Over the Cuckoo's Nest;* 1983, *Terms of Endearment*)

Meryl Streep, Basking Ridge, 1951 (1979, *Kramer vs. Kramer;* 1982, *Sophie's Choice*)

Linda Hunt, Morristown, b. 1945 (1983, *The Year of Living Dangerously*)

Michael Douglas, New Brunswick, b. 1945 (1987, *Wall Street*)

New York

Alice Brady, New York City, b. 1892, d. 1939 (1937, *In Old Chicago*)

James Cagney, New York City, b. 1899, d. 1986 (1942, *Yankee Doodle Dandy*)

Teresa Wright, New York City, b. 1918 (1942, *Mrs. Miniver*)

James Dunn, New York City, b. 1905, d. 1967 (1945, *A Tree Grows in Brooklyn*)

Ann Revere, New York City, b. 1923 (1945, *National Velvet*)

Celeste Holm, New York City, b. 1919 (1947, *Gentlemen's Agreement*)

Claire Trevor, New York City, b. 1909 (1948, *Key Largo*)

Judy Holliday, New York City, b. 1922, d. 1965 (1950, *Born Yesterday*)

Humphrey Bogart, New York City, b. 1899, d. 1957 (1951, *The African Queen*)

Shirley Booth, New York City, b. 1907 (1952, *Come Back, Little Sheba*)

Edmund O'Brien, New York City, b. 1915, d. 1985 (1954, *The Barefoot Contessa*)

Red Buttons, New York City, b. 1918 (1957, *Sayonara*)

Susan Hayward, Brooklyn, b. 1918, d. 1975 (1958, *I Want to Live*)

Burt Lancaster, New York City, b. 1913 (1960, *Elmer Gantry*)

Anne Bancroft, The Bronx, b. 1931 (1962, *The Miracle Worker*)

Patty Duke, Elmhurst, b. 1946 (1962, *The Miracle Worker*)

Lee Marvin, New York City, b. 1924, d. 1987 (1965, *Cat Ballou*)

Martin Balsam, New York City, b. 1919 (1965, *A Thousand Clowns*)

Walter Matthau, New York City, b. 1920 (1966, *The Fortune Cookie*)

George Kennedy, New York City, b. 1925 (1967, *Cool Hand Luke*)

Rod Steiger, Westhampton, b. 1925 (1967, *In the Heat of the Night*)

Barbra Streisand, Brooklyn, b. 1942 (1968, *Funny Girl*)

Jane Fonda, New York City, b. 1937 (1971, *Klute;* 1978, *Coming Home*)

Art Carney, Mount Vernon, b. 1918 (1974, *Harry and Tonto*)

Robert De Niro, New York City, b. 1943 (1974, *The Godfather, Part II;* 1980, *Raging Bull*)

George Burns, New York City, b. 1896 (1975, *The Sunshine Boys*)

Lee Grant, New York City, b. 1926 (1975, *Shampoo*)

Beatrice Straight, Old Westbury, b. 1918 (1976, *Network*)

Richard Dreyfuss, Brooklyn, b. 1947 (1977, *The Goodbye Girl*)

Jon Voight, Yonkers, b. 1938 (1976, *Coming Home*)

Christopher Walken, Queens, b. 1943 (1978, *The Deer Hunter*)

Maureen Stapleton, Troy, b. 1925 (1981, *Reds*)

Lou Gossett, Jr., New York City, b. 1936 (1982, *An Officer and a Gentleman*)

Jodie Foster, The Bronx, b. 1962 (1988, *The Accused*)

Denzel Washington, Mount Vernon, b. 1954 (1989, *Glory*)

Ohio

Warner Baxter, Columbus, b. 1889, d. 1951 (1928–1929, *In Old Arizona*)

Clark Gable, Cadiz, b. 1901, d. 1960 (1934, *It Happened One Night*)

Dean Jagger, Lima, b. 1903 (1949, *Twelve O'Clock High*)

George Chakiris, Norwood, b. 1933 (1961, *West Side Story*)
Joel Grey, Cleveland, b. 1932 (1972, *Cabaret*)
Eileen Heckart, Columbus, b. 1919 (1972, *Butterflies Are Free*)
Paul Newman, Cleveland, b. 1925 (1986, *The Color of Money*)

Oklahoma
Van Heflin, Walters, b. 1910, d. 1971 (1942, *Johnny Eager*)
Jennifer Jones, Tulsa, b. 1919 (1943, *The Song of Bernadette*)
Ben Johnson, Foreaker, b. 1919 (1971, *The Last Picture Show*)

Pennsylvania
Janet Gaynor, Philadelphia, b. 1906, d. 1984 (1927–1928, *Sunrise, Seventh Heaven,* and *Street Angel*)
Lionel Barrymore, Philadelphia, B. 1878, d. 1954 (1930–1931, *A Free Soul*)

James Stewart, Indiana, b. 1908 (1940, *The Philadelphia Story*)

Ethel Barrymore, Philadelphia, b. 1879, d. 1959 (1944, *None But the Lonely Heart*)

Broderick Crawford, Philadelphia, b. 1911, d. 1986 (1949, *All the King's Men*)

Grace Kelly, Philadelphia, b. 1928, d. 1982 (1954, *The Country Girl*)

Shirley Jones, Smithton, b. 1934 (1960, *Elmer Gantry*)

F. Murray Abraham, Pittsburgh, b. 1940 (1984, *Amadeus*)

Texas

Joan Crawford, San Antonio, b. 1906, d. 1977 (1945, *Mildred Pierce*)

Sissy Spacek, Quitman, b. 1949 (1980, *Coal Miner's Daughter*)

Utah

Loretta Young, Salt Lake City, b. 1913 (1947, *The Farmer's Daughter*)

Virginia

Shirley MacLaine, Richmond, b. 1934 (1983, *Terms of Endearment*)

Washington

Bing Crosby, Tacoma, b. 1904, d. 1977 (1944, *Going My Way*)

West Virginia

George C. Scott, Wise, b. 1927 (1970, *Patton*)

Wisconsin

Fredric March, Racine, b. 1897, d. 1975 (1931–1932, *Dr. Jekyll and Mr. Hyde;* 1946, *The Best Years of Our Lives*)

Spencer Tracy, Milwaukee, b. 1900, d. 1967 (1937, *Captains Courageous;* 1938, *Boys' Town*)

Don Ameche, Kenosha, b. 1908 (1985, *Cocoon*)

Writers

American writers have made major contributions to world literature since colonial times. Here is a selective list of them, arranged by the states in which they were born, with their home towns, dates of birth and death, and best-known works.

Alabama

Harper Lee, novelist (Monroeville, b. 1926, *To Kill a Mockingbird*)

California

Joan Didion, novelist (Sacramento, b. 1934, *Play It As It Lays*)

Robert Frost, poet (San Francisco, b. 1874, d. 1963, four-time Pulitzer Prize winner, *New Hampshire*)

Ursula Le Guin, novelist (Berkeley, b. 1929, *Left Hand of Darkness*)

Jack London, novelist (San Francisco, b. 1876, d. 1916, *The Call of the Wild*)

Rod McKuen, poet (San Francisco, b. 1938, *Come to Me in Silence*)

William Saroyan, playwright (Fresno, b. 1908, d. 1981, Pulitzer Prize winner, *The Time of Your Life*)

Jean Stafford, short-story writer (Covina, b. 1915, d. 1979, Pulitzer Prize winner, *Collected Stories*)

John Steinbeck, novelist (Salinas, b. 1902, d. 1968, Pulitzer Prize winner, *The Grapes of Wrath*)

Irving Stone, novelist (San Francisco, b. 1903, *The Agony and the Ecstasy*)

Colorado

Ken Kesey, novelist (La Junta, b. 1935, *One Flew Over the Cuckoo's Nest*)

Connecticut

Harriet Beecher Stowe, novelist (Litchfield, b. 1811, d. 1896, *Uncle Tom's Cabin*)

Thomas Tryon, novelist (Hartford, b. 1926, *The Other*)

Sloan Wilson, novelist (Norwalk, b. 1920, *The Man in the Gray Flannel Suit*)

Delaware

John P. Marquand, novelist (Wilmington, b. 1893, d. 1960, Pulitzer Prize winner, *The Late George Apley*)

Georgia

Erskine Caldwell, novelist (White Oak, b. 1903, d. 1987, *Tobacco Road*)

James Dickey, novelist (Atlanta, b. 1923, *Deliverance*)

Joel Chandler Harris, short-story writer (Eatonton, b. 1848, d. 1908, *Uncle Remus and Br'er Rabbit*)

Carson McCullers, novelist (Columbus, b. 1917, d. 1967, *A Member of the Wedding*)

Margaret Mitchell, novelist (Atlanta, b. 1900, d. 1949, *Gone With the Wind*)

Idaho

Erza Pound, poet (Hailey, b. 1885, d. 1972, *Cantos*)

Illinois

Richard Bach, novelist (Oak Park, b. 1936, *Jonathan Livingston Seagull*)

Ray Bradbury, novelist (Waukegan, b. 1920, *Fahrenheit 451*)

Michael Crichton, novelist (Chicago, b. 1942, *The Marathon Man*)

John Dos Pasos, novelist (Chicago, b. 1896, d. 1970, *USA*)

James T. Farrell, novelist (Chicago, b. 1904, d. 1979, *Young Lonigan*)

Lorraine Hansbury, playwright (Chicago, b. 1930, d. 1965, *A Raisin in the Sun*)

Ernest Hemingway, novelist (Oak Park, b. 1899, d. 1961, Nobel Prize winner, *For Whom the Bell Tolls*)

James Jones, novelist (Robinson, b. 1921, d. 1977, *From Here to Eternity*)

Carl Sandburg, poet (Galesburg, b. 1878, d. 1967, Pulitzer Prize winner, *The People, Yes*)

Sidney Sheldon, novelist (Chicago, b. 1917, *Bloodline*)

Irving Wallace, novelist (Chicago, b. 1916, *The Man*)

Indiana

Lloyd C. Douglas, novelist (Columbia City, b. 1877, d. 1951, *The Robe*)

Theodore Dreiser, novelist (Terre Haute, b. 1871, d. 1945, *An American Tragedy*)

James Whitcomb Riley, poet (Greenfield, b. 1849, d. 1916, *The Old Swimmin' Hole and 'Leven More Poems*)

Booth Tarkington, novelist (Indianapolis, b. 1869, d. 1946, two-time Pulitzer Prize winner, *The Magnificent Ambersons*)

Kurt Vonnegut, novelist (Indianapolis, b. 1922, *Slaughterhouse Five*)

Lew Wallace, novelist (Brookville, b. 1827, d. 1905, *Ben Hur*)

Iowa

Eugene Burdick, novelist (Sheldon, b. 1918, d. 1965, *Fail-Safe*)

McKinley Kantor, novelist (Webster City, b. 1904, d. 1977, Pulitzer Prize winner, *Andersonville*)

Kansas

William Inge, playwright (Independence, b. 1913, Pulitzer Prize winner, *Picnic*)

Edgar Lee Masters, poet (Garnett, b. 1869, d. 1950, *Spoon River Anthology*)

Damon Runyan, short-story writer (Manhattan, b. 1884, d. 1946, *Guys and Dolls*)

Kentucky

John Patrick, playwright (Louisville, b. 1905, Pulitzer Prize winner, *The Teahouse of the August Moon*)

Robert Penn Warren, novelist (Guthrie, b. 1905, three-time Pulitzer Prize winner, *All the King's Men*)

Louisiana

Truman Capote, novelist (New Orleans, b. 1924, d. 1984, *In Cold Blood*)

Shirley Ann Grau, novelist (New Orleans, b. 1929, Pulitzer Prize winner, *The Keepers of the House*)

Lillian Hellman, playwright (New Orleans, b. 1907, d. 1984, *Watch on the Rhine*)

Maine

Stephen King, novelist (Portland, b. 1947, *The Shining*)

Henry Wadsworth Longfellow, poet (Portland, b. 1807, d. 1882, *Evangeline*)

Edna St. Vincent Millay, poet (Rockland, b. 1892, d. 1950, Pulitzer Prize winner, *The Harp Weaver*)

Kenneth Roberts, novelist (Kennebunk, b. 1885, d. 1957, Pulitzer Prize winner, *Northwest Passage*)

Maryland

John Barth, novelist (Cambridge, b. 1930, *The Sot-Weed Factor*)

James M. Cain, novelist (Annapolis, b. 1892, d. 1977, *The Postman Always Rings Twice*)

Leon Uris, novelist (Baltimore, b. 1924, *Exodus*)

Massachusetts

William Cullen Bryant, poet (Cummington, b. 1794, d. 1878, *Thanatopsis*)

John Cheever, novelist (Quincy, b. 1912, d. 1983, *Bullet Park*)

e. e. cummings, poet (Cambridge, b. 1894, d. 1962, *95 Poems*)

Emily Dickinson, poet (Amherst, b. 1830, d. 1886, *Collected Poems*)

Ralph Waldo Emerson, essayist (Boston, b. 1803, d. 1882, *Essays*)

Theodore "Doctor Seuss" Geisel, writer and illustrator (Springfield, b. 1904, *The Cat in the Hat*)

Nathaniel Hawthorne, novelist (Salem, b. 1804, d. 1864, *The Scarlet Letter*)

Amy Lowell, poet (Brookline, b. 1874, d. 1925, Pulitzer Prize winner, *What's O'Clock*)

William Manchester, historian (Attleboro, b. 1922, *The Death of a President*)

Sylvia Plath, novelist (Boston, b. 1932, d. 1963, *The Bell Jar*)

Edgar Allen Poe, poet and short-story writer (Boston, b. 1809, d. 1849, *The Murders in the Rue Morgue*)

John Greenleaf Whittier, poet (Haverhill, b. 1807, d. 1892, *Snow-Bound*)

Michigan

Nelson Algren, novelist (Detroit, b. 1909, d. 1981, *The Man with the Golden Arm*)

Edna Ferber, novelist (Kalamazoo, b. 1885, d. 1968, *Giant*)

Ring Lardner, short-story writer (Niles, b. 1885, d. 1933, *You Know Me, Al*)

Theodore Roethke, poet (Saginaw, b. 1908, d. 1963, Pulitzer Prize winner, *Words for the Wind*)

Minnesota

F. Scott Fitzgerald, novelist (St. Paul, b. 1896, d. 1940, *The Great Gatsby*)

Garrison Keillor, short-story writer (Anoka, b. 1942, *A Prairie Home Companion*)

Sinclair Lewis, novelist (Sauk Centre, b. 1885, d. 1951, *Elmer Gantry*)

Mississippi

William Faulkner, novelist (New Albany, b. 1897, d. 1962, Nobel Prize winner, *Intruder in the Dust*)

Tennessee Williams, playwright (Columbus, b. 1911, d. 1983, Pulitzer Prize winner, *Cat on a Hot Tin Roof*)

Richard Wright, novelist (near Natchez, b. 1908, d. 1960, *Native Son*)

Missouri

Zoe Akins, playwright (Humansville, b. 1886, d. 1958, *The Old Maid*)

Sally Benson, novelist (St. Louis, b. 1900, d. 1972, *Meet Me in St. Louis*)

Eugene Field, poet (St. Louis, b. 1850, d. 1895, *Little Boy Blue*)

Langston Hughes, poet (Joplin, b. 1902, d. 1967, *Weary Blues*)

Marianne Moore, poet (St. Louis, b. 1887, d. 1972, Pulitzer Prize winner, *Observations*)

Sara Teasdale, poet (St. Louis, b. 1884, d. 1933, *Love Songs*)

Mark Twain, novelist (Florida, b. 1835, d. 1910, *The Adventures of Huckleberry Finn*)

Nebraska

Ernest K. Gann, novelist (Lincoln, b. 1910, *The High and the Mighty*)

New Hampshire

John Irving, novelist (Exeter, b. 1942, *The World According to Garp*)

New Jersey

Judy Blume, novelist (Elizabeth, b. 1938, *Wifey*)

James Fenimore Cooper, novelist (b. 1789, d. 1851, *The Last of the Mohicans*)

Stephen Crane, novelist (Newark, b. 1871, d. 1900, *The Red Badge of Courage*)

Norman Mailer, novelist (Long Branch, b. 1923, *The Naked and the Dead*)

Philip Roth, novelist (Newark, b. 1933, *Goodbye, Columbus*)

New York

Louis Auchincloss, novelist (Lawrence, b. 1917, *The Rector of Justin*)

James Baldwin, novelist (New York City, b. 1924, d. 1987, *The Fire Next Time*)

L. Frank Baum, novelist (Chittenango, b. 1856, d. 1919, *The Wonderful Wizard of Oz*)

E. L. Doctorow, novelist (New York City, b. 1931, *Ragtime*)

Alex Haley, novelist (Ithaca, b. 1921, *Roots*)

Joseph Heller, novelist (Brooklyn, b. 1923, *Catch-22*)

Washington Irving, short-story writer (New York City, b. 1783, d. 1859, *The Legend of Sleepy Hollow*)

Henry James, novelist (New York City, b. 1843, d. 1916, *The Turn of the Screw*)

Ira Levin, novelist (New York City, b. 1929, *Rosemary's Baby*)

Bernard Malamud, novelist (Brooklyn, b. 1914, d. 1986, Pulitzer Prize winner, *The Natural*)

Herman Melville, novelist (New York City, b. 1819, d. 1891, *Moby Dick*)

James A. Michener, novelist (New York City, b. 1907, *Hawaii*)

Arthur Miller, playwright (New York City, b. 1915, *Death of a Salesman*)

Joyce Carol Oates, novelist (Lockport, b. 1938, *Them*)

Eugene O'Neill, playwright (New York City, b. 1888, d. 1953, Nobel Prize winner, *The Iceman Cometh*)

Chaim Potok, novelist (New York City, b. 1929, *The Chosen*)

Mario Puzo, novelist (New York City, b. 1920, *The Godfather*)

Judith Rossner, novelist (New York City, b. 1935, *Looking for Mr. Goodbar*)

J. D. Salinger, novelist (New York City, b. 1919, *The Catcher in the Rye*)

Irwin Shaw, novelist (New York City, b. 1913, d. 1984, *Rich Man, Poor Man*)

Neil Simon, playwright (New York City, b. 1927, *The Odd Couple*)

Gore Vidal, novelist and playwright (West Point, b. 1925, *Burr*)

Edith Wharton, novelist (New York City, b. 1862, d. 1937, *The Age of Innocence*)

E. B. White, novelist (Mount Vernon, b. 1899, d. 1985, *Charlotte's Web*)

Walt Whitman, poet (West Hills, b. 1819, d. 1892, *Leaves of Grass*)

Herman Wouk, novelist (New York City, b. 1915, *The Winds of War*)

North Carolina

O. Henry, short-story writer (Greensboro, b. 1862, d. 1910, *The Gift of the Magi*)

Robert Ruark, novelist (Wilmington, b. 1915, d. 1965, *Something of Value*)

Thomas Wolfe, novelist (Asheville, b. 1900, d. 1938, *You Can't Go Home Again*)

Ohio

Sherwood Anderson, novelist (Camden, b. 1876, d. 1941, *Winesburg, Ohio*)

Louis Bromfield, novelist (Mansfield, b. 1896, d. 1956, Pulitzer Prize winner, *Early Autumn*)

Russell Crouse, playwright (Findlay, b. 1893, d. 1966, *The Sound of Music*)

Zane Grey, novelist (Zanesville, b. 1872, d. 1939, *Riders of the Purple Sage*)

James Thurber, humorist (Columbus, b. 1894, d. 1961, *My Life and Hard Times*)

Oklahoma

John Berryman, poet (McAlester, b. 1914, d. 1972, Pulitzer Prize winner, *Dreamsongs*)

Ralph Ellison, novelist (Oklahoma City, b. 1914, *The Invisible Man*)

Oregon

Edwin C. Markham, poet (Oregon City, b. 1852, d. 1940, *Lincoln and Other Poems*)

Phyllis McGinley, poet (Ontario, b. 1905, d. 1978, Pulitzer Prize winner, *Selected Verse from Three Decades*)

Pennsylvania

Louisa May Alcott, novelist (Germantown, b. 1832, d. 1888, *Little Women*)

Maxwell Anderson, playwright (Atlantic, b. 1888, d. 1959, Pulitzer Prize winner, *Winterset*)

Stephen Vincent Benét, poet and short-story writer (Bethlehem, b. 1898, d. 1943, two-time Pulitzer Prize winner, *John Brown's Body*)

George S. Kaufman, playwright (Pittsburgh, b. 1889, d. 1961, two-time Pulitzer Prize winner, *You Can't Take It with You*)

Jean Kerr, humorist (Scranton, b. 1923, *Please Don't Eat the Daisies*)

Clifford Odets, playwright (Philadelphia, b. 1906, d. 1963, *The Country Girl*)

John O'Hara, novelist (Pottsville, b. 1905, d. 1970, *Butterfield 8*)

Gertrude Stein, poet and biographer (Allegheny, b. 1874, d. 1946, *Four Saints in Three Acts*)

Wallace Stevens, poet (Reading, b. 1879, d. 1955, Pulitzer Prize winner, *Collected Poems*)

John Updike, novelist (Shillington, b. 1932, *Rabbit, Run*)

Joseph Waumbaugh, novelist (East Pittsburgh, b. 1937, *The Onion Field*)

Rhode Island

H. P. Lovecraft, novelist (Providence, b. 1890, d. 1937, *The Dunwich Horror*)

Edwin O'Connor, novelist (Providence, b. 1918, d. 1968, *The Last Hurrah*)

Tennessee

Randall Jarrell, novelist (Nashville, b. 1914, d. 1965, *The Lost World*)

John Crowe Ransom, poet (Pulaski, b. 1888, d. 1965, *Chills and Fever*)

Texas

Alan Drury, novelist (Houston, b. 1918, *Advise and Consent*)

Patricia Highsmith, novelist (Fort Worth, b. 1921, *Strangers on a Train*)

Terry Southern, screenwriter (Alvarado, b. 1928, *Easy Rider*)

Virginia

Willa Cather, novelist (Winchester, b. 1876, d. 1947, Pulitzer Prize winner, *Death Comes for the Archbishop*)

Ellen Glasgow, novelist (Richmond, b. 1874, d. 1945, Pulitzer Prize winner, *In This Our Life*)

William Styron, novelist (Newport News, b. 1925, Pulitzer Prize winner, *Sophie's Choice*)

Tom Wolfe, novelist (Richmond, b. 1931, *Bonfire of the Vanities*)

Washington

Max Brand, novelist (Seattle, b. 1892, d. 1944, *Destry Rides Again*)

Mary McCarthy, novelist (Seattle, b. 1912, d. 1989, *The Group*)

West Virginia

Pearl S. Buck, novelist (Hillsboro, b. 1892, d. 1973, Nobel Prize winner, *The Good Earth*)

John Knowles, novelist (Fairmont, b. 1926, *A Separate Peace*)

Wisconsin

Hamlin Garland, novelist (West Salem, b. 1860, d. 1940, Pulitzer Prize winner, *A Daughter of the Middle Border*)

Laura Ingalls Wilder, novelist (Lake Pepin, b. 1867, d. 1957, *Little House on the Prairie*)

Thornton Wilder, novelist and playwright (Madison, b. 1897, d. 1975, Pulitzer Prize winner, *Our Town*)

The Census in History

The first census of the United States was taken in 1790, and it has been taken every ten years since then. The total population of the country, from one decade to the next, has progressed in this way:

U.S. Population	Year	U.S. Population	Year
3,929,214	1790	62,979,766	1890
5,308,483	1800	76,212,624	1900
7,239,881	1810	92,228,496	1910
9,638,453	1820	106,012,537	1920
12,860,702	1830	123,202,624	1930
17,063,353	1840	132,164,569	1940
23,191,876	1850	151,325,798	1950
31,443,321	1860	179,323,175	1960
38,558,371	1870	203,302,031	1970
50,189,209	1880	226,542,518	1980

☆ 12 ☆
A Little Geography

The United States is a gold mine of geographical contrasts. It has some of the highest and lowest places on earth. Vast distances extend from north to south and from east to west. The weather ranges from tropical to Arctic, and seasonal storms, tornadoes, hurricanes, and other weather phenomena can be awesome. Here are some geographical facts and figures.

Largest and Smallest

• The largest county in the United States is San Bernardino County, California: it extends from the suburbs of Los Angeles to the Arizona border, and takes in most of the Mojave Desert.

• The smallest county in the country is New York County, which is really Manhattan Island—and it is also the most populous.

• The largest city in area is Jacksonville, Florida, at 760 square miles—the equivalent of 62 percent of the entire area of the state of Rhode Island.

• The largest island in the United States is Long Island, New York, at 1,401 square miles.

• The smallest island is Santa Barbara Island off the California coast—two square miles.

Extremes of Latitude and Longitude

• The northernmost point in the country is at Point Barrow, Alaska.

• The southernmost point is at Ka Lae, or South Cape, on the island of Hawaii.

• The easternmost point is at West Quoddy Head, Maine.

• The westernmost point is at Cape Wrangell, on Attu Island, in the Aleutians of Alaska.

Weather Bits

• The highest wind velocity in the United States can be found atop Mt. Washington in New Hampshire—in 1934 it hit 231 miles per hour.

• The windiest city in the country is not Chicago—it is Great Falls, Montana.

• Iowa gets the greatest number of tornadoes—15 for every 50 square miles each year.

The Highest

The highest point in the 48 contiguous states, Mt. Whitney, California, and the lowest point in the country, Zabriskie Point in Death Valley, California, are less than 80 miles apart. The highest city in the country is Leadville, Colorado—at 10,200 feet. Here are the highest points in each state, along with their nearby towns.

Alabama:	Cheaha Mountain, Anniston	2,704	feet
Alaska:	Mt. McKinley, Anchorage	20,320	
Arizona:	Humphreys Peak, Flagstaff	12,633	
Arkansas:	Magazine Mountain, Waveland	2,753	
California:	Mt. Whitney, Lone Pine	14,494	
Colorado:	Mt. Elbert, Leadville	14,433	
Connecticut:	Mt. Frissell, Canaan	2,380	
Delaware:	near Wilmington	422	
Florida:	near Crestview	345	
Georgia:	Brasstown Bald, Blairsville	4,784	
Hawaii:	Mauna Kea, Hilo	13,796	
Idaho:	Borah Peak, Mackey	12,662	
Illinois:	Charles Mound, Galena	1,235	

Indiana:	near Richmond	1,257 feet
Iowa:	near Sibley	1,670
Kansas:	Mt. Sunflower, Goodland	4,039
Kentucky:	Black Mountain, Harlan	4,139
Louisiana:	Driskill Mountain, Monroe	535
Maine:	Mt. Katahdin, Millinocket	5,267
Maryland:	Backbone Mountain, Oakland	3,360
Massachusetts:	Mt. Greylock, Adams	3,487
Michigan:	Mt. Curwood, Skanee	1,979
Minnesota:	Eagle Mountain, Grand Marais	2,301
Mississippi:	Woodall Mountain, Iuka	806
Missouri:	Taum Sauk Mountain, Marble Hill	1,772
Montana:	Granite Peak, Red Lodge	12,799
Nebraska:	near Kimball	5,426
Nevada:	Boundary Peak, Minden	13,140
New Hampshire:	Mt. Washington, Bretton Woods	6,288
New Jersey:	High Point, Sussex	1,803
New Mexico:	Wheeler Peak, Taos	13,161
New York:	Mt. Marcy, Westport	5,344
North Carolina:	Mt. Mitchell, Asheville	6,684
North Dakota:	White Butte, Amidon	3,506
Ohio:	Campbell Hill, Bellefontaine	1,549
Oklahoma:	Black Mesa, Boise City	4,973
Oregon:	Mt. Hood, Gresham	11,239
Pennsylvania:	Mt. Davis, Somerset	3,213
Rhode Island:	Jerimoth Hill, North Foster	812
South Carolina:	Sassafras Mountain, Pickens	3,560
South Dakota:	Harney Peak, Custer	7,242
Tennessee:	Clingmans Dome, Knoxville	6,643
Texas:	Guadalupe Peak, El Paso	8,749
Utah:	Kings Peak, Vernal	13,528
Vermont:	Mt. Mansfield, Essex Junction	4,393
Virginia:	Mt. Rogers, Hillsville	5,729
Washington:	Mt. Rainier, Puyallup	14,410
West Virginia:	Spruce Knob, Franklin	4,861
Wisconsin:	Timms Hill, Merrill	1,951
Wyoming:	Gannett Peak, Jackson	13,804

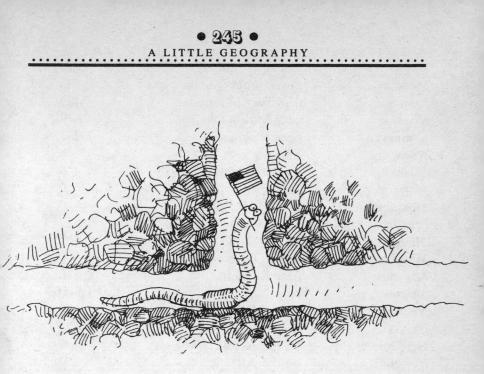

The Lowest

Here are the lowest points in each state with their locations. Of course, all states that border on an ocean except Louisiana and California will have a low mark on the seashore of 0 feet above sea level.

Alabama:	on the Gulf of Mexico	0 feet
Alaska:	on the Pacific Ocean	0
Arizona:	near Yuma	70
Arkansas:	near Crossett	55
California:	Death Valley, Panamint Springs	−282
Colorado:	near Lamar	3,350
Connecticut:	on Long Island Sound	0
Delaware:	on the Atlantic Ocean	0
Florida:	on the Atlantic and the Gulf	0
Georgia:	on the Atlantic	0
Hawaii:	on the Pacific	0
Idaho:	near Lewiston	710
Illinois:	near Mounds	279

Indiana:	near Mount Vernon	320 feet
Iowa:	near Fort Madison	480
Kansas:	near Burlington	679
Kentucky:	near Hickman	257
Louisiana:	Spanish Fort	−8
Maine:	on the Atlantic	0
Maryland:	on the Atlantic	0
Massachusetts:	on the Atlantic	0
Michigan:	near Monroe	572
Minnesota:	near Duluth	602
Mississippi:	on the Gulf of Mexico	0
Missouri:	near Kennett	230
Montana:	near Libby	1,800
Nebraska:	near Fall City	840
Nevada:	near Boulder City	479
New Hampshire:	on the Atlantic	0
New Jersey:	on the Atlantic	0
New Mexico:	near Carlsbad	2,842
New York:	on the Atlantic	0
North Carolina:	on the Atlantic	0
North Dakota:	near Drayton	750
Ohio:	near Cincinnati	455
Oklahoma:	near Idabel	269
Oregon:	on the Pacific	0
Pennsylvania:	near Philadelphia	0
Rhode Island:	on the Atlantic	0
South Carolina:	on the Atlantic	0
South Dakota:	near Sisseton	966
Tennessee:	near Memphis	178
Texas:	on the Gulf of Mexico	0
Utah:	near Saint George	2,000
Vermont:	near Saint Albans	95
Virginia:	on the Atlantic	0
Washington:	on the Pacific	0
West Virginia:	near Charles Town	240
Wisconsin:	near Milwaukee	581
Wyoming:	near Sundance	3,099

Geographical Centers

The geograpical center of the United States, including Alaska and Hawaii, is in South Dakota—Butte County, west of Castle Rock. The geograpical center of the 48 contiguous states is in Kansas—Smith County, near Lebanon. The geographical center of the North American continent is in North Dakota—Pierce County, six miles west of Balta. Here are the geographical centers of each state.

Alabama: Chilton County, 12 miles southwest of Clanton
Alaska: About 60 miles northwest of Mt. McKinley
Arizona: Yavapai County, 55 miles east-southeast of Prescott
Arkansas: Pulaski County, 12 miles northwest of Little Rock
California: Madera County, 38 miles east of Madera
Colorado: Park County, 30 miles northwest of Pikes Peak
Connecticut: Hartford County, in East Berlin
Delaware: Kent County, 11 miles south of Dover
District of Columbia: Near 4th and L Streets, NW
Florida: Hernando County, 12 miles north-northwest of Brooksville
Georgia: Twiggs County, 18 miles southeast of Macon
Hawaii: Island of Maui, off-shore
Idaho: Custer County, at Custer, southwest of Challis
Illinois: Logan County, 28 miles northeast of Springfield
Indiana: Boone County, 14 miles north-northwest of Indianapolis

Iowa: Story County, five miles northeast of Ames
Kansas: Barton County, 15 miles northeast of Great Bend
Kentucky: Marion County, three miles north-northwest of Lebanon
Louisiana: Avoyelles Parish, three miles southeast of Marksville
Maine: Piscataquis County, 18 miles north of Dover
Maryland: Prince Georges County, 4.5 miles northwest of Davidsonville
Massachusetts: Worcester, in the northwest part of the city
Michigan: Wexford County, five miles north-northwest of Cadillac
Minnesota: Crow Wing County, ten miles southwest of Brainerd
Mississippi: Leake County, nine miles west-northwest of Carthage
Missouri: Miller County, 20 miles southwest of Jefferson City
Montana: Fergus County, 11 miles west of Lewistown
Nevada: Lander County, 26 miles southeast of Austin
New Hampshire: Belknap County, three miles east of Ashland
New Jersey: Mercer County, five miles southeast of Trenton
New Mexico: Torrance County, 12 miles south-southwest of Willard
New York: Madison County, 12 miles south of Oneida and 26 miles southwest of Utica
North Carolina: Chatham County, ten miles northwest of Sanford
North Dakota: Sheridan County, five miles southwest of McClusky
Ohio: Delaware County, 25 miles north-northeast of Columbus
Oklahoma: Oklahoma County, eight miles north of Oklahoma City
Oregon: Crook County, 25 miles south-southeast of Prineville
Pennsylvania: Centre County, 2.5 miles southwest of Bellefonte
Rhode Island: Kent County, one mile south-southwest of Crompton
South Carolina: Richland County, 13 miles southeast of Columbia
South Dakota: Hughes County, eight miles northeast of Pierre
Tennessee: Rutherford County, five miles northeast of Murfreesboro
Texas: McCulloch County, 15 miles northeast of Brady
Utah: Sanpete County, three miles north of Manti
Vermont: Washington County, three miles east of Roxbury
Virginia: Buckingham County, five miles southwest of Buckingham
Washington: Chelan County, ten miles west-southwest of Wenatchee
West Virginia: Braxton County, four miles east of Sutton
Wisconsin: Wood County, nine miles southeast of Marshfield
Wyoming: Fremont County, 58 miles east-northeast of Lander

Hot Spots

Temperatures vary widely in the United States. The hottest temperature ever recorded was 134° Fahrenheit in California in 1913.
Here are the states and their highest-ever temperatures, arranged
from highest to lowest, and the dates and places of the temperature
reading.

1. *California:*
   134° in Death Valley on July 10, 1913
2. *Arizona:*
   127° in Parker on July 7, 1905
3. *Alabama:*
   122° in Centreville on September 5, 1925 (tie)
4. *Nevada:*
   122° in Overton on June 23, 1954 (tie)
   122° near Tonopah on August 12 and 18, 1914 (tic)
5. *Kansas:*
   121° in Fredonia on July 18, 1936 (tie)
   121° near Alton on July 24, 1936 (tie)
6. *North Dakota:*
   121° in Steele on July 6, 1936 (tie)
7. *Arkansas:*
   120° in Ozark on August 10, 1936 (tie)
8. *Oklahoma:*
   120° in Alva on July 18, 1936 (tie)
   120° in Altus on July 19 and August 12, 1936 (tie)
   120° in Poteau on August 10, 1936 (tie)
   120° in Tishomingo on July 26, 1943 (tie)

9. *South Dakota:*
   120° in Gannvalley on July 5, 1936 (tie)
10. *Texas:*
   120° in Seymour on August 12, 1936
11. *Oregon:*
   119° in Prineville on July 29, 1898
   119° in Pendleton on August 10, 1898
12. *Colorado:*
   118° in Bennett on July 11, 1888 (tie)
13. *Idaho:*
   118° in Orofino on July 28, 1934
14. *Iowa:*
   118° in Keokuk on July 20, 1934 (tie)
15. *Missouri:*
   118° in Clinton on July 15, 1936 (tie)
   118° in Lamar on July 18, 1936 (tie)
   118° in Union and Warsaw on July 14, 1954 (tie)
16. *Nebraska:*
   118° in Minden on July 24, 1936 (tie)
   118° in Hartington on July 17, 1936 (tie)
   118° in Geneva on July 15, 1934 (tie)
17. *Washington:*
   118° near Ephrata on July 24, 1928 (tie)
   118° at Ice Harbor Dam on August 5, 1961 (tie)
18. *Illinois:*
   117° in East St. Louis on July 14, 1954 (tie)
19. *Montana:*
   117° in Glendive on July 20, 1893 (tie)
   117° in Medicine Lake on July 5, 1937 (tie)
20. *Indiana:*
   116° in Collegeville on July 14, 1936 (tie)
21. *New Mexico:*
   116° in Orogrande on July 14, 1934 (tie)
   116° in Artesia on June 29, 1918 (tie)
22. *Utah:*
   116° in St. George on June 28, 1892 (tie)
23. *Mississippi:*
   115° in Holly Springs on July 29, 1930 (tie)

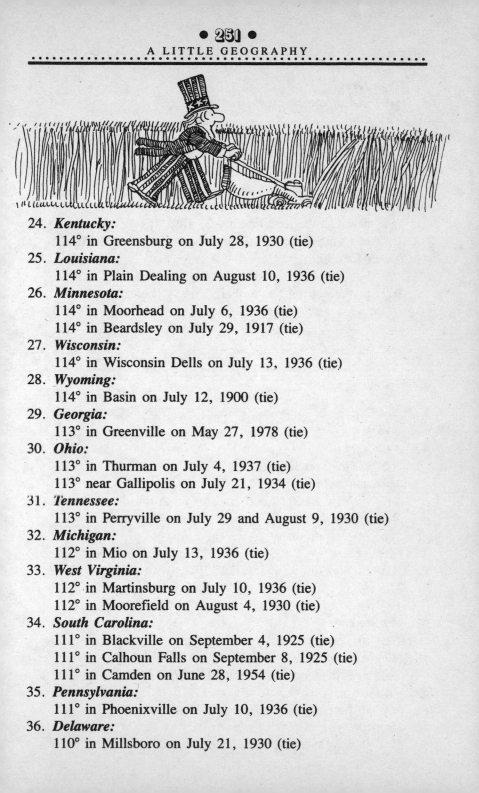

24. *Kentucky:*
     114° in Greensburg on July 28, 1930 (tie)
25. *Louisiana:*
     114° in Plain Dealing on August 10, 1936 (tie)
26. *Minnesota:*
     114° in Moorhead on July 6, 1936 (tie)
     114° in Beardsley on July 29, 1917 (tie)
27. *Wisconsin:*
     114° in Wisconsin Dells on July 13, 1936 (tie)
28. *Wyoming:*
     114° in Basin on July 12, 1900 (tie)
29. *Georgia:*
     113° in Greenville on May 27, 1978 (tie)
30. *Ohio:*
     113° in Thurman on July 4, 1937 (tie)
     113° near Gallipolis on July 21, 1934 (tie)
31. *Tennessee:*
     113° in Perryville on July 29 and August 9, 1930 (tie)
32. *Michigan:*
     112° in Mio on July 13, 1936 (tie)
33. *West Virginia:*
     112° in Martinsburg on July 10, 1936 (tie)
     112° in Moorefield on August 4, 1930 (tie)
34. *South Carolina:*
     111° in Blackville on September 4, 1925 (tie)
     111° in Calhoun Falls on September 8, 1925 (tie)
     111° in Camden on June 28, 1954 (tie)
35. *Pennsylvania:*
     111° in Phoenixville on July 10, 1936 (tie)
36. *Delaware:*
     110° in Millsboro on July 21, 1930 (tie)

37. *New Jersey:*
110° in Runyon on July 10, 1936 (tie)
38. *Virginia:*
110° in Columbia on July 5, 1900 (tie)
110° near Glasgow on July 15, 1954 (tie)
39. *Florida:*
109° in Monticello on June 29, 1931 (tie)
40. *Maryland:*
109° near Cumberland on July 3, 1898 (tie)
109° in Cumberland and Frederick on July 10, 1936 (tie)
41. *North Carolina:*
109° in Albemarle on July 28, 1940 (tie)
109° in Weldon on September 7, 1954 (tie)

42. *New York:*
108° in Troy on July 22, 1926
43. *Massachusetts:*
107° in New Bedford and Chester on August 2, 1975 (tie)
44. *New Hampshire:*
106° in Nashua on July 4, 1911
45. *Connecticut:*
105° in Waterbury on July 22, 1926 (tie)
46. *Maine:*
105° in North Bridgton on July 10, 1911 (tie)
47. *Vermont:*
105° in Vernon on July 4, 1911 (tie)
48. *Rhode Island:*
104° in Providence on August 2, 1975
49. *Alaska:*
100° in Fort Yukon on June 27, 1915 (tie)
50. *Hawaii:*
100° in Pahala on April 27, 1931 (tie)

Ice Boxes

The coldest temperature ever recorded in the United States was −80° Fahrenheit in Alaska—112 degrees below the freezing point of water. Here are the states and their lowest-ever temperatures, arranged from lowest to highest, and the dates and places of the temperature readings.

1. *Alaska:*
   −80° near Barrow on January 23, 1971
2. *Montana:*
   −70° in Warsaw on February 13, 1905
3. *Wyoming:*
   −63° in Moran on February 9, 1933
4. *Colorado:*
   −61° in Maybell on February 1, 1985
5. *Idaho:*
   −60° at Island Park Dam on January 18, 1943 (tie)
6. *North Dakota:*
   −60° in Parshall on February 15, 1936 (tie)
7. *Minnesota:*
   −59° at Pokegama Dam on February 16, 1903
   −59° at Leech Lake Dam on February 9, 1899
8. *South Dakota:*
   −58° in McIntosh on February 17, 1936

9. *Oregon:*
   - −54° in Ukiah on February 9, 1933 (tie)
   - −54° in Seneca on February 10, 1933 (tie)
10. *Wisconsin:*
   - −54° in Danbury on January 24, 1922 (tie)
11. *New York:*
   - −52° in Old Forge on February 18, 1979

12. *Michigan:*
   - −51° in Vanderbilt on February 9, 1934
13. *Nevada:*
   - −50° in San Jacinto on January 8, 1937 (tie)
14. *New Mexico:*
   - −50° in Gavilan on February 1, 1951 (tie)
15. *Utah:*
   - −50° in Woodruff on February 6, 1899 (tie)
   - −50° near Provo on January 5, 1913 (tie)
16. *Vermont:*
   - −50° in Bloomfield on December 30, 1933 (tie)
17. *Maine:*
   - −48° in Van Buren on January 19, 1925 (tie)
18. *Washington:*
   - −48° in Mazama and Winthrop on December 30, 1968 (tie)
19. *Iowa:*
   - −47° in Washta on January 12, 1912 (tie)
20. *Nebraska:*
   - −47° near Northport on February 12, 1899 (tie)
21. *New Hampshire:*
   - −46° in Pittsburg on January 28, 1925
22. *California:*
   - −45° near Truckee on January 20, 1937

23. *Pennsylvania:*
   −42° in Smethport on January 5, 1904
24. *Arizona:*
   −40° in Hawley Lake on January 7, 1971 (tie)
25. *Kansas:*
   −40° in Lebanon on February 13, 1905 (tie)
26. *Maryland:*
   −40° in Oakland on January 13, 1912 (tie)
27. *Missouri:*
   −40° in Warsaw on February 13, 1905 (tie)
28. *Ohio:*
   −39° near New Lexington on February 10, 1899
29. *West Virginia:*
   −37° in Lewisburg on December 30, 1917
30. *Illinois:*
   −35° in Mount Carroll on January 22, 1930 (tie)
31. *Indiana:*
   −35° in Greensburg on February 2, 1951 (tie)
32. *Kentucky:*
   −34° in Cynthiana on January 28, 1963 (tie)
33. *Massachusetts:*
   −34° at Birch Hill Dam on January 18, 1957 (tie)
34. *New Jersey:*
   −34° in River Vale on January 5, 1904 (tie)
35. *Connecticut:*
   −32° in Falls Village on February 16, 1943 (tie)
36. *Tennessee:*
   −32° in Mountain City on December 30, 1917 (tie)
37. *Arkansas:*
   −29° near Bentonville on February 13, 1905 (tie)
38. *North Carolina:*
   −29° in Mount Mitchell on January 30, 1966 (tie)
39. *Virginia:*
   −29° in Monterey on February 10, 1899 (tie)
40. *Alabama:*
   −27° in New Market on January 30, 1966 (tie)
41. *Oklahoma:*
   −27° in Vinita on February 13, 1905 (tie)
   −27° in Watts on January 18, 1930 (tie)

42. *Rhode Island:*
    −23° in Kingston on January 11, 1942 (tie)

43. *Texas:*
    −23° in Julia on February 12, 1899 (tie)
    −23° in Seminole on February 8, 1933 (tie)

44. *South Carolina:*
    −20° in Caesar's Head on January 18, 1977

45. *Mississippi:*
    −19° in Corinth on January 30, 1966

46. *Delaware:*
    −17° in Millsboro on January 17, 1893 (tie)

47. *Georgia:*
    −17° near Rome on January 27, 1940 (tie)

48. *Louisiana:*
    −16° in Minden on February 13, 1899

49. *Florida:*
    −2° in Tallahassee on February 13, 1899

50. *Hawaii:*
    14° at Haleakala Crater on January 2, 1961

When It Rains, It Pours

Here is a list of rainfall records. Arranged from wettest to least wet, it gives each state's record rainfall in inches, in a single 24-hour period, with the name of the weather station reporting it and the date of occurrence.

1. *Texas:* 43.00 at Alvin on July 25–26, 1979
2. *Florida:* 38.70 at Yankeetown on September 5, 1950
3. *Hawaii:* 38.00 at Kilauea Plantation on January 24–25, 1956
4. *Pennsylvania:* 34.50 at Smethport on July 17, 1942
5. *Virginia:* 27.00 in Nelson County on August 20, 1969
6. *California:* 26.12 at Hoegees Camp on January 22–23, 1943
7. *North Carolina:* 22.22 at Altapass on July 15–16, 1916
8. *Alabama:* 20.33 at Axis on April 13, 1955
9. *Louisiana:* 22.00 at Hackberry on August 28–29, 1962
10. *West Virginia:* 19.00 at Rockport on July 18, 1989
11. *Missouri:* 18.18 at Edgarton on July 20, 1965
12. *Massachusetts:* 18.15 at Westfield on August 18–19, 1955
13. *Georgia:* 18.00 at St. George on August 28, 1911
14. *Iowa:* 16.70 in Decatur County on August 5–6, 1959
15. *Illinois:* 16.54 at East St. Louis on June 14–15, 1957
16. *Mississippi:* 15.68 at Columbus on July 9, 1968
17. *Oklahoma:* 15.50 at Sapulpa on September 3–4, 1940
18. *Alaska:* 15.20 at Angoon on October 12, 1982
19. *New Jersey:* 14.81 at Tuckerton on August 19, 1939
20. *Maryland:* 14.75 at Jewell on July 26–27, 1897
21. *Arkansas:* 14.06 at Big Fork on December 3, 1982
22. *South Carolina:* 13.25 at Effingham on July 14–15, 1916
23. *Nebraska:* 13.15 at York on July 8–9, 1950
24. *Connecticut:* 12.77 at Burlington on August 19, 1955
25. *Kansas:* 12.59 at Burlington on May 31–June 1, 1941
26. *Rhode Island:* 12.13 at Westerly on September 16–17, 1932
27. *Washington:* 12.00 at Quinault on January 21, 1935
28. *Wisconsin:* 11.72 at Mellen on June 24, 1946
29. *Montana:* 11.50 at Circle on June 20, 1921
30. *Arizona:* 11.40 at Workman Creek on September 4–5, 1970
31. *New Mexico:* 11.28 at Lake Maloya on May 18–19, 1955
32. *New York:* 11.17 at New York City on October 9, 1903
33. *Colorado:* 11.08 at Holly on June 17, 1965
34. *Tennessee:* 11.00 at McMinnville on March 28, 1902
35. *Minnesota:* 10.84 at Fort Ripley on July 21–22, 1972
36. *Ohio:* 10.51 at Sandusky on July 12, 1966
37. *Indiana:* 10.50 at Princeton on October 6, 1905
38. *Kentucky:* 10.40 at Dunmor on June 28, 1960

39. *New Hampshire:* 10.38 at Mt. Washington on February 10–11, 1970
40. *Oregon:* 10.17 at Glenora on December 21, 1915
41. *Michigan:* 9.78 at Bloomingdale on August 31–September 1, 1914
42. *Vermont:* 8.77 at Somerset on November 3–4, 1927
43. *Delaware:* 8.50 at Dover on July 13, 1975
44. *North Dakota:* 8.10 at Litchville on June 29, 1975
45. *Maine:* 8.05 at Brunswick on September 11, 1954
46. *South Dakota:* 8.00 at Elk Point on September 10, 1900
47. *Nevada:* 7.40 at Lewer's Ranch on March 19, 1907
48. *Idaho:* 7.17 at Rattlesnake Creek on November 23, 1909
49. *Wyoming:* 6.06 at Cheyenne on August 1, 1985
50. *Utah:* 6.00 at Bug Point on September 5, 1970

Let It Snow

Here are the snowiest 51 cities and towns in the country, arranged in descending order with the record number of inches of snow per year.

1. *Stampede Pass, Washington:* 431.9
2. *Valdez, Alaska:* 303.9
3. *Mt. Washsington, New Hampshire:* 253.5
4. *Blue Canyon, California:* 240.8
5. *Yakutat, Alaska:* 204.5
6. *Marquette, Michigan:* 123.5
7. *Sault Ste. Marie, Michigan:* 115.5
8. *Caribou, Maine:* 111.7
9. *Syracuse, New York:* 109.9
10. *Talkeetna, Alaska:* 108.1
11. *Mt. Shasta, California:* 104.9
12. *Lander, Wyoming:* 104.6
13. *Juneau, Alaska:* 98.3
14. *Sexton Summit, Oregon:* 97.8
15. *Muskegon, Michigan:* 97.2
16. *Flagstaff, Arizona:* 97.1
17. *Buffalo, New York:* 91.5
18. *McGrath, Alaska:* 90.3
19. *Rochester, New York:* 88.3
20. *Alpena, Michigan:* 85.0
21. *Erie, Pennsylvania:* 84.4
22. *Binghamton, New York:* 82.9
23. *Casper, Wyoming:* 80.9
24. *Bettles, Alaska:* 78.5
25. *Burlington, Vermont:* 77.6
26. *Houghton Lake, Michigan:* 77.2

27. *Kodiak, Alaska: 76.8*
28. *Duluth, Minnesota: 76.7*
29. *Elkins, West Virginia: 74.2*
30. *South Bend, Indiana: 72.0*
31. *Grand Rapids,*
    Michigan: 71.3
32. *Portland, Maine: 71.2*
33. *Sheridan, Wyoming: 70.7*
34. *Worcester,*
    Massachusetts: 69.2
35. *Anchorage, Alaska: 68.5*
36. *Albany, New York: 65.3*
37. *Fairbanks, Alaska: 65.0*
38. *Kalispell, Montana: 64.6*
39. *Concord,*
    New Hampshire: 64.2
40. *Cold Bay, Alaska: 61.6*
41. *International Falls,*
    Minnesota: 61.3
42. *Beckley, West Virginia: 61.0*
43. *Denver, Colorado: 60.0*
44. *Blue Hill,*
    Massachusetts: 59.9
45. *Homer, Alaska: 58.6*
46. *Great Falls, Montana: 58.3*
47. *Salt Lake City, Utah: 58.2*
48. *St. Paul Island,*
    Alaska: 56.5 (tie)
49. *Youngstown,*
    Ohio: 56.5 (tie)
50. *Billings, Montana: 56.4*
51. *Nome, Alaska: 55.1*

The More It Blows

Here are 45 of the windiest places in the country, arranged from highest to lowest average daily speeds in miles per hour.

1. *Mt. Washington,*
   New Hampshire: 35.2
2. *Casper, Wyoming: 12.9*
3. *Boston,*
   Massachusetts: 12.5
4. *Buffalo, New York: 12.0*
5. *Milwaukee, Wisconsin: 11.6*
6. *Honolulu, Hawaii: 11.5*
7. *Cape Hatteras,*
   North Carolina: 11.2

8. *Galveston, Texas:* 11.0
9. *Dallas, Texas:* 10.9
10. *Kansas City, Missouri:* 10.8
11. *Minneapolis, Minnesota:* 10.6 (tie)
12. *Omaha, Nebraska:* 10.6 (tie)
13. *Bismarck, North Dakota:* 10.3 (tie)
14. *Chicago, Illinois:* 10.3 (tie)
15. *Cleveland, Ohio:* 10.3 (tie)
16. *Detroit, Michigan:* 10.3 (tie)
17. *St. Louis, Missouri:* 9.7
18. *Indianapolis, Indiana:* 9.6
19. *Philadelphia, Pennsylvania:* 9.5

27. *Albuquerque, New Mexico:* 9.0 (tie)
28. *Mobile, Alabama:* 9.0 (tie)
29. *Seattle, Washington:* 9.0 (tie)
30. *Memphis, Tennessee:* 8.9
31. *Salt Lake City, Utah:* 8.8 (tie)
32. *Spokane, Washington:* 8.8 (tie)
33. *Denver, Colorado:* 8.7 (tie)
34. *San Francisco, California:* 8.7 (tie)
35. *Louisville, Kentucky:* 8.3
36. *New Orleans, Louisiana:* 8.2
37. *Jacksonville, Florida:* 8.0
38. *Little Rock, Arkansas:* 7.9 (tie)

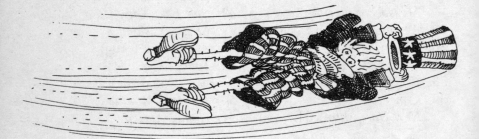

20. *New York, New York:* 9.4
21. *Lexington, Kentucky:* 9.3 (tie)
22. *Miami, Florida:* 9.3 (tie)
23. *Washington, D.C.:* 9.3 (tic)
24. *Baltimore, Maryland:* 9.2
25. *Atlanta, Georgia:* 9.1 (tie)
26. *Pittsburgh, Pennsylvania:* 9.1 (tie)

39. *Portland, Oregon:* 7.9 (tie)
40. *Helena, Montana:* 7.8 (tie)
41. *Houston, Texas:* 7.8 (tie)
42. *Anchorage, Alaska:* 6.9 (tie)
43. *San Diego, California:* 6.9 (tie)
44. *Phoenix, Arizona:* 6.3
45. *Los Angeles, California:* 6.2

Big Blasts

The following windy places have had their big blows. For example, the figure for Galveston, Texas, is an estimate, because the measuring anemometer blew away when the wind hit 100 miles per hour. Here are the biggest gusts per place, ranked from highest to lowest in miles per hour.

1. *Mt. Washington,*
   New Hampshire: 231
2. *Galveston, Texas: 120*
3. *Cape Hatteras,*
   North Carolina: 110
4. *Omaha, Nebraska: 109*
5. *New Orleans, Louisiana: 98*
6. *Minneapolis, Minnesota: 92*
7. *Buffalo, New York: 91*
8. *Albuquerque,*
   New Mexico: 90
9. *Portland, Oregon: 88*
10. *Phoenix, Arizona: 86*
11. *Jacksonville, Florida: 82*
12. *Casper, Wyoming: 81*
13. *Baltimore, Maryland: 80*
14. *Washington, D.C.: 78*
15. *Cleveland, Ohio: 74 (tie)*
16. *Miami, Florida: 74 (tie)*
17. *Dallas, Texas: 73 (tie)*
18. *Helena, Montana: 73 (tie)*
19. *Philadelphia, Pennsylvania:*
    73 (tie)
20. *Bismarck, North Dakota:*
    72
21. *Salt Lake City, Utah: 71*
22. *Kansas City, Missouri:*
    70 (tie)
23. *New York City: 70 (tie)*
24. *Honolulu, Hawaii: 67*
25. *Seattle, Washington: 66*
26. *Little Rock, Arkansas: 65*
27. *Anchorage, Alaska: 64*
28. *Mobile, Alabama: 63*
29. *Boston, Massachusetts:*
    61 (tie)
30. *Louisville, Kentucky:*
    61 (tie)
31. *Atlanta, Georgia: 60 (tie)*
32. *St. Louis, Missouri: 60 (tie)*
33. *Spokane, Washington: 59*
34. *Chicago, Illinois: 58 (tie)*
35. *Pittsburgh, Pennsylvania:*
    58 (tie)
36. *Denver, Colorado: 56 (tie)*
37. *San Diego, California:*
    56 (tie)
38. *Milwaukee, Wisconsin: 54*
39. *Houston, Texas: 51*
40. *Los Angeles, California:*
    49
41. *Detroit, Michigan: 48*
42. *San Francisco, California:*
    47
43. *Indianapolis, Indiana:*
    46 (tie)
44. *Lexington, Kentucky:*
    46 (tie)
45. *Memphis, Tennessee:*
    46 (tie)

★ 13 ★
Down On the Farm

The United States is still a country of vast farmlands and small truck farms, raising great numbers of chickens, cattle, pigs, sheep, and other livestock. It is truly the food capital of the world. The following breakdown shows the states that can claim to be number one in farming along with those that are least agricultural.

Number of Farms

There are 2,173,000 farms in the United States. Here are the states with the most and the fewest farms, respectively.

   1. Texas: 186,000
  50. Alaska: 600

Total Farm Income

Farmers in the United States have a combined annual income of $139,468,400.

   1. California: $16,598,300
  50. Alaska: $30,200

Total Crop Income

Crops in the United States earn $72,569,000 every year. Major
U.S. crops include corn, wheat, soybeans, barley, oats, and potatoes.
   1. California: $11,894,500
   50. Alaska: $20,400

Total Livestock and Livestock Products Income

Livestock and their products in the United States earn $78,861,700.
   1. Texas: $6,498,200
   50. Alaska: $9,800

Farm Acreage

Total farm area in the United States stands at 991,000,000 acres.
   1. Texas: 132,000,000 acres
   50. Connecticut: 444,000 acres

Acreage per Farm

The average farm in the United States is 456 acres in extent.
   1. Arizona: 5,080 acres
   50. Rhode Island: 95 acres

Egg Production

An astronomical number of eggs is produced annually in the
United States—69,476,000,000.
   1. California: 7,718,000,000
   50. Alaska: 1,700,000

Total Acreage of Harvest Crops

Harvest crops in the United States cover 290,077,000 acres.
1. Iowa: 23,042,000 acres
50. Rhode Island: 11,000 acres

Crop Leaders

Here are the totals for various crops produced annually on American farms, with the leading state for each crop.

Barley
United States: 290,505,000 bushels
Idaho: 51,000,000 bushels

Corn and Grain
United States: 4,921,191,000 bushels
Iowa: 898,800,000 bushels

Cotton
United States: 15,446,000 bales
Texas: 5,260,000 bales

Hay
United States: 126,817,000 tons
California: 8,652,000 tons

Oats
United States: 218,773,000 bushels
Kansas: 26,400,000 bushels

Potatoes
United States: 349,973,000 hundredweight
Idaho: 99,320,000 hundredweight

Soybeans
United States: 1,538,666,000 bushels
Iowa: 248,000,000 bushels

Tobacco
United States: 1,369,662,000 pounds
North Carolina: 553,627,000 pounds

Wheat
United States: 1,811,261,000 bushels
Kansas: 323,000,000 bushels

☆ Index ☆

Academy Award winners, 221–30
Air fair. *See* State air fair
Alabama, 176, 181, 212–13; attractions, 118, 128, 141, 144, 159, 164; celebrated persons, 219, 221, 230; education, 112–16; emblems and symbols, 184, 186, 191, 196, 198, 200, 202–3, 205; geography, 243, 245, 247; names/nicknames, 62, 71, 98–99, 103; origin and history, 3, 31–32, 58, 61, 92; weather, 249, 255, 257, 260–61
Alaska, 156, 176, 212–13, 262–63; attractions, 118, 121, 138, 145, 159, 165; education, 112–15, 117; emblems and symbols, 184, 186, 191, 197–98, 201–2, 204–5; geography, 242–43, 245, 247; names/nicknames, 62, 72, 98, 103; origin and history, 4, 32, 58–83, 91, 99–100; weather, 252–53, 257-58, 259–61
Alaska Purchase, 58
Albany, New York, 85
American Exploration, 58
Amusement/Theme parks, 121–28
Annapolis, Maryland, 85
Animals. *See* State animal; State bug; State cat; State crustacean; State dog; State domestic animal; State fish; State horse; State insect; State mammal; State reptile
Arizona, 156, 177, 212–13, 263; attractions, 118, 121, 129, 138, 145, 160, 165; celebrated persons, 219, 222; education, 112–13, 117; emblems and symbols, 184, 186, 191, 198, 202, 205; geography, 243, 245, 247; names/nicknames, 62, 72, 99, 103; origin and history, 4–5, 32–33, 58–59, 82, 93; weather, 249, 255, 257–58, 260–61

Arkansas, 156, 177, 212–13; attractions, 118, 121, 129, 138, 145, 160, 165; celebrated persons, 220; education, 112–15, 117; emblems and symbols, 184, 186, 191, 195, 198, 200–203, 205; geography, 243, 245, 247; names/nicknames, 63, 72, 98, 103; origin and history, 5, 33, 57, 59–61, 83, 92, 103; weather, 249, 255, 257
Atlanta, Georgia, 85
Augusta, Maine, 86
Austin, Texas, 86

Baton Rouge, Louisiana, 86
Birds. *See* State birds
Bismarck, North Dakota, 87
Boise, Idaho, 87
Boston, Massachusetts, 87

California, 104, 156, 177, 212–13, 262–64; attractions, 118, 121, 129, 139, 141, 145, 160, 165–66; celebrated persons, 214, 220, 222, 230; education, 112–15, 117; emblems and symbols, 184, 186, 191, 194, 197–98, 200–205; geography, 241–43, 245, 247; names/nicknames, 63, 72, 98, 103; origin and history, 5–6, 33, 58–61, 83, 95; weather, 249, 254, 257–58, 260–61
Capitals. *See* State capitals
Carson City, Nevada, 87
Census (U.S.), 240
Charleston, West Virginia, 87
Cheyenne, Wyoming, 88
Colorado, 104, 156, 177, 212–13; attractions, 118, 122, 129, 139, 141, 145–46, 160, 166; celebrated persons, 220, 231; education, 112–15, 117;

Colorado (con't.)
  emblems and symbols, 184, 186, 191,
  194, 198, 201, 205; geography, 243,
  245, 247; names/nicknames, 63, 72, 98;
  origin and history, 6–7, 34, 57, 59–61,
  83, 89; weather, 250, 253, 257, 259–61
Columbia, South Carolina, 88
Columbus, Ohio, 88
Concord, New Hampshire, 88
Confederate States of America, 3, 82
Connecticut, 104–5, 156, 177, 212–13, 263;
  attractions, 118, 146, 160, 166;
  celebrated persons, 217, 220, 222;
  education, 111–15, 117, 130; emblems
  and symbols, 184, 186, 191, 194, 200,
  202, 205; geography, 243, 245, 247;
  names/nicknames, 64, 72–73, 99; origin
  and history, 7, 34, 57, 59–61, 83, 90,
  100; weather, 252, 255, 257
Crustacean. See State crustacean
Cultural organizations, 159–64

Dance. See State dance; State folk dance
Delaware, 177, 212–13; attractions, 119,
  146; celebrated persons, 231; education,
  111–16, 130; emblems and symbols,
  184, 186, 191, 195–97, 202, 205;
  geography, 243, 245, 247; names/
  nicknames, 64, 73; origin and history,
  8, 34–35, 57, 59–61, 83, 89, 99–100;
  weather, 251, 256, 258
Denver, Colorado, 89
Des Moines, Iowa, 89
District of Columbia, 105; attractions, 146,
  160, 166; celebrated persons, 220, 222;
  education, 113–15; emblems and
  symbols, 184, 187, 191; origin and
  history, 35, 64, 100–101; weather, 260–61
Dover, Delaware, 89

Education: enrollments, 112–14; graduates,
  114–15; public school beginnings, 111

Fairs. See State fairs
Farm profiles, 262–65
Festivals, 144–55, 203
First Ladies, 217–19
Florida, 101, 105, 156, 177, 212–13;
  attractions, 119, 122, 130, 139, 141,
  146, 160, 167; celebrated persons, 222;
  education, 112–15, 117; emblems and
  symbols, 184, 187, 192, 194–95,
  197–98, 201, 203, 205; geography, 241,
  243, 245, 247; names/nicknames, 64,
  73, 103; origin and history, 8–9, 36,
  58–61, 83, 97; weather, 252, 256–57,
  260–61
Flowers. See State flowers
Folk art symbol. See State folk art symbol
Frankfort, Kentucky, 89

Geographical centers, 241–48
Georgia, 101, 105, 156, 177, 212–13;
  attractions, 119, 123, 130, 146, 160,
  167; celebrated persons, 214, 217, 220,
  223, 231; education, 112–16; emblems
  and symbols, 184, 187, 192, 195,
  197–98, 200–202, 205–6; geography,
  243, 245, 247; names/nicknames, 64,
  73, 99, 103; origin and history, 9, 36,
  57, 59–61, 82–83, 85; weather, 251,
  256–57, 260–61

Halls of Fame, 141–44
Harrisburg, Pennsylvania, 89
Hartford, Connecticut, 90
Hawaii, 101, 105, 156, 177, 212–13;
  attractions, 119, 123, 139, 147, 160,
  167; education, 112–15, 117; emblems
  and symbols, 184, 187, 192, 196, 206;
  geography, 243, 245, 247; names/
  nicknames, 64, 73, 98; origin and
  history, 9–10, 37, 58–61, 83, 90, 99;
  weather, 250, 253, 258
Hawaiian Annexation, 58
Helena, Montana, 90
Historic attractions, 128–38
Honolulu, Hawaii, 90
Horses. See State horse

Idaho, 105, 156, 177, 212–13, 264–65;
  attractions, 119, 147, 160; celebrated
  persons, 232; education, 112–15, 117;
  emblems and symbols, 184, 187, 192,
  198, 200, 206; geography, 243, 245,
  247; names/nicknames, 65, 73, 99;
  origin and history, 10, 37, 58–61, 83,
  87; weather, 250, 253
Illinois, 105, 156, 177, 212–13; attractions,
  119, 123, 130, 147, 161, 167–68;

celebrated persons, 214, 217, 220, 223, 232; education, 112–15, 117; emblems and symbols, 184, 187, 192, 194, 200–202, 206; geography, 243, 245, 247; names/nicknames, 65, 74, 99; origin and history, 10–11, 37–38, 57, 59–61, 84, 96; weather, 250, 255, 257, 260–61

Indiana, 101, 106, 156, 177, 212–13; attractions, 119, 123, 131, 142, 147, 161, 168; celebrated persons, 223, 232–33; education, 111–16; emblems and symbols, 184, 187, 192, 201–2, 204, 206; geography, 244, 246–47; names/ nicknames, 65, 74, 99, 103; origin and history, 11, 38, 57, 59–61, 84, 90; weather, 250, 255, 257, 259–61

Indianapolis, Indiana, 90

Insects. See State insect

Iowa, 106, 177–78, 212–13, 264–65; attractions, 119, 124, 131, 148, 161, 168; celebrated persons, 214, 217, 223, 233; education, 112–15, 117; emblems and symbols, 184, 187, 192, 203, 206; geography, 244, 246; names/nicknames, 65, 74, 99, 103; origin and history, 11–12, 38–39, 57, 59–61; weather, 242, 250, 254, 257

Jackson, Mississippi, 91

Jefferson City, Missouri, 91

Juneau, Alaska, 91

Kansas, 106, 157, 178, 212–13, 265; attractions, 119, 124, 131, 142, 148, 161, 168; celebrated persons, 220, 223, 233; education, 112–15, 117; emblems and symbols, 185, 188, 192, 194, 200, 206; geography, 244, 246, 248; names/ nicknames, 65, 74–75, 99; origin and history, 12, 39, 57, 59–61, 84, 97; weather, 249, 255, 257

Kentucky, 106, 157, 178, 212–13; attractions, 119, 124, 131–32, 139, 148, 161, 169; celebrated persons, 214, 217, 223, 233; education, 112–15, 117; emblems and symbols, 185, 188, 192, 201, 206; geography, 244, 246, 248; names/nicknames, 65, 75, 99; origin and history, 12–13, 39, 57, 59–61, 84; weather, 251, 255, 257, 260–61

Language. See State language

Lansing, Michigan, 91

Laws, 103–10

Lincoln, Nebraska, 92

Litter. See State Litter control symbol

Little Rock, Arkansas, 92

Louisiana, 101, 106, 157, 178, 182, 212–13; attractions, 119, 124, 132, 148, 161, 169; celebrated persons, 233–34; education, 111–15, 117; emblems and symbols, 185, 188, 192, 195–98, 207; geography, 244, 246, 248; names/ nicknames, 66, 75, 99, 103; origin and history, 13, 39–40, 57, 59–61, 84, 86, 92; weather, 251, 256–57, 260

Louisiana Purchase, 57

Madison, Wisconsin, 92

Maine, 101, 106–7, 178, 212–13; attractions, 119, 124, 132, 139, 148, 161; celebrated persons, 234; education, 112–15, 117; emblems and symbols, 185, 188, 192, 194, 196, 198, 200, 202, 207; geography, 242, 244, 246, 248; names/nicknames, 66, 75; origin and history, 13–14, 40, 57, 59–61, 84, 86; weather, 252, 254, 258–59

Mammal. See State mammal; State land mammal; State saltwater mammal

Maryland, 107, 178, 212–13; attractions, 119, 124, 132, 142, 148–49, 161, 169; celebrated persons, 217, 234; education, 111–15, 17; emblems and symbols, 185, 188, 192, 197, 200, 203–4, 207; geography, 244, 246, 248; names/ nicknames, 66, 76, 99; origin and history, 14, 40, 57, 59–61, 84–85, 100; weather, 252, 255, 257, 260–61

Massachusetts, 101, 107, 178, 212–13; attractions, 119, 132, 142, 149, 161, 169; celebrated persons, 214–15, 217, 223, 234–35; education, 111–15, 117; emblems and symbols, 185, 188, 192, 195–98, 200–203; geography, 244, 246, 248; names/nicknames, 66, 76, 99; origin and history, 14–15, 40–41, 57–61, 84, 87, 100; weather, 252, 255, 257, 259, 261

Mexican War, 58

Michigan, 107, 157, 178, 212–13;

Michigan (con't.)
attractions, 119, 124, 132, 139, 142, 149, 161, 170; celebrated persons, 220, 224, 235; education, 111–16; emblems and symbols, 185, 188, 192, 197–98, 204, 207; geography, 244, 246, 248; names/nicknames, 66, 76, 99; origin and history, 15, 41–42, 57, 59–61, 84, 91–92; weather, 251, 254, 258, 260–61

Minerals. See State mineral

Minnesota, 108, 157, 178, 212–13; attractions, 119, 124, 133, 139, 142, 150, 161, 170; celebrated persons, 220, 224, 235; education, 112–15, 117; emblems and symbols, 185, 188, 192, 195, 197–99, 202, 207; geography, 244, 246, 248; names/nicknames, 66, 76, 99–100, 103; origin and history, 16, 42, 57, 59–61, 84, 95; weather, 251, 253, 257, 259–61

Miss Americas, 219–20

Mississippi, 108, 157, 178, 182, 212–13; attractions, 119, 133, 150, 161, 170; celebrated persons, 220, 235; education, 112–15, 117; emblems and symbols, 185, 188, 192, 195, 197, 201, 203–4, 208; geography, 244, 246, 248; names/ nicknames, 66–67, 76–77, 99–100; origin and history, 16, 42–43, 57, 59–61, 82, 84, 91; weather, 250, 256–57

Missouri, 157, 178–79, 212–13; attractions, 119, 124, 133, 142, 150, 161, 170; celebrated persons, 215, 218, 220, 225, 235; education, 112–15, 117; emblems and symbols, 185, 188, 192, 202–3, 208; geography, 244, 246, 248; names/ nicknames, 67, 77, 99–100; origin and history, 17, 43, 57, 59–61, 84, 91; weather, 250, 255, 257, 260–61

Montana, 157, 179, 212–13; attractions, 119, 133, 139, 150; celebrated persons, 225; education, 112–15, 117; emblems and symbols, 185, 188, 192, 194, 197–99, 208; geography, 244, 246, 248; names/nicknames, 67, 77, 103; origin and history, 17, 43, 57, 59–61, 84, 90; weather, 242, 250, 253, 257, 259, 261

Montgomery, Alabama, 92

Montpelier, Vermont, 93

Mottoes. See State mottoes

Movies, 155–59

Mushrooms. See State mushroom

Nashville, Tennessee, 93

National Parks, 138–41

Nebraska, 101, 108, 157, 179, 212–13; attractions, 119, 133, 150, 161, 171; celebrated persons, 215, 226, 236; education, 112–15, 117; emblems and symbols, 185, 188–89, 192, 198–99, 201, 203, 208; geography, 244, 246, 248; names/nicknames, 18, 67, 77, 99–100, 103; origin and history, 18, 44, 57, 59–61, 84, 92, 101; weather, 250, 254, 257, 260–61

Nevada, 101, 108, 158, 179, 212–13; attractions, 119, 124, 133, 139, 151, 162, 171; celebrated persons, 218; education, 112–15, 117; emblems and symbols, 185, 188–89, 192, 198–99, 201, 203, 208; geography, 244, 246, 248; names/nicknames, 67, 77, 100, 103; origin and history, 18, 44, 58–61, 84, 87, 101; weather, 249, 254, 258

New Hampshire, 101, 158, 179, 212–13; attractions, 119, 125, 133, 151; celebrated persons, 215, 218, 236; education, 111–15, 117; emblems and symbols, 185, 189, 192, 195, 201, 208; geography, 244, 246, 248; names/ nicknames, 67, 77; origin and history, 19, 45, 57, 58–61, 84, 88, 101; weather, 242, 252, 254, 258–59, 261

New Jersey, 108, 179, 212–13; attractions, 119, 125, 134, 151, 171; celebrated persons, 215, 218, 220, 226, 236; education, 111–16; emblems and symbols, 185, 189, 192, 195, 201; geography, 244, 246, 248; names/ nicknames, 67, 78; origin and history, 19, 45, 57, 59–61, 84, 97; weather, 252, 255, 257

New Mexico, 108, 158, 179, 182, 212–13; attractions, 119, 134, 140, 143, 151, 162; education, 112–15, 117; emblems and symbols, 185, 189, 193, 195, 198–99, 204, 208; geography, 244, 246, 248; names/nicknames, 68, 78; origin and history, 20, 46, 58–61, 84, 96; weather, 250, 254, 257, 260–61

New York, 108, 179, 212–13; attractions, 119, 125, 134–35, 143, 152, 162, 171–72; celebrated persons, 215, 218, 220, 226, 236–37; education, 111–16; emblems and symbols, 185, 189, 193, 195, 197–99, 201, 208; geography, 241–42, 244, 246, 248; names/ nicknames, 68, 78, 99; origin and history, 20, 46, 57, 59–61, 84–85; weather, 252, 254, 257–59, 260–61

Nicknames. *See* State nicknames

North Carolina, 108, 158, 179, 212–13, 254; attractions, 119, 125, 135, 140, 143, 152, 162, 172; celebrated persons, 215, 218, 220, 237; education, 111–16; emblems and symbols, 185, 189, 193, 196, 201, 203–4, 208; geography, 244, 246, 248; names/nicknames, 68, 78, 99, 103; origin and history, 21, 47, 57, 59–61, 84, 94–95; weather, 252, 255, 257, 259, 261

North Dakota, 108, 158, 179, 212–13; attractions, 119, 135, 140, 152, 172; education, 112–15, 117; emblems and symbols, 185, 189, 193, 195, 198–99, 201, 208; geography, 244, 246, 248; names/nicknames, 68, 78–79, 99, 103; origin and history, 21, 47, 57, 59–61, 84, 87; weather, 249, 253, 258, 260–61

"Odds and Ends," 98–103

Ohio, 179, 212–13; attractions, 119, 125, 135, 143, 152, 162, 172–73; celebrated persons, 215, 218, 220, 227, 237–38; education, 111–15, 117; emblems and symbols, 185, 189, 193, 195, 199, 208; geography, 244, 246, 248; names/ nicknames, 68, 79, 99; origin and history, 22, 48, 57, 59–61, 84, 88; weather, 251, 255, 257, 259–61

Oklahoma, 101–2, 109, 158, 179, 212–13; attractions, 119, 126, 135, 143, 152, 163, 173; celebrated persons, 220, 228, 238; education, 112–15, 117; emblems and symbols, 185, 189, 193, 195–97, 199, 202–3, 208; geography, 244, 246, 248; names/nicknames, 68, 79, 99–100, 103; origin and history, 22–23, 48, 57, 59–61, 84, 93; weather, 249, 255, 257

Oklahoma City, Oklahoma, 93

Olympia Washington, 93

Oregon, 101, 109, 158, 179–80, 212–13; attractions, 119, 126, 135, 140, 152–53, 163, 173; celebrated persons, 238; education, 112–15, 117; emblems and symbols, 185, 189, 193, 195, 197, 200–201, 203, 209; geography, 244, 246, 248; names/nicknames, 68–69, 79; origin and history, 23, 49, 58–61, 84, 96, 102; weather, 250, 254, 260–61

Parks. *See* National Parks

Pennsylvania, 109, 180, 212–13; attractions, 119, 126, 135–36, 143, 153, 163, 173–74; celebrated persons, 216, 218, 220, 228–29, 238; education, 111–15, 117; emblems and symbols, 185, 187, 193, 195, 197, 201; geography, 244, 246, 248; names/nicknames, 69, 79, 99, 103; origin and history, 23–24, 49, 57, 59–61, 84, 89, 100; weather, 251, 255, 257 58, 260 61

Phoenix, Arizona, 93

Pierre, South Dakota, 94

Pledges to the Flag, 181–82

Poems. *See* State poem

Population, 211–13

Presidents (U.S.), 214–16

Providence, Rhode Island, 94

Rain, 256–58

Raleigh, North Carolina, 94

Reptile. *State* reptile

Revolutionary War, 57

Rhode Island, 180, 212–13, 263–64; attractions, 119, 127, 136, 144, 153, 163, 174; celebrated persons, 238–39; education, 111–15, 117; emblems and symbols, 185, 187, 193–94, 202–3, 209; geography, 241, 244, 246, 248; names/ nicknames, 69, 79, 102; origin and history, 24, 49–50, 57, 59–61, 84, 96; weather, 252, 256–57

Richmond, Virginia, 95

Rock. *See* State building and monument stone; State explorer rock; State rock

Sacramento, California, 95

St. Paul, Minnesota, 95

Salem, Oregon, 96

Salt Lake City, Utah, 96
Sante Fe, New Mexico, 96
Seminole Wars, 58
Ships. *See* State ship
Snow, 258–59
Soil. *See* State soil
Songs. *See* State songs
South Carolina, 109, 158, 180, 182,
    212–13; attractions, 119, 136, 144, 153,
    163; celebrated persons, 216, 220;
    education, 111–16; emblems and
    symbols, 186, 189, 193, 195–99, 201,
    203–4, 209; geography, 244, 246, 248;
    names/nicknames, 69, 80, 99, 103;
    origin and history, 24–25, 50–51, 57,
    59–61, 84, 88; weather, 251, 256–57
South Dakota, 102, 109, 158, 180, 212–13;
    attractions, 119, 127, 136, 140, 153,
    163; education, 112–15, 117; emblems
    and symbols, 186, 190, 193, 195, 197,
    199, 201–2, 209; geography, 244, 246,
    248; names/nicknames, 70, 80, 99, 103;
    origin and history, 25, 51, 57, 59–61,
    84, 94, 102; weather, 250, 253, 258
Sporting events, 164–74
Springfield, Illinois, 96
State air fair, 194
State American folk art symbol, 194
State animal, 194–95
State art gallery, 195
State atlas, 195
State baked goods, 195
Stae beautification and conservation plant,
    195
State beverage/drink, 195
State bird, 183–86
State bug, 196
State building and monument stone, 196
State capitals, 83–97
State cat, 196
State color, 196
State crustacean, 196
State dance, 196
State dog, 197
State domestic animal, 197
State emblem, 197
State explorer rock, 197
State fairs, 118–20, 194
State festival, 197
State fine art, 197

State fish, 197–98; *see also* State freshwater
    fish; State saltwater fish
State flowers, 191–93
State fossil, 198
State fossil shell, 198
State folk dance, 198
State freshwater fish, 198
State fruit, 198
State gem, 198–99
State grain, 199
State grass, 199
State heroine, 199
State historical rock, 199
State horse, 200
State hostess, 200
State insect, 200–201
State language, 201
State land mammal, 201
State litter control symbol, 201
State mammal, 201
State marine mammal, 201
State metal, 201
State mineral, 202
State mottoes, 176–81
State mushroom, 202
State musical instrument, 202
State neckwear, 202
State nicknames, 71–82
State pageant, 202
State play, 202
State poem, 202
State populations, 212–13
State railroad museum, 202
State reptile, 202
State rock, 203
State saltwater fish, 203
State saltwater mammal, 203
State Shakespeare festival, 203
State shell, 203
State ship, 203
State soil, 203
State songs, 204–10
State trees, 186–90
State universities, 115–17
Stone. *See* State building and monument
    stone; State rock
        Symbols, 194–204

Tallahassee, Florida, 97
Tennessee, 110, 158, 180, 212–13;

attractions, 119, 127, 136, 144, 153, 163, 174; celebrated persons, 218, 220, 239; education, 112–16; emblems and symbols, 186, 190, 193, 197, 199, 201–4, 209; geography, 244, 246, 248; names/nicknames, 70, 80, 99; origin and history, 25–26, 51, 57, 59–61, 84, 93, 100; weather, 251, 255, 257, 260–61

Texas, 110, 158–59, 180, 182, 212–13, 262–64; attractions, 120, 127, 136–37, 140, 144, 153–54, 164, 174; celebrated persons, 220, 230; education, 112–15, 117; emblems and symbols, 186, 190, 193, 202, 209; geography, 244, 246, 248; names/nicknames, 70, 80, 99; origin and history, 26, 52, 58–61, 84, 86, 102; weather, 250, 256–57, 260–61

Texas Revolution, 58

Topeka, Kansas, 97

Treaty with England, 58

Trees. See State trees

Trenton, New Jersey, 97

Universities. See State universities

Utah, 102, 110, 180, 212–13; attractions, 120, 128, 137, 140, 144, 154, 164, 174; celebrated persons, 220, 230; education, 112–15, 117; emblems and symbols, 186, 190, 193, 195, 197, 199, 201, 209; geography, 244, 246, 248; names/nicknames, 70, 80–81, 99–100, 102; origin and history, 26–27, 52–53, 59–61, 84, 96; weather, 250, 254, 258–61

Vermont, 110, 180, 212–13; attractions, 120, 128, 137, 154; celebrated persons, 216, 219; education, 111–16; emblems and symbols, 186, 190, 193, 195, 197, 199, 201, 209; geography, 244, 246, 248; names/nicknames, 70, 81, 99; origin and history, 27, 53, 57, 59–61, 84, 93; weather, 252, 254, 258

Virginia, 110, 159, 180, 212–13; attractions, 120, 128, 137, 140, 154, 164, 175; celebrated persons, 216, 219–20, 230, 239; education, 112–16; emblems and

symbols, 186, 190, 193, 195, 197, 203, 209; geography, 244, 246, 248; names/nicknames, 70, 81, 99, 103; origin and history, 27–28, 54, 57–61, 82, 84, 95, 100; weather, 252, 255, 257

War of 1812, 58

Washington, 110, 180, 212–13; attractions, 120, 128, 137, 140–41, 154, 164, 175; celebrated persons, 230, 239; education, 112–15, 117; emblems and symbols, 186, 190, 193, 196–97, 199, 209; geography, 244, 246, 248; names/nicknames, 71, 81, 99; origin and history, 28, 55, 58–61, 84, 93; weather, 250, 254, 257–61

Weather, temperature extremes, 249–56; see also Rain; Snow; Wind

West Virginia, 110, 180, 212–13; attractions, 120, 137, 154, 175; celebrated persons, 230, 240; education, 112–15, 117; emblems and symbols, 186, 190, 193, 195, 197–98, 210; geography, 244, 246, 248; names/nicknames, 71, 81, 99, 103; origin and history, 29, 55, 57, 59–61, 84, 87; weather, 251, 255, 257, 259

Wind, 259–61

Wisconsin, 110, 180–181, 212–13; attractions, 120, 128, 137–38, 144, 155, 164, 175; celebrated persons, 220, 230, 240; education, 112–15, 117; emblems and symbols, 186, 190, 193, 195, 197–98, 201–4, 210; geography, 244, 246, 248; names/nicknames, 71, 81, 99–100; origin and history, 29–30, 55–57, 59–61, 84, 92; weather, 251, 254, 257, 259, 261

Writers, 230–240

Wyoming, 110, 155, 181, 212–13; attractions, 120, 138, 141, 159; education, 112–15, 117; emblems and symbols, 186, 190, 193, 199, 210; geography, 244, 246, 248; names/nicknames, 71, 82, 99; origin and history, 30, 56–57, 59–61, 82, 84, 88; weather, 251, 253, 258–59, 261

The Kids' World

Once you have one Kids' World Almanac book...

THE KIDS' WORLD ALMANAC OF RECORDS AND FACTS
by Margo McLoone-Basta and Alice Siegel

THE SECOND KIDS' WORLD ALMANAC OF RECORDS AND FACTS
by Margo McLoone-Basta and Alice Siegel

THE KIDS' WORLD ALMANAC OF ANIMALS & PETS
by Deborah Felder

THE KIDS' WORLD ALMANAC OF BASEBALL
by Thomas G. Aylesworth

Almanac®

...you'll want to have them all!

●●●

THE KIDS' WORLD ALMANAC OF THE UNITED STATES
by Thomas G. Aylesworth

Please send me...

QUANTITY   TOTAL

____ KIDS' WORLD ALMANAC OF RECORDS AND FACTS (pb) @ $6.95 ea.   ____

____ THE SECOND KIDS' WORLD ALMANAC OF RECORDS AND FACTS (pb) @ $6.95 ea.   ____

____ THE KIDS' WORLD ALMANAC OF ANIMALS AND PETS (pb) @ $6.95 ea.   ____

____ THE KIDS' WORLD ALMANAC OF BASEBALL (pb) @ $6.95 ea.   ____

____ THE KIDS' WORLD ALMANAC OF THE UNITED STATES (pb) @ $6.95 ea.   ____

Subtotal ____

Plus $1.50 per book shipping ____

Total ____

Name _____

Address _____

City _____ State _____ Zip _____

Please enclose a check or money order payable to PHAROS BOOKS for the total amount and return to: Pharos Books, 200 Park Avenue, New York, NY 10166